Assembly Language

From Basics to Expert Proficiency

Contents

Introduction

Assembly language, often considered the most fundamental form of computer programming, serves as the essential bridge between human understanding and machine execution. This book, "Assembly Language: From Basics to Expert Proficiency," is meticulously crafted to provide a comprehensive guide to mastering assembly language programming. Whether you are a beginner delving into the world of low-level programming or an experienced programmer seeking to deepen your understanding, this book aims to equip you with the knowledge and skills necessary to excel.

Assembly language holds a unique place in the spectrum of programming languages. Unlike high-level languages that abstract away the hardware details, assembly provides a clear and direct mapping to the underlying machine code instructions executed by the processor. This characteristic makes it invaluable for tasks that require fine-grained control over hardware resources, high performance, or detailed understanding of system internals.

Historically, assembly language has played a crucial role in the development of software and computing technology. From the early days of computing, where every instruction had to be meticulously hand-coded, to the modern era where it is used for optimization, embedded systems, and performance-critical applications, assembly language has continually proven its relevance and power.

In modern computing, assembly language remains pivotal. It is used in various domains such as operating system kernels, device drivers, embedded systems, and real-time applications. The knowledge of assembly language provides a deeper understanding of how software interacts with hardware, which is indispensable for debugging, optimizing, and developing high-performance applications.

This book compares assembly language with high-level languages to highlight its distinct advantages and its role in performance-critical and resource-constrained environments. While high-level languages offer ease and productivity, assembly language programming fosters a thorough understanding of low-level operations, enabling precise control and optimization that high-level languages cannot afford.

Throughout this book, we will introduce key low-level programming concepts that are fundamental to writing efficient and effective assembly language programs. You will learn how to structure an assembly language program, understand the basic syntax and conventions, and get acquainted with the tools of the trade, including assemblers, linkers, and debuggers.

Our journey begins with a step-by-step guide to writing your first assembly language program, laying a strong foundation for more advanced topics. You will explore the common scenarios where assembly language excels and understand its applications in the real world.

The focus remains on accessibility and clarity, ensuring that complex concepts are explained in a detailed and comprehensible manner. The content is organized in a logical sequence, where later chapters build upon the knowledge gained in earlier ones, enabling a smooth learning curve.

By the end of this book, you will have a solid understanding of both the theoretical and practical aspects of assembly language programming. You will be equipped with the proficiencies to write, debug, and optimize assembly programs, making you adept in a skill that remains essential in the ever-evolving landscape of computer science.

Chapter 1

Introduction to Assembly Language

This chapter covers the essential foundations of assembly language programming, including its definition, historical context, and significance in modern computing. It provides a clear comparison between assembly language and high-level languages, introduces fundamental low-level programming concepts, and explains the basic structure and syntax of an assembly language program. Additionally, the chapter includes a practical guide to writing a first assembly language program and discusses its common use cases and applications.

1.1 What is Assembly Language?

Assembly language is a low-level programming language that provides a direct interface between the programmer and the machine's hardware architecture. Unlike high-level languages (HLL) such as Python, Java, or C++, which abstract the hardware details and provide syntactic constructs to manage data and control program flow, assembly language offers precise control over the machine's resources through mnemonic representations of the machine instructions.

At its core, assembly language instructions translate directly to machine code instructions that a computer's processor executes. Each assembly language is unique to a given computer architecture, reflecting its specific instruction set and operational capabilities. This architecture-specific nature of assembly language means that programs written for one type of processor cannot be directly executed on another type without modification or reassembly.

The primary advantage of using assembly language lies in its ability to exploit the full potential of the processor, enabling optimizations that are often impossible to achieve with high-level languages. This capability is essential in scenarios where performance and resource utilization are critical, such as embedded systems, real-time applications, and systems programming.

- **Instruction Set Architecture (ISA)**: Each assembly language corresponds to a specific Instruction Set Architecture. The ISA defines the set of instructions supported by the processor, the data types, the registers, the addressing modes, and the memory architecture. For example, the x86 and ARM architectures have distinct ISAs, and consequently, the assembly languages for these architectures are different.
- **Mnemonics**: Assembly languages use mnemonics, which are human-readable representations of machine instructions. For example, the Intel x86 assembly language uses the mnemonic MOV to represent the "move" instruction, which transfers data from one location to another.
- **Registers**: Assembly language provides direct control over the processor's registers, which are small, fast storage locations within the CPU. Effective use of registers is crucial for writing efficient assembly programs. For instance, in x86 assembly language, common registers include EAX, EBX, ECX, and EDX.
- **Addressing Modes**: Assembly language supports various addressing modes that define how the operand of an instruction is accessed. These modes include immediate, direct, indirect, register, and indexed addressing, each offering different levels of flexibility and complexity.

To understand how assembly language operates in practice, consider the simple task of adding two numbers and storing the result. In high-level languages, this can be accomplished with a single line of code. However, in assembly language, this task requires multiple instructions to load data into registers, perform the addition, and store the result back to memory. Below is an example in the x86 assembly language:

```
section .data
    num1 db 5 ; Define byte data num1 with value 5
    num2 db 3 ; Define byte data num2 with value 3

section .text
    global _start ; Entry point for the program

_start:
    mov al, [num1] ; Load value of num1 into register AL
    add al, [num2] ; Add value of num2 to register AL
    ; Result of addition is now in AL
```

In this example, the mov instruction loads the value of num1 into the AL register, and the add instruction adds the value of num2 to AL. The result of the addition is stored in the AL register. Assembly language programming requires meticulous attention to the flow of data and the manipulation of processor registers.

Despite its advantages in performance and control, assembly language programming is labor-intensive and prone to errors. The lack of abstraction means that the programmer must manage every detail of the program's operation, including memory allocation and hardware-specific details. This complexity makes assembly language less accessible and more cumbersome for general application development.

Nevertheless, the use of assembly language remains indispensable in certain domains. For instance, in systems programming, writing operating system kernels, device drivers, and firmware often necessitates direct hardware manipulation, for which assembly language is ideally suited. Additionally, in areas like game development, performance-critical sections of code (such as graphics rendering) are sometimes optimized using assembly language.

зыклbThe advent of modern high-level languages and sophisticated compilers has reduced the necessity for writing entire applications in assembly language. These tools can generate highly optimized machine code from more abstract and readable source code. However, a foundational understanding of assembly language remains crucial for understanding the inner workings of computer systems, debugging low-level errors, and conducting performance optimizations.

1.2 History and Evolution of Assembly Language

Assembly language has a rich history that dates back to the early days of computing. Understanding the evolution of assembly language is crucial for appreciating its contemporary applications and significance in modern computing.

In the late 1940s and early 1950s, the first digital computers were developed. These early machines, such as the Electronic Numerical Integrator and Computer (ENIAC) and the Manchester Small-Scale Experimental Machine (SSEM), were programmed using machine code. Machine code consists of binary instructions that are directly executed by the computer's central processing unit (CPU). Programming in machine code is error-prone and extremely tedious due to its low-level nature and lack of abstraction, as every instruction must be written in binary format.

Recognizing the need for a more human-readable and manageable way to program computers, assembly language was introduced. Assembly language provides a symbolic representation of machine code, making it easier to read, write, and debug. Each instruction in an assembly language program corresponds directly to a machine instruction, allowing programmers to write code that closely aligns with the hardware's operation.

The first widely used assembly language was created for the EDSAC (Electronic Delay Storage Automatic Calculator) in 1949. The EDSAC assembly language used mnemonics, which are human-readable symbols, to represent machine instructions. For example, an addition operation could be represented by the mnemonic ADD instead of a binary opcode. This innovation significantly improved the programming process by reducing the complexity of writing and understanding instructions.

Throughout the 1950s and 1960s, assembly languages were developed for various computer architectures. Notable examples include the assembly languages for IBM's Series 7000 computers and the assembly language for Digital Equipment Corporation's PDP-8. Each assembly language was tailored to the specific architecture of the computer it was designed for, which means that assembly languages were not standardized across different machines. Consequently, programmers had to learn and use different assembly languages for different hardware platforms.

The development of higher-level programming languages in the late 1950s, such as Fortran and COBOL, marked a significant evolution in programming. These languages provided greater abstraction, allowing programmers to write code that was more portable and easier to understand. However, assembly language remained essential for tasks that required direct hardware manipulation, optimization, or control over system resources.

In the 1970s and 1980s, assembly language continued to evolve alongside the rapid advancements in computer hardware. The proliferation of microprocessors, such as the Intel 8080, Motorola 6800, and Zilog Z80, led to the creation of new assembly languages tailored to these architectures. During this time, assembly language became a critical tool for developing operating systems, compilers, and embedded systems.

The introduction of the x86 architecture by Intel in 1978 marked a turning point for assembly language programming. The x86 assembly language, designed for the Intel 8086 microprocessor, became widely adopted due to the success and popularity of the x86 hardware platform. This architecture has evolved over the decades, but the fundamental principles of x86 assembly language have remained relatively consistent. As a result, x86 assembly language has become one of the most well-documented and widely studied assembly languages.

The assembly language landscape further diversified with the emergence of Reduced Instruction Set Computing (RISC) architectures in the 1980s. RISC architectures, exemplified by the MIPS and ARM processors, focus on a small set of simple instructions that can execute very quickly. The corresponding assembly languages for RISC processors are designed to leverage these simple and fast instructions, providing a different approach compared to the more complex instruction sets of CISC (Complex Instruction Set Computing) architectures like x86.

Despite the growing dominance of high-level programming languages, assembly language remains relevant in modern computing. It is essential for performance-critical applications, such as real-time systems, device drivers, and certain types of scientific computing. Assembly language is also indispensable for reverse engineering and security research, where understanding the low-level operations of software and hardware is crucial.

The continued advancement of computing technology and the development of new processors ensure that assembly language will remain a vital skill for certain specialized domains. Modern assemblers, integrated development environments (IDEs), and debugging tools have significantly improved the usability and efficiency of assembly language programming, making it accessible to a new generation of programmers.

Understanding the history and evolution of assembly language provides valuable insights into the fundamental principles of computer architecture and programming. This knowledge is instrumental in leveraging the power of assembly language to optimize performance, ensure precise control over hardware, and develop robust and efficient software solutions.

1.3 The Role of Assembly Language in Modern Computing

Assembly language retains a critical role in modern computing, despite the proliferation of higher-level programming languages. This significance spans various domains, including systems programming, embedded systems, and performance-critical applications. Understanding the impact and necessity of assembly language in contemporary computing environments highlights its enduring relevance.

Assembly language operates at a low level, interfacing directly with a computer's hardware. This characteristic confers several advantages:

- **Fine-grained control over hardware:** Assembly language enables programmers to manipulate hardware resources such as CPU registers, memory addresses, and I/O ports directly. This control is pivotal in systems programming, where efficiency and optimization are paramount.
- **Performance optimization:** Given its proximity to machine code, assembly language allows for finely-tuned and highly optimized code, essential for time-critical applications like real-time systems or high-frequency trading platforms.
- **Minimal overhead:** Compared to high-level languages, assembly language incurs minimal abstraction overhead. This characteristic is particularly valuable in resource-constrained environ-

ments, such as embedded systems, where maximizing available resources is critical.

- **Deep understanding of system architecture:** Learning and using assembly language fosters a deep understanding of a computer's architecture and operation, which can enhance a programmer's ability to debug and optimize high-level code.

To illustrate the practical application of assembly language in modern computing, consider the following scenarios:

1. System Boot Process: During system startup, the initial code executed is typically written in assembly language. The low-level control necessary to initialize hardware components, such as the processor and memory, and to load the operating system kernel, requires the precision and efficiency of assembly language.

2. Device Drivers: Device drivers, which facilitate communication between the operating system and hardware devices, often contain assembly language routines. These routines are used to execute time-sensitive tasks, manage interrupts, and interface directly with hardware registers.

3. Embedded Systems: In embedded systems, assembly language is frequently employed to manage hardware resources efficiently. Given the limited computational power and memory in many embedded devices, assembly language's low overhead is invaluable. Consider, for example, the software controlling an automotive engine control unit (ECU), which demands precise timing and resource management.

4. Performance Critical Applications: Applications that demand high performance, such as video codecs, game engines, and scientific computations, often incorporate assembly language to optimize sections of code where maximal performance is essential. These optimizations can involve leveraging specific CPU instructions or executing operations in parallel.

In modern high-performance computing (HPC) environments, vectorized operations utilizing Single Instruction, Multiple Data (SIMD) instructions are frequently implemented in assembly language to maximize computational throughput. For example, utilizing the Advanced Vector Extensions (AVX) instruction set on x86 processors can achieve significant performance improvements in vector and matrix operations.

Algorithm 1: Vector Addition with AVX in Assembly Language

Data: Vector lengths n, vectors a and b
Result: Vector c where $c\_i = a\_i + b\_i$ for all i in {0, 1, ..., n-1}

```
mov rcx, n;
for i = 0 to n-1 4 do
    vmovaps ymm0, [a + 4*i];
    vmovaps ymm1, [b + 4*i];
    vaddps ymm0, ymm0, ymm1;
    vmovaps [c + 4*i], ymm0;
end
```

The algorithm above demonstrates a typical use case for assembly language in performance-critical vector computations. The vector addition task leverages AVX instructions to add elements of two vectors, a and b, storing the result in vector c. By using SIMD instructions, four floating-point numbers are processed simultaneously, thereby enhancing computational efficiency.

Despite these applications, assembly language is not without its drawbacks. Code written in assembly language can be more challenging to read and maintain due to its low-level nature and lack of abstraction. Consequently, it is often used in conjunction with high-level languages, with critical sections of code manually optimized in assembly.

Within an integrated development environment (IDE), developers can use inline assembly to embed assembly code within a high-level language, such as C or C++. This approach provides a balance between the readability and abstract power of high-level languages and the performance optimization potential of assembly language. The following example illustrates the use of inline assembly within a C program:

```
#include <stdio.h>

int main() {
    int a = 10, b = 20, c;

    __asm__ volatile (
        "movl %1, %%eax;\n"
        "addl %2, %%eax;\n"
        "movl %%eax, %0;\n"
        : "=r"(c) /* output */
        : "r"(a), "r"(b) /* inputs */
        : "%eax" /* clobbered register */
    );

    printf("Result: %d\n", c);
    return 0;
}
```

The code snippet above showcases an implementation of the addition operation using inline assembly within a C program. The assembly code operates directly on the CPU registers, achieving efficient computation while maintaining the structure of the high-level C language for broader program logic.

Integrating high-level languages with assembly language allows leveraging the advantages of both paradigms, ensuring code maintains high performance where necessary but remains comprehensible and maintainable. Enablement of this hybrid approach has contributed significantly to the continued relevance of assembly language in modern computing development practices.

1.4 Comparison Between Assembly Language and High-Level Languages

Assembly language and high-level languages are integral components of the programming landscape, each with unique characteristics and applications. Understanding the distinctions between these two paradigms is essential for comprehending their respective roles and utilities in software development.

Abstraction Level: High-level languages, such as Python, Java, and C++, are designed to provide an abstraction layer over the hardware. They enable developers to write code using syntax and constructs that are closer to human languages and abstract away the hardware details. This abstraction allows for easier programming, enhanced readability, and quicker development cycles.

Conversely, assembly language operates at a low level, providing a direct interface to the hardware. Each assembly instruction corresponds closely to machine code instructions executed by the CPU. The syntax and structure closely mirror the architecture's instruction set, offering precise control over the hardware but requiring detailed understanding of the underlying system.

Development Complexity: High-level languages significantly reduce development complexity by offering built-in functions, libraries, and frameworks that handle common programming tasks. Error handling, memory management, and other utilities are often abstracted, enabling developers to focus on application logic rather than system-specific intricacies.

Assembly language, however, demands precise and meticulous attention to detail. Developers must manage all aspects of the program, including memory allocation, instruction sequencing, and system-level interactions. This detailed oversight allows for optimized performance but typically requires more time and expertise to develop and maintain.

Portability: One of the significant advantages of high-level languages is their portability. High-level code can often be compiled or interpreted to run on multiple platforms with little to no modification, thanks to compilers and interpreters that translate high-level instructions into machine code suitable for different architectures.

In contrast, assembly language is inherently specific to a particular CPU architecture. An assembly program written for one type of processor will not run on another without significant modifications to account for different instruction sets and hardware characteristics. This platform-specific nature makes assembly less suitable for applications requiring cross-platform compatibility.

Performance: Performance is one area where assembly language can outperform high-level languages due to its low-level proximity to machine code. By allowing direct manipulation of hardware, assembly programs can be highly optimized for speed and resource efficiency. Critical system components such as operating system kernels, device drivers, and hardware control routines often leverage assembly for this reason.

High-level languages, while generally slower due to abstraction layers and additional overhead, benefit from sophisticated compiler optimizations and advancements in just-in-time (JIT) compilation techniques. For most applications, the performance trade-off is acceptable in light of the increased productivity and code maintainability offered by high-level languages.

Debugging and Maintenance: High-level languages simplify debugging and maintenance through modern integrated development environments (IDEs), which offer powerful tools such as debugging interfaces, code highlighting, and automated refactoring. These features allow developers to identify and fix errors more efficiently, contributing to faster development cycles and more robust software.

Assembly language lacks these advanced tools, making debugging and maintenance a more challenging endeavor. Errors in assembly code can be subtler and harder to diagnose, often requiring a deep understanding of the hardware and system architecture. Furthermore, maintaining assembly code can become cumbersome due to its complexity and lack of abstraction.

Educational Aspects: High-level languages serve as an excellent starting point for learners due to their simplicity and user-friendly syntax. These languages introduce fundamental programming concepts without overwhelming beginners with intricate details of the hardware.

Assembly language, though more complex, is equally valuable educationally for understanding low-level operations, memory management, and CPU functioning. Learning assembly language provides insight into the inner workings of computers, revealing how high-level language constructs are translated into machine-level instructions.

Use Cases: High-level languages are predominantly used for application development, including web applications, mobile apps, and enterprise software. The emphasis on rapid development, code readability, and maintainability aligns well with the needs of these domains.

Assembly language finds its niche in areas where direct hardware control or maximum performance is crucial. Typical use cases include systems programming, embedded systems, real-time processing applications, and situations requiring precise timing and resource management.

The distinct characteristics of assembly language and high-level languages illustrate the broad spectrum of programming paradigms, each suited to specific contexts and requirements. By leveraging the strengths of both, developers can create efficient, versatile, and high-performance software solutions.

1.5 Understanding Low-Level Programming Concepts

To fully grasp assembly language, it is crucial to understand the underlying low-level programming concepts that form the foundation of this language category. Low-level programming deals directly with the hardware, offering greater control over computing resources and mechanisms. This section will delve into fundamental low-level programming concepts, including memory addressing, instruction sets, and processor registers.

Memory Addressing

Memory addressing is a pivotal concept in low-level programming. It refers to the way data is accessed and stored in the computer's memory. In high-level languages, memory management is abstracted, but in assembly language, programmers must handle it explicitly. Understanding how memory addresses work enables the efficient manipulation of data at a granular level.

Memory is organized in a linear sequence of bytes, each having a unique address. These addresses are typically presented in hexadecimal format. For instance, the address 0x1000 might hold a specific value. Access and modification of memory locations are done through these addresses.

Consider the following assembly code snippet that moves the value 5 into a memory location:

```
MOV AX, 5
MOV [0x1000], AX
```

In this example, AX is a register loaded with the value 5. The instruction MOV [0x1000], AX places this value into the memory address 0x1000.

Instruction Sets

Instruction sets are a collection of instructions that a processor can execute. Each CPU family has its own instruction set architecture (ISA), which defines how operations are performed. Common ISAs include x86, ARM, and MIPS. The instructions within an ISA can be categorized as data transfer, arithmetic, logic, control, and input/output operations.

For example, in the x86 instruction set, the following categories exist:

- **Data Transfer Instructions:** These include MOV, PUSH, POP, and similar operations.
- **Arithmetic Instructions:** These include ADD, SUB, MUL, DIV, and others.
- **Logic Instructions:** These include AND, OR, XOR, and NOT.
- **Control Instructions:** These include JMP, CALL, RET, and CMP.
- **Input/Output Instructions:** These include IN and OUT.

Consider the following assembly code demonstrating arithmetic instructions:

```
MOV AX, 10
MOV BX, 5
ADD AX, BX
```

Here, the value 10 is moved into the AX register, and the value 5 into the BX register. The instruction ADD AX, BX adds the value in BX to AX, resulting in AX holding the value 15.

Processor Registers

Registers are small, fast storage locations within the CPU. They are used to hold instructions, data, and addresses. Registers play a critical role in execution speed and efficiency, as accessing data from registers is faster than accessing data from memory. Common types of registers include general-purpose registers, segment registers, and control registers.

In the x86 architecture, several general-purpose registers are commonly used:

- AX, BX, CX, DX: These are general-purpose registers used for a variety of tasks.
- SP (Stack Pointer): Points to the top of the stack.
- BP (Base Pointer): Used to point to the base of the stack.
- SI (Source Index) and DI (Destination Index): Used in string operations.

The following assembly code snippet utilizes the stack pointer and base pointer registers:

```
PUSH AX
MOV BP, SP
POP AX
```

In this code, the PUSH AX instruction stores the value of AX on the stack. The MOV BP, SP instruction copies the stack pointer into the base pointer for referencing stack frames, and the POP AX instruction retrieves the value back from the stack into AX.

Understanding these low-level programming concepts provides the foundation needed to effectively write and optimize assembly language programs, leveraging the full potential of the computer's hardware resources. Techniques such as memory addressing, utilizing various instruction sets, and effectively managing processor registers enable precise and efficient control over program execution.

1.6 The Structure of an Assembly Language Program

An assembly language program is structured in a way that reflects the underlying architecture and operational flow of the computer. Understanding this structure is vital for writing efficient and error-free code. An assembly language program is typically divided into several key sections, each serving a specific purpose.

1. The Data Section:

The data section is used to define variables and constants that the program will use. It is where memory for data storage is allocated. Data segments can be divided into initialized data, uninitialized data (bss), and read-only data. Here is an example of a data section in the x86 assembly language:

```
section .data
    message db 'Hello, World!', 0
    num1 db 5
    num2 db 10

section .bss
    buffer resb 64
```

In this example, message is a string of characters ending with a null byte, num1 and num2 are initialized byte-sized variables, and buffer is a reserved space in memory for a buffer.

2. The Code Section:

The code section contains the executable instructions of the program. This section starts with a label to indicate the entry point of the program (e.g., _start). The instructions in this section are written using the mnemonic forms of the machine language instructions of the specific CPU architecture. Here's an example of a code section:

```
section .text
global _start

_start:
    mov eax, 4
    mov ebx, 1
    mov ecx, message
    mov edx, 13
    int 0x80

    mov eax, 1
    xor ebx, ebx
    int 0x80
```

This program moves the necessary values into the appropriate registers to invoke the system call for writing to standard output, then performs another system call to exit the program.

3. Comments Section:

Comments are crucial in assembly language to provide clarity and context to the code. Single-line comments typically use a semicolon (;):

```
; This is a single-line comment
mov eax, 4 ; System call for sys_write
```

Comments do not affect the execution of the program but help in documenting the functionality of code segments.

4. Directives:

Directives provide instructions to the assembler itself and are not converted into machine language instructions. Common directives include global, extern, and section.

```
global _start ; Indicates the entry point for the linker
extern printf ; Tells the assembler that printf is an external function
section .data ; Defines the data section
```

5. Variables and Constants:

Assembly language programs define variables using mnemonics such as db (define byte), dw (define word), and dd (define double word). Constants are often defined using the equ directive:

```
section .data
    var1 db 10
    var2 dw 2000
    PI equ 3.14159
```

In this example, var1 and var2 are variables, while PI is a constant.

Putting It All Together:

The following is a skeleton structure of a simple assembly language program:

```
section .data
    ; Data declarations
    message db 'Hello, World!', 0

section .bss
    ; Uninitialized data
    buffer resb 64

section .text
global _start
```

```
_start:
    ; Code to execute
    mov eax, 4 ; Write system call
    mov ebx, 1 ; File descriptor (stdout)
    mov ecx, message ; Pointer to message
    mov edx, 13 ; Length of message
    int 0x80 ; Interrupt to call kernel

    mov eax, 1 ; Exit system call
    xor ebx, ebx ; Return 0 status
    int 0x80 ; Interrupt to call kernel
```

This structured approach ensures that the program is organized, readable, and maintainable. Each section of the program has a distinct role, and adherence to these conventions is crucial for successful assembly programming. By carefully defining the data, understanding directives, and structuring the executable code, programmers can create assembly language programs that are both efficient and effective.

1.7 Basic Syntax and Conventions

Assembly language programming necessitates a meticulous understanding of its syntax and conventions. These foundational elements ensure the correct interpretation and execution of commands by the assembler. This section delineates the key aspects of assembly language syntax to provide a clear grasp of how to correctly structure and write assembly code.

Assembly language syntax generally comprises instructions, labels, comments, and directives. Each of these components has a specific role and syntax that must be adhered to precisely for the program to function as intended.

- **Instructions:** The instructions represent the actual operations that the CPU will execute. Each instruction typically comprises an opcode (operation code) and operands. The instruction format can vary based on the assembler and the target architecture. A standard structure of an instruction in x86 assembly language would be:

  ```
  MOV AX, BX ; Moves the content of BX register into AX register
  ```

  In this example, MOV is the opcode, and AX, BX are operands.

- **Labels:** Labels serve the purpose of marking a position within a program. They can be used to define addresses for branching, looping, or data locations. Labels are followed by a colon (':'). For example:

```
START:
```

Here, START is a label.

- **Comments:** Comments provide explanations or annotations within the assembly code, making it easier to understand. They are ignored by the assembler. In x86 assembly language, comments are typically introduced with a semicolon (';'). For example:

```
; This is a comment
MOV AX, BX ; Move BX to AX
```

- **Directives:** Directives (or pseudo-operations) give instructions to the assembler itself, not the CPU. They define data sections, allocate memory, set alignment, and more. Common directives include SEGMENT, DB (Define Byte), DW (Define Word), and others. For example:

```
SEGMENT .data
msg DB "Hello World",0 ; Define a null-terminated string
```

This defines a data segment with a string.

By exploring the basic syntax and conventions, the subsequent lines of the assembly language program naturally fall into place, maintaining clarity and function.

Spaces or tabs typically separate the different parts of an instruction (opcode, operands). However, the exact rules can vary slightly depending on the assembler being used. Below is an example of a simple assembly language program that demonstrates the use of instructions, labels, comments, and directives:

```
SECTION .data ; Data segment
hello_msg db 'Hello',0 ; Null-terminated string
world_msg db 'World',0 ; Null-terminated string

SECTION .bss ; Uninitialized data segment
SECTION .text ; Code segment

global _start ; Entry point for the program
_start: ; Label marking the start of the program
    ; System call to write to stdout
    MOV EAX, 4 ; sys_write system call number
    MOV EBX, 1 ; File descriptor (stdout)
    MOV ECX, hello_msg ; Pointer to the message
    MOV EDX, 5 ; Length of the message
    INT 0x80 ; Trigger the system call
```

```
; System call to write to stdout
MOV EAX, 4 ; sys_write system call number
MOV EBX, 1 ; File descriptor (stdout)
MOV ECX, world_msg ; Pointer to the message
MOV EDX, 5 ; Length of the message
INT 0x80 ; Trigger the system call

; System call to exit
MOV EAX, 1 ; sys_exit system call number
XOR EBX, EBX ; Exit code 0
INT 0x80 ; Trigger the system call
```

Understanding the rules for the typical assembly language syntax, as well as the nuances of specific assemblers, is necessary for writing functioning and efficient assembly code. Taking special note of the aforementioned components will aid in mastering the essential structure of an assembly program. This knowledge equips you with the ability to diagnose and fix errors stemming from syntactical misunderstandings.

1.8 Introduction to Assemblers, Linkers, and Debuggers

In any assembly language programming endeavor, the tools that facilitate the conversion of human-readable assembly code into machine-executable code are indispensable. This process involves several stages and employs specific tools known as assemblers, linkers, and debuggers. Understanding the functions and operational mechanisms of these tools is crucial for effective assembly language programming.

Assemblers are specialized programs that convert assembly language code into machine code. Assembly language, being a low-level programming language, provides a more human-readable format compared to binary machine code but still maintains a close relationship with the hardware instructions of a computer. An assembler translates each assembly language instruction into a corresponding binary instruction that the processor can execute directly. This process is known as the assembly process. Assemblers also handle symbolic labels, macros, and pseudo-instructions, which help simplify coding.

```
// Example Assembly Code for an assembler
section .data
    msg db 'Hello, world!', 0

section .text
```

```
    global _start

_start:
    ; system call to write the message
    mov eax, 4 ; syscall number for sys_write
    mov ebx, 1 ; file descriptor (stdout)
    mov ecx, msg ; pointer to the message
    mov edx, 13 ; message length
    int 0x80 ; call kernel

    ; system call to exit
    mov eax, 1 ; syscall number for sys_exit
    xor ebx, ebx ; exit status 0
    int 0x80 ; call kernel
```

The assembler takes this source code and generates an object file, which consists of the machine code instructions corresponding to the assembly code and various data structures necessary for the linking process.

Linkers then come into play after the assembler has generated object files. The primary role of a linker is to combine one or more object files into a final executable. This involves several tasks:

- **Symbol Resolution:** The linker resolves symbolic references between object files. For example, one object file may refer to a function or variable defined in another.
- **Relocation:** The linker adjusts the addresses in the code and data sections. Since each object file may be compiled with position-independent code, the linker adjusts these addresses so that the final executable can run correctly.
- **Library Handling:** The linker can also link in pre-compiled libraries (both static and dynamic). Static libraries are directly included in the final executable, while dynamic libraries are linked at runtime.

```
# Example of linking using GNU linker ld
ld -o program file1.o file2.o
```

In this command, file1.o and file2.o are object files produced by the assembler, and program is the final executable produced by the linker.

Debuggers are essential tools for inspecting the behavior of an executable during runtime. They help in identifying and troubleshooting logical errors, execution flow anomalies, and other issues in a program. A debugger allows a programmer to execute their code line-by-line, set breakpoints, watch variables, and inspect memory contents. Some of the most commonly used debuggers for assembly language include GDB (GNU Debugger) for Unix-like systems and WinDbg for Windows systems.

```
(gdb) break _start
Breakpoint 1 at 0x80483f6
(gdb) run
Starting program: /path/to/program

Breakpoint 1, 0x080483f6 in _start ()
(gdb) next
(gdb) print $eax
$1 = 4
(gdb) continue
```

In this example with GDB, the command break _start sets a breakpoint at the start of the program. The run command initiates the program execution until it hits the breakpoint. The next command runs the next line of the assembly code. Using the print command, we can inspect the value of registers or variables.

Assemblers, linkers, and debuggers collectively contribute to transforming assembly source code into a functioning executable and ensuring its correctness. Each tool has a distinct role but is part of an interconnected workflow essential for effective assembly language programming. Understanding their functions and how they interact is fundamental in the development of efficient and reliable low-level code.

1.9 First Assembly Language Program: A Step-by-Step Guide

Writing your first assembly language program involves understanding the fundamental instructions and syntax. We will walk through a basic program that outputs a simple string, ensuring clarity and comprehension at each step.

Step 1: Setting Up the Development Environment

Before you begin, ensure your environment is configured correctly. You need an assembler (such as NASM for x86 architecture) and a linker to combine object files into an executable.

Step 2: Writing the Assembly Code

We will write a program to print "Hello, World!" to the console. Create a file named hello.asm.

```
section .data
    hello db 'Hello, World!',0 ; The string to be printed

section .text
    global _start ; Required by linker

_start:
    ; Write the string to stdout
    mov eax, 4 ; syscall: sys_write
    mov ebx, 1 ; file descriptor: stdout
    mov ecx, hello ; pointer to the string
    mov edx, 13 ; number of bytes
    int 0x80 ; call kernel

    ; Exit the process
    mov eax, 1 ; syscall: sys_exit
    xor ebx, ebx ; status: 0
    int 0x80 ; call kernel
```

Step 3: Understanding the Code

- section .data - Defines a data section to store data such as strings.
- hello db 'Hello, World!',0 - Declares a string 'Hello, World!' ending with a null byte.
- section .text - Defines a text section for code.
- global _start - Indicates the entry point of the program.
- _start: - Label marking the beginning of the execution.
- mov eax, 4 - Moves the value 4 (syscall number for sys_write) into the EAX register.
- mov ebx, 1 - Moves the value 1 (file descriptor for stdout) into the EBX register.
- mov ecx, hello - Moves the address of the string into the ECX register.
- mov edx, 13 - Moves the value 13 (number of bytes to write) into the EDX register.
- int 0x80 - Interrupt to invoke a system call.
- mov eax, 1 - Moves the value 1 (syscall number for sys_exit) into the EAX register.
- xor ebx, ebx - Zeroes the EBX register for a status code of 0.
- int 0x80 - Interrupt to invoke a system call.

Step 4: Assembling the Code

To assemble the code, use the NASM assembler, generating an object file hello.o:

```
nasm -f elf hello.asm -o hello.o
```

Step 5: Linking the Object File

Link the object file to create an executable. Use a linker like ld:

```
ld -m elf_i386 -s -o hello hello.o
```

Step 6: Running the Program

Once linked, run your executable:

./helloYou should see the output:

```
Hello, World!
```

Analyzing the Execution Flow

1. The program starts execution at the _start label. 2. The first system call, sys_write, is invoked to output the string to the console. 3. Next, the program exits gracefully using the sys_exit system call.

Understanding the registers involved:

- EAX - Stores the system call number.
- EBX - Stores parameters for the system call (file descriptor in sys_write).
- ECX - Points to the data to be written.
- EDX - Holds the size of the data.

Handling Common Errors

1. Incorrect syscall numbers lead to undefined behavior. Ensure correct values based on the syscall table. 2. Segmentation faults occur if pointers (e.g., hello) are incorrect or data sections are mishandled.

Optimization Tips

1. Use macros for repetitive tasks to improve readability. 2. Minimize the number of instructions in critical sections for performance. 3. Use meaningful labels to keep code maintainable.

Writing and executing assembly language programs requires an understanding of hardware-specific details and system call interfaces. By meticulously assembling, linking, and debugging, you can control the execution flow and manage low-level operations effectively.

1.10 Common Use Cases and Applications of Assembly Language

Assembly language, although less frequently used than higher-level languages, is indispensable in specific applications where low-level hardware interaction, performance optimization, or direct control of computer resources is crucial. This section elucidates various common use cases and applications where assembly language proves to be a formidable choice, providing insights into scenarios where its utilization significantly benefits computing processes.

1. System Programming

System programming, which includes writing operating systems, device drivers, and system utilities, often necessitates close interaction with hardware. Assembly language provides an unparalleled level of control over the system's resources, enabling programmers to write highly efficient and optimally performing code.

```
section .data
    msg db 'Hello, Kernel!',0x0

section .text
    global _start

_start:
    mov edx, 14 ; message length
    mov ecx, msg ; message to write
    mov ebx, 1 ; file descriptor (stdout)
    mov eax, 4 ; system call number (sys_write)
    int 0x80 ; call kernel

    mov eax, 1 ; system call number (sys_exit)
    int 0x80 ; call kernel
```

This program outputs "Hello, Kernel!" to the terminal using direct system calls, demonstrating the low-level control afforded by assembly language.

2. Embedded Systems

Embedded systems, such as microcontrollers and real-time embedded systems, frequently leverage assembly language due to their stringent performance and memory constraints. Assembly provides deterministic execution times and minimal overhead, crucial in contexts where timing precision and resource usage are critical.

```
section .data
    port_base equ 0x378

section .text
    global _start

_start:
    mov al, 0x01 ; data to send
    out dx, al ; write data to port
    hlt ; halt CPU
```

This minimalistic code writes data to an I/O port on, for example, a microcontroller, showcasing the direct hardware interfacing capability.

3. Performance Optimization

One of the prominent use cases of assembly language is in performance-critical applications. High-performance computing applications, such as scientific computations, game development, and multimedia processing, often require fine-tuned code to maximize efficiency.

```
section .data
    array db 1, 2, 3, 4, 5
    result db 0

section .text
    global _start

_start:
    mov ecx, 5 ; counter
    xor ebx, ebx ; sum = 0
    lea esi, [array] ; load address of the array

loop_start:
    add bl, [esi] ; sum += array[i]
    inc esi ; next element
    loop loop_start ; decrement ecx and loop if not zero

    mov [result], bl ; store result

    mov eax, 1 ; system call number (sys_exit)
    int 0x80 ; call kernel
```

The loop in this program efficiently sums the elements of an array, illustrating potential performance gains over higher-level language implementations.

4. Reverse Engineering and Malware Analysis

Reverse engineering often involves disassembling compiled binaries to understand their functionality. Assembly language is the native language of disassembled code, making it essential for reverse engineering tasks such as security analysis, ethical hacking, and malware dissection.

```
section .data
    secret_msg db 'You have hacked this code',0

section .text
    global _start

_start:
    ; Assume some complex operations to reach here
    lea eax, [secret_msg]
    call print_message

print_message:
    ; Code to print the message to stdout
    ret
```

Understanding such snippets helps cybersecurity experts analyze and interpret the workings of potentially malicious software.

5. Bootloaders and Firmware

Bootloaders and firmware are typically written in assembly language due to their necessity for direct hardware manipulation and a very small footprint. A bootloader's primary function is to initialize system hardware and load the operating system kernel.

```
section .text
    org 0x7C00

Start:
    mov ah, 0x0E ; BIOS teletype output function
    mov al, '!' ; Character to print
    int 0x10 ; BIOS interrupt
    hlt ; Halt the CPU

times 510-($-$$) db 0 ; Pad with zeroes
dw 0xAA55 ; Boot sector signature
```

This minimalist bootloader prints a character to the screen, demonstrating foundational boot process elements.

6. Real-Time Operating Systems (RTOS)

Real-time operating systems within various industrial and automotive applications rely on precise timing and concurrency control. Assembly language ensures predictable execution, which is paramount in systems where timing is critical.

```
section .data
    timer_value dw 0

section .text
    global _start
```

```
_start:
    mov dx, 0x40 ; Timer port
    in al, dx ; Read current timer value into al
    mov [timer_value], al

    ; Further RTOS timer handling code here

    hlt
```

This snippet reads from a hardware timer, typical in real-time operations requiring exact intervals.

Assembly language's specificity, control, and efficiency make it indispensable in various computing domains, solidifying its relevance despite the prevalence of high-level languages.

Chapter 2

Basic Assembly Language Instructions

This chapter delves into the core instructions fundamental to assembly language programming. It covers data transfer, arithmetic, bitwise, shift, and comparison instructions, along with the implementation of conditional and unconditional branching. Emphasis is also placed on stack operations, string manipulation, and the use of assembly language directives, providing a comprehensive understanding of performing basic operations efficiently in assembly language.

2.1 Introduction to Basic Instructions

Assembly language instructions form the foundational building blocks of low-level programming, providing a direct interface to the underlying hardware. This section introduces the basic instructions essential for performing fundamental operations in assembly language. Each instruction type is designed to accomplish specific tasks, ranging from data transfer to arithmetic calculations, and from logic operations to conditional branching. Understanding these instructions is crucial for developing efficient and effective assembly language programs.

Data Transfer Instructions

Data transfer instructions move data between registers, memory, and

I/O ports. The MOV instruction is the most commonly used data transfer instruction. Here is an example of how to use the MOV instruction:

```
MOV AX, BX ; Move the content of register BX into register AX
MOV AL, 34H ; Move the immediate value 34H into the lower byte of register AX
MOV [SI], AX ; Move the content of AX into the memory location pointed to by SI
```

The MOV instruction has various forms, allowing data transfer between different types of operands, such as register-to-register, register-to-memory, memory-to-register, and immediate-to-register.

Arithmetic Instructions

Arithmetic instructions perform basic mathematical operations. The ADD and SUB instructions execute addition and subtraction, respectively:

```
ADD AX, BX ; Add the content of BX to AX and store the result in AX
SUB CX, DX ; Subtract the content of DX from CX and store the result in CX
```

For multiplication and division, the MUL and DIV instructions are used:

```
MUL BX ; Multiply AX by BX; result stored in DX:AX
DIV CX ; Divide DX:AX by CX; quotient in AX, remainder in DX
```

These instructions allow for efficient handling of numerical data within registers.

Bitwise Instructions

Bitwise instructions perform logical operations on binary values. The essential bitwise instructions include AND, OR, XOR, and NOT:

```
AND AX, BX ; Perform bitwise AND between AX and BX, store result in AX
OR CX, DX ; Perform bitwise OR between CX and DX, store result in CX
XOR AX, AX ; Perform bitwise XOR between AX and AX (clears AX)
NOT BX ; Perform bitwise NOT on BX; invert all bits in BX
```

These instructions are vital for manipulating individual bits and are widely used in tasks such as setting, clearing, toggling, and testing specific bits in a value.

Shift and Rotate Instructions

Shift and rotate instructions are used to move bits within a register to the left or right. The common instructions include SHL, SHR, ROL, and ROR:

```
SHL AX, 1 ; Shift all bits in AX left by 1 position; zero fill the least significant bit
SHR BX, 2 ; Shift all bits in BX right by 2 positions; zero fill the most significant bits
ROL CX, 1 ; Rotate bits in CX left by 1 position; wrap around the most significant bit
    to the least significant bit
ROR DX, 3 ; Rotate bits in DX right by 3 positions; wrap around the least significant
```

```
bit to the most significant bit
```

These instructions are particularly useful for performing operations such as multiplication and division by powers of two, bit masks, and circular buffering.

Comparison and Test Instructions

Comparison and test instructions evaluate the relationship between two operands. The CMP instruction compares two values and sets the flags register based on the result, while the TEST instruction performs a bitwise AND operation without affecting the destination operand:

```
CMP AX, BX ; Compare AX with BX, set flags accordingly
TEST AX, AX ; Perform bitwise AND between AX and AX, set flags based on the
    result
```

These instructions do not store the result of the operation but update the status flags, which are then used by conditional branching instructions to alter program flow.

Branching Instructions

Branching instructions change the flow of execution based on specific conditions. They include both conditional and unconditional jumps. Examples are JMP, JE, JNE, JG, and JL:

```
JMP LABEL ; Unconditionally jump to the instruction at LABEL
JE LABEL ; Jump to LABEL if the Zero Flag (ZF) is set (equality)
JNE LABEL ; Jump to LABEL if the Zero Flag (ZF) is not set (inequality)
JG LABEL ; Jump to LABEL if the result is greater (signed comparison)
JL LABEL ; Jump to LABEL if the result is less (signed comparison)
```

These instructions are crucial for implementing decision-making in programs, such as loops and conditional statements.

Stack Operations

Stack operations are used for managing data in a last-in, first-out (LIFO) manner. The primary stack instructions are PUSH and POP:

```
PUSH AX ; Push the content of AX onto the stack
POP BX ; Pop the top value from the stack into BX
```

These operations are integral to subroutine handling, parameter passing, and local variable storage.

String Manipulation Instructions

String manipulation instructions operate on sequences of bytes or words. These include instructions such as MOVSB, MOVSW, LODSB,

LODSW, STOSB, and STOSW:

```
MOVSB ; Move byte from address DS:SI to ES:DI
MOVSW ; Move word from address DS:SI to ES:DI
LODSB ; Load byte at DS:SI into AL
LODSW ; Load word at DS:SI into AX
STOSB ; Store byte in AL at ES:DI
STOSW ; Store word in AX at ES:DI
```

These instructions are effective for block transfers, initialization, and handling character strings.

Conditional Execution

Conditional execution refers to the execution of instructions only if certain conditions are met, as determined by the status flags. Instructions like JNZ (Jump if Not Zero) and JZ (Jump if Zero) are key components of conditional execution:

```
JNZ NEXT ; Jump to NEXT if the Zero Flag (ZF) is not set
JZ END ; Jump to END if the Zero Flag (ZF) is set
```

Utilizing conditional execution improves program logic and efficiency by allowing different paths of execution based on runtime conditions.

Assembly Language Directives

Directives are special commands that provide instructions to the assembler on how to process the source code. Directives such as SEGMENT, ENDS, and DB define memory segments, mark the end of segments, and allocate memory, respectively:

```
SEGMENT DATASEG
DB 100h ; Define a byte with the value 100h
ENDS
```

Directives are pivotal in organizing code, memory management, and defining constants and variables, aiding in the clarity and structure of assembly programs.

2.2 MOV Instruction: Data Transfer

The MOV instruction is one of the most fundamental and frequently used instructions in assembly language. It serves the essential purpose of transferring data from one location to another within the CPU's registers, memory locations, or between a register and a memory location. Understanding the MOV instruction is crucial as it forms the basis for manipulating data in an assembly program.

The general syntax for the MOV instruction is:

```
MOV destination, source
```

In this syntax, destination refers to the location where the data is to be copied, and source is the location from which the data is to be copied. The MOV instruction copies the value from the source to the destination, leaving the source value unchanged.

Several types of operands can be used with MOV instructions, including immediate values, register names, and memory addresses. Let us examine each type in detail:

- **Immediate to Register Transfer**

  The MOV instruction can transfer an immediate value directly into a register. An immediate value is a constant value provided directly in the instruction. The example below demonstrates this operation:

  ```
  MOV AX, 5 ; Load the value 5 into register AX
  ```

- **Register to Register Transfer**

  The MOV instruction can transfer data from one register to another register. This type of data transfer is common in assembly programming. The following example shows such a transfer:

  ```
  MOV BX, AX ; Copy the contents of register AX into register BX
  ```

- **Memory to Register Transfer**

  The MOV instruction can transfer data from a memory location to a register. This involves accessing the content at a specific memory address and loading it into a register. Consider the following example:

  ```
  MOV AX, [1234h] ; Load the value at memory address 1234h into register
      AX
  ```

  When specifying a memory address, square brackets [] are used to denote that the operand is a memory location.

- **Register to Memory Transfer**

  The MOV instruction can also transfer data from a register to a memory location. This involves storing the content of a register into a specified memory address as shown below:

```
MOV [5678h], CX ; Store the value in register CX into memory address 5678
    h
```

- **Immediate to Memory Transfer**

  Immediate values can also be transferred directly to memory locations. The example below demonstrates this operation:

```
MOV [1234h], 6 ; Store the value 6 into the memory address 1234h
```

The flexibility of the MOV instruction allows for a wide range of data transfer operations, and its efficient use is critical for optimizing the performance of assembly programs. However, it is important to comply with operand size compatibility rules to avoid errors. For instance, transferring data between registers of different sizes without appropriate operations or modifying entity size is problematic.

```
MOV AX, BX ; Correct: Both AX and BX are 16-bit registers.
MOV AL, [1234h] ; Correct: Accessing an 8-bit memory value into 8-bit AL register.
MOV DX, 12345h ; Incorrect: Immediate value exceeds the size of register DX (16-bit).
```

In addition to simple data transfers, the MOV instruction is instrumental in preparing operands for arithmetic or logical operations, configuring pointers for indirect addressing modes, and initializing values in memory during program setup. It is essential to diligently manage the content of registers and memory locations as the improper use of the MOV instruction can lead to unintended data overwrites, causing erroneous program behavior.

2.3 Arithmetic Instructions: ADD, SUB, MUL, DIV

Arithmetic instructions form the backbone of computation in an assembly language. These instructions are used to perform basic mathematical operations on integer operands. The primary arithmetic instructions in assembly language are ADD, SUB, MUL, and DIV, each serving a distinct purpose.

ADD Instruction

The ADD instruction adds the source operand to the destination operand, storing the result in the destination operand. The syntax for the ADD instruction is as follows:

```
ADD destination, source
```

The destination operand can be a register or a memory location. The source operand can be a register, memory location, or an immediate value. Consider the following example:

```
MOV AX, 5
ADD AX, 10
```

This code moves the value 5 into the AX register and then adds 10 to AX. After execution, the AX register contains the value 15.

SUB Instruction

The SUB instruction subtracts the source operand from the destination operand, storing the result in the destination operand. The syntax for the SUB instruction is:

```
SUB destination, source
```

Similar to the ADD instruction, the destination operand can be a register or a memory location, and the source operand can be a register, memory location, or an immediate value. For instance:

```
MOV BX, 20
SUB BX, 5
```

This code moves the value 20 into the BX register and then subtracts 5 from BX. After this operation, the BX register will contain the value 15.

MUL Instruction

The MUL instruction performs an unsigned multiplication of the source operand and the accumulator register. The result of the multiplication is stored in a combination of AX, DX:AX, or EAX, depending on the size of the operand. The syntax for the MUL instruction is:

```
MUL source
```

For an 8-bit operand, the multiplicand is assumed to be in AL, and the product is stored in AX. For a 16-bit operand, the multiplicand is in AX, and the product is stored in DX:AX. For a 32-bit operand, the multiplicand is in EAX, and the result is stored in EDX:EAX. Example:

```
MOV AL, 10
MOV BL, 3
MUL BL
```

Here, AL is multiplied by BL, and the 16-bit result is stored in AX. If AL contains 10 and BL contains 3, AX will have 30.

DIV Instruction

The DIV instruction performs an unsigned division of the accumulator register by the source operand. The syntax for the DIV instruction is:

```
DIV source
```

For an 8-bit operand, the dividend is assumed to be in AX, with the quotient stored in AL and the remainder in AH. For a 16-bit operand, the dividend is in DX:AX, and the quotient is stored in AX with the remainder in DX. For a 32-bit operand, the dividend is in EDX:EAX, and the quotient is stored in EAX with the remainder in EDX. Consider the following code:

```
MOV AX, 30
MOV BL, 5
DIV BL
```

Here, AX (having 30) is divided by BL (containing 5). After division, AL will contain the quotient (6), and AH will contain the remainder (0).

Each of these arithmetic instructions is critical for performing fundamental mathematical operations in assembly language. Efficient coding with these instructions demands a thorough understanding of operand types and sizes, the specific registers used for storing results, and how to manage the instructions' effects on the flags in the status register.

Executing arithmetic operations is essential for nearly all programming tasks, making mastery of these instructions foundational for further study and application in assembly language programming. Understanding how the CPU interprets and executes these instructions provides deeper insights into system-level optimizations and performance enhancements.

2.4 Bitwise Instructions: AND, OR, XOR, NOT

Bitwise instructions are vital in assembly language as they allow direct manipulation of individual bits within registers. These operations are foundational for low-level programming, including tasks such as setting, clearing, toggling, and testing bits. Here, we will delve into the fundamental bitwise instructions: AND, OR, XOR, and NOT.

The AND Instruction: The AND instruction performs a bitwise AND operation between two operands. Each bit of the result is set to 1 only if the corresponding bits of both operands are also 1. This is useful for masking operations, where specific bits of an operand are cleared, leaving the desired bits unchanged.

```
; Example of AND instruction in NASM assembly
section .data
    value1 db 0b11001100
    mask db 0b10101010

section .text
global _start
_start:
    mov al, [value1] ; Load value1 into AL
    and al, [mask] ; Perform AND operation with mask
    ; Resultant AL = 0b10001000
```

The above example demonstrates loading a byte from value1 into the AL register and then performing a bitwise AND operation with the mask. The result, stored in AL, will be 0b10001000.

The OR Instruction: The OR instruction executes a bitwise OR operation between two operands. Each bit in the result is set to 1 if at least one of the corresponding bits of either operand is 1. This is particularly useful for setting specific bits within a register.

```
; Example of OR instruction in NASM assembly
section .data
    value1 db 0b11001100
    mask db 0b10101010

section .text
global _start
_start:
    mov al, [value1] ; Load value1 into AL
    or al, [mask] ; Perform OR operation with mask
    ; Resultant AL = 0b11101110
```

In this example, the byte from value1 is loaded into AL, and a bitwise OR operation is performed with the mask. Consequently, the result in AL will be 0b11101110.

The XOR Instruction: The XOR instruction implements a bitwise exclusive OR (XOR) between two operands. Each bit of the result is set to 1 if the corresponding bits of the operands are different. This operation is valuable for toggling bits and can also be used to zero out a register by XOR-ing it with itself.

```
; Example of XOR instruction in NASM assembly
section .data
```

```
    value1 db 0b11001100
    mask db 0b10101010

section .text
global _start
_start:
    mov al, [value1] ; Load value1 into AL
    xor al, [mask] ; Perform XOR operation with mask
    ; Resultant AL = 0b01100110
```

Here, the byte value1 is loaded into AL, and a bitwise XOR operation is applied with the mask. The resulting AL will hold 0b01100110.

The NOT Instruction: The NOT instruction performs a bitwise negation (inversion) on a single operand. Each bit in the operand is inverted, turning 1s into 0s and vice versa. This operation is useful for reversing bit patterns.

```
; Example of NOT instruction in NASM assembly
section .data
    value1 db 0b11001100

section .text
global _start
_start:
    mov al, [value1] ; Load value1 into AL
    not al ; Invert the bits in AL
    ; Resultant AL = 0b00110011
```

In this instance, value1 is loaded into the AL register, and the bits in AL are inverted using the NOT instruction. The final result in AL will be 0b00110011.

These fundamental bitwise operations, AND, OR, XOR, and NOT, form the core toolkit for manipulating bits directly. Such instructions enable precise control over data at the binary level, which is essential for various low-level programming tasks in assembly language. Proper understanding and usage of these instructions are crucial for achieving expert proficiency in assembly language programming.

2.5 Shift and Rotate Instructions

Shift and rotate instructions are essential operations in assembly language, frequently utilized for bit-level manipulation. These instructions operate at a lower level than arithmetic operations, directly influencing the individual bits within a register or memory location. Here, we will explore the various shift and rotate instructions available in assembly language, along with their syntactic and functional details.

Assembly language provides two primary categories of bitwise shift instructions: logical shifts and arithmetic shifts. Additionally, rotate instructions can be classified into rotate without carry and rotate through carry operations.

Logical Shifts

Logical shift instructions move bits left or right within a register, filling the vacated positions with zeros. The syntax for logical shift left and logical shift right are as follows:

```
; Logical shift left (SHL)
SHL destination, count

; Logical shift right (SHR)
SHR destination, count
```

The destination operand can be a register or memory location, and count specifies the number of positions to shift. For example:

```
MOV AL, 0b10101010 ; AL = 10101010
SHL AL, 1 ; AL = 01010100
```

This example demonstrates a logical shift left by one position. The Most Significant Bit (MSB) is discarded, and a zero is inserted at the Least Significant Bit (LSB) position.

Arithmetic Shifts

Arithmetic shifts behave similarly to logical shifts but preserve the sign bit during the shift operation. This is especially useful for signed binary numbers. The syntax for arithmetic shifts are:

```
; Arithmetic shift right (SAR)
SAR destination, count
```

An example of arithmetic shift right:

```
MOV AL, 0b11001010 ; AL = -54 as a signed integer
SAR AL, 1 ; AL = 11100101 (preserving the sign bit)
```

When performing an arithmetic shift right, the sign bit (MSB) is replicated to preserve the number's sign, making this instruction vital for signed arithmetic operations.

Rotate Instructions

Rotate instructions cyclically shift bits within a register, wrapping around the vacated positions. Rotate instructions come in two variations: rotate without carry (ROL and ROR) and rotate through carry (RCL and RCR).

```
; Rotate left without carry (ROL)
ROL destination, count

; Rotate right without carry (ROR)
ROR destination, count
```

In the rotate left operation (ROL), the MSB is moved to the LSB position, while all other bits are shifted left. Here's an example:

```
MOV AL, 0b10101010 ; AL = 10101010
ROL AL, 1 ; AL = 01010101
```

For the rotate right (ROR), the LSB is moved to the MSB position, while all other bits are shifted right:

```
MOV AL, 0b10101010 ; AL = 10101010
ROR AL, 1 ; AL = 01010101
```

Rotate through carry instructions incorporate the carry flag (CF) as an additional bit during the rotation:

```
; Rotate left through carry (RCL)
RCL destination, count

; Rotate right through carry (RCR)
RCR destination, count
```

An example of rotate left through carry:

```
MOV AL, 0b10101010 ; AL = 10101010
STC ; Set Carry Flag to 1
RCL AL, 1 ; AL = 01010100, CF = 1
```

After the operation, the carry flag is rotated into the LSB position, and the original MSB is moved to the carry flag. This makes rotate through carry useful for extended precision arithmetic operations.

Shifting and rotating instructions are crucial when performing low-level manipulation of data. Understanding their usage and effects on register and memory values is fundamental for efficient assembly language programming.

2.6 Comparison and Test Instructions: CMP, TEST

Comparison and test instructions are essential in assembly language as they dictate the flow of control by evaluating expression outcomes.

The CMP and TEST instructions are fundamental tools used to compare values and test conditions, yielding flags that drive branching decisions.

CMP (Compare) is utilized to compare two operands by subtracting the second operand from the first operand, whereas the actual results are not stored; only the condition flags are affected. These flags include the Zero Flag (ZF), Sign Flag (SF), Overflow Flag (OF), and Carry Flag (CF). The instruction syntax is as follows:

```
CMP operand1, operand2
```

Here, operand1 is typically the destination operand, and operand2 is the source operand. The operands can be registers, immediate values, or memory locations. The result of CMP operand1, operand2 can be interpreted based on the flags:

- $ZF = 1$: operand1 equals operand2
- $CF = 1$: operand1 is less than operand2 (unsigned comparison)
- $SF \neq OF$: operand1 is less than operand2 (signed comparison)
- $SF = OF$: operand1 is greater than or equal to operand2 (signed comparison)

Consider the following example where we compare two register values:

```
MOV AX, 5
MOV BX, 10
CMP AX, BX
```

In this example, the operation subtracts BX from AX without storing the result, only affecting the flags. Since AX (5) is less than BX (10):

- ZF is cleared (0)
- CF is set (1)
- SF is set (1)

The use of comparison results in the subsequent branching instructions such as JE (Jump if Equal), JNE (Jump if Not Equal), JG (Jump if Greater), JL (Jump if Less), which rely on these flags to determine the execution path.

TEST performs a bitwise AND operation between two operands and sets the flags accordingly, without storing the result. Its syntax is:

```
TEST operand1, operand2
```

This instruction is commonly employed to test specific bits within a register or a memory location. If any bit position of the result is non-zero, the Zero Flag (ZF) is cleared (0). If all bit positions are zero, the Zero Flag (ZF) is set (1).

Consider testing the state of specific bits:

```
MOV AX, 5 ; AX = 0000 0101b
TEST AX, 1 ; AND AX with 0000 0001b
```

In this case, the least significant bit (LSB) of AX is 1, so:

- ZF is cleared (0)

However, if testing a bit pattern that results in zero:

```
MOV AX, 4 ; AX = 0000 0100b
TEST AX, 1 ; AND AX with 0000 0001b
```

The result of TEST is 0, clearing the zero flag:

- ZF is set (1)

An example contributing to conditional execution could be:

```
MOV AX, 4
TEST AX, 1
JZ label ; Jump if Zero Flag set
‘‘;
code1
LABEL: code2
```

In this example, execution will jump to LABEL if the lowest bit of AX is 0 (indicating an even number), based on the Zero Flag from the TEST instruction.

Efficiently combining CMP and TEST instructions with appropriate branching instructions enhances control over program flow and lays the foundation for implementing complex conditional logic.

2.7 Branching Instructions: JMP, JE, JNE, JG, JL

Branching instructions in assembly language control the flow of execution by allowing jumps to different segments of the code based on conditioned or unconditioned criteria. This aids in constructing loops, conditional statements, and other control structures. In this section, we will explore various branching instructions including JMP, JE, JNE, JG, and JL, and how they alter the flow of execution in a program.

JMP (Jump):

The JMP instruction unconditionally transfers the execution to a specified address. This instruction does not consider any flags and is straightforward.

```
JMP target_label
```

Here, the execution jumps to the address labeled target_label.

JE (Jump if Equal):

The JE instruction transfers control to a specified address if the Zero Flag (ZF) is set. This typically means the two values compared earlier are equal.

```
cmp eax, ebx
JE equal_label
```

In this example, if eax is equal to ebx, the execution will jump to equal_label.

JNE (Jump if Not Equal):

The JNE instruction jumps to a given address if the Zero Flag (ZF) is clear, indicating that the comparison yielded non-equal results.

```
cmp eax, ebx
JNE not_equal_label
```

Here, if eax is not equal to ebx, execution jumps to not_equal_label.

JG (Jump if Greater):

The JG instruction checks if the destination operand is strictly greater than the source operand. It jumps if the Zero Flag (ZF) is clear and the Sign Flag (SF) equals the Overflow Flag (OF), indicating a greater-than condition in signed arithmetic.

```
cmp eax, ebx
JG greater_label
```

In this code, if eax is greater than ebx, it jumps to greater_label.

JL (Jump if Less):

The JL instruction performs a signed comparison. It jumps to the specified address if the Sign Flag (SF) is not equal to the Overflow Flag (OF), indicating a less-than condition for signed numbers.

```
cmp eax, ebx
JL less_label
```

Here, if eax is less than ebx, the control jumps to less_label.

Consider a practical example demonstrating some of these branching instructions:

```
section .text
    global _start

_start:
    mov eax, 10 ; EAX = 10
    mov ebx, 20 ; EBX = 20
    cmp eax, ebx ; Compare EAX and EBX
    JG greater_than ; Jump if EAX > EBX
    JL less_than ; Jump if EAX < EBX
    JE equal_to ; Jump if EAX == EBX

greater_than:
    ; Code for EAX > EBX
    JMP end_program

less_than:
    ; Code for EAX < EBX
    JMP end_program

equal_to:
    ; Code for EAX == EBX

end_program:
    ; Exit program
```

In this example, depending on the values of eax and ebx, the control jumps to the appropriate section of the code and executes the corresponding block. This illustrates the use of branching instructions to manage different execution paths based on comparisons. Structuring the control flow using these instructions leads to more dynamic and efficient programs.

These instructions serve as the foundation for implementing if-else conditions, loops, and other control structures in assembly language. Their mastery is essential for programming at the lower-level and understanding how high-level constructs are translated into assembly language operations.

2.8 Stack Operations: PUSH, POP

Stack operations in assembly language are essential for managing function calls, local variables, and temporary data storage within a program. The primary instructions for stack manipulation are PUSH and POP. These instructions interact with the stack, a Last-In-First-Out (LIFO) data structure which operates at a specific memory region defined by the stack pointer (SP) or extended stack pointer (ESP).

The PUSH instruction places data onto the top of the stack, while the POP instruction removes data from the top of the stack. To understand these operations precisely, let us delve into their mechanics and utilize examples to demonstrate their practical application.

PUSH Instruction

The PUSH instruction decrements the stack pointer register (ESP) by the size of the operand (typically 4 bytes for 32-bit or 8 bytes for 64-bit architectures) and then moves the operand to the memory location pointed to by ESP. The syntax for PUSH is as follows:

```
PUSH operand
```

For example, consider the following:

```
PUSH EAX
```

If the current ESP is 0x1000, after execution of PUSH EAX, the ESP will be decremented by 4 (assuming a 32-bit system) to 0x0FFC, and the value of EAX will be stored at this new stack address.

```
Before PUSH:
ESP = 0x1000
EAX = 0x12345678

After PUSH:
ESP = 0x0FFC
Memory[0x0FFC] = 0x12345678
```

POP Instruction

The POP instruction performs the inverse operation of PUSH. It reads the value at the memory location pointed to by ESP into the destination register or memory operand, and then increments ESP by the size of the operand. The syntax for POP is:

```
POP operand
```

For example, consider the stack state from the previous PUSH EAX example. If we now execute:

```
POP EBX
```

The value at the top of the stack (currently at address 0x0FFC) will be moved into the EBX register, and ESP will be incremented back to 0x1000:

```
Before POP:
ESP = 0x0FFC
Memory[0x0FFC] = 0x12345678

After POP:
ESP = 0x1000
EBX = 0x12345678
```

Usage in Function Calls

Stack operations are integral to function calls. When a function is called, the return address (the address to which the control will return after the function completes) is automatically PUSHed onto the stack by the CALL instruction. The RET instruction subsequently POPs this address to return control to the calling function.

For instance:

```
CALL MyFunction
...
MyFunction:
    ; Function body
    RET
```

The CALL instruction pushes the return address onto the stack before transferring control to MyFunction. Upon completion, the RET instruction pops this return address from the stack, allowing the program to continue execution from the point following the CALL instruction.

PUSH and POP can also save and restore register states to ensure that registers used within a function do not alter the values needed by the calling function. For example:

```
MyFunction:
    PUSH EBP ; Save base pointer
    MOV EBP, ESP ; Set base pointer to current stack pointer
    PUSH EAX ; Save EAX register
    ; Function body
    POP EAX ; Restore EAX register
    POP EBP ; Restore base pointer
    RET
```

In this example, PUSH instructions are used at the start of the function to save the current state of EBP and EAX. Before the function returns, POP instructions restore these saved values. This ensures that the calling function's context remains intact.

The proper use of PUSH and POP instructions is vital in maintaining a well-structured and bug-free assembly language program. By managing stack operations effectively, programmers can implement complex function calls, handle local variables, and preserve register states with precision.

2.9 String Manipulation Instructions

In assembly language, string manipulation is a crucial aspect of handling sequences of characters stored in contiguous memory locations. String operations help in performing tasks such as copying, comparing, searching, and moving substrings. This section will cover a variety of instructions tailored for efficient string manipulation, primarily found in Intel x86 assembly language. The key instructions include MOVSB/MOVSW/MOVSD, CMPSB/CMPSW/CMPSD, SCASB/SCASW/SCASD, and LODSB/LODSW/LODSD.

MOVSB, MOVSW, MOVSD: These instructions move data from the source string to the destination string. The suffix SB, SW, and SD refer to moving 8-bit bytes, 16-bit words, and 32-bit double words, respectively.

The general syntax for these instructions is as follows:

```
MOVSB ; Move byte from [ESI] to [EDI]
MOVSW ; Move word from [ESI] to [EDI]
MOVSD ; Move doubleword from [ESI] to [EDI]
```

Before executing these instructions, the source index (ESI) and destination index (EDI) must point to the source and destination memory locations, respectively. The direction flag (DF) controls the increment or decrement of these pointers. If DF is clear (CLD), pointers increment; if set (STD), pointers decrement.

Example Usage:

```
cld ; Clear direction flag to increment
mov esi, source ; Load source address into ESI
mov edi, dest ; Load destination address into EDI
mov ecx, length ; Load the length of the string into ECX
rep movsb ; Repeat MOVSB ECX times
```

In this example, CLD ensures that the pointers increment. The rep prefix repeats the MOVSB instruction ECX times.

CMPSB, CMPSW, CMPSD: These instructions compare the elements of two strings. The suffix SB, SW, and SD correspond to comparing 8-bit bytes, 16-bit words, and 32-bit double words, respectively. The comparison subtracts the data in ESI from that in EDI.

Syntax:

```
CMPSB ; Compare byte at [EDI] with byte at [ESI]
CMPSW ; Compare word at [EDI] with word at [ESI]
CMPSD ; Compare doubleword at [EDI] with doubleword at [ESI]
```

Example:

```
cld ; Clear direction flag to increment
mov esi, string1 ; Load address of first string
mov edi, string2 ; Load address of second string
mov ecx, length ; Load length of strings into ECX
repe cmpsb ; Repeat while equal and ECX != 0
jnz not_equal ; Jump if the strings are not equal
equal:
; Code to execute if strings are equal
not_equal:
; Code to execute if strings are not equal
```

In this example, repe continues the comparison as long as the elements are equal and ECX is not zero. The jnz instruction branches to the not_equal label if a mismatch is found.

SCASB, SCASW, SCASD: These instructions scan a string for a specific value. The suffix SB, SW, and SD denote scanning for 8-bit bytes, 16-bit words, and 32-bit double words, respectively.

Syntax:

```
SCASB ; Scan byte at [EDI] for AL
SCASW ; Scan word at [EDI] for AX
SCASD ; Scan doubleword at [EDI] for EAX
```

Example:

```
cld
mov edi, string ; Load string address into EDI
mov al, value ; Load byte to scan for into AL
mov ecx, length ; Load length of the string into ECX
repe scasb ; Repeat while equal and ECX != 0
jnz found ; Jump if the value is found
; Code to execute if value is not found
found:
; Code to execute if value is found
```

In this example, repe continues scanning the string until the value in AL is found or ECX is zero.

LODSB, LODSW, LODSD: These instructions load a value from the source string into the accumulator register. The suffix SB, SW, and SD refer to loading 8-bit bytes into AL, 16-bit words into AX, and 32-bit double words into EAX.

Syntax:

```
LODSB ; Load byte at [ESI] into AL
LODSW ; Load word at [ESI] into AX
LODSD ; Load doubleword at [ESI] into EAX
```

Example:

```
cld
mov esi, string ; Load string address into ESI
mov ecx, length ; Load length of the string into ECX
repeat_lods:
lodsb ; Load byte at [ESI] into AL and increment ESI
; Process the loaded byte in AL
loop repeat_lods; Decrement ECX and repeat
```

In this example, the LODSB instruction loads bytes from the string into the AL register one at a time, and each byte is processed in a loop until the full length of the string is processed.

The instructions and examples illustrated in this section highlight the efficiency and control provided by assembly language for handling string data. These fundamental string manipulation instructions are essential for tasks that require direct memory operations and performance optimization.

2.10 Introduction to Conditional Execution

In assembly language, conditional execution is a mechanism that allows the control flow of a program to be altered based on certain conditions. These conditions are typically the result of comparison or test instructions, such as CMP and TEST, which set certain flags in the processor's status register. Conditional execution is essential in programming, as it provides the means to implement decision-making processes, loop constructs, and other control structures crucial to complex algorithms.

Conditional execution in assembly language is achieved primarily through conditional jump instructions. These instructions cause the processor to continue execution from a different place in the code if specified conditions are met. The conditions are evaluated based on the status flags, including Zero Flag (ZF), Sign Flag (SF), Carry Flag (CF), Overflow Flag (OF), and Parity Flag (PF). Let's explore the usage of these flags in determining whether to alter the control flow using jump instructions.

Zero Flag (ZF):

The Zero Flag is set if the result of an arithmetic or logical operation is zero. It can be used to determine equality or whether a given operation yielded no results. For example,

CMP EAX, 0

When this operation is executed, if the value in the EAX register is zero, the Zero Flag will be set.

Sign Flag (SF):

The Sign Flag is set if the result of an operation is negative. This flag helps in deciding signed comparisons.

Carry Flag (CF):

The Carry Flag is set during arithmetic operations that produce a carry or borrow out of the most significant bit. It is useful for unsigned arithmetic comparisons.

Overflow Flag (OF):

The Overflow Flag is relevant in signed arithmetic operations and is set when the result of a signed operation is too large to be represented.

With the flags and their implications understood, the following table lists some common conditional jump instructions and their meanings:

- JE (Jump if Equal): Jumps if ZF is set.
- JNE (Jump if Not Equal): Jumps if ZF is not set.
- JG (Jump if Greater): Jumps if ZF is not set and SF equals OF.
- JL (Jump if Less): Jumps if SF does not equal OF.
- JGE (Jump if Greater or Equal): Jumps if SF equals OF.
- JLE (Jump if Less or Equal): Jumps if ZF is set or SF does not equal OF.
- JA (Jump if Above): Jumps if CF is not set and ZF is not set (unsigned greater).

- JB (Jump if Below): Jumps if CF is set (unsigned less).
- JAE (Jump if Above or Equal): Jumps if CF is not set.
- JBE (Jump if Below or Equal): Jumps if CF is set or ZF is set.

Each of these instructions allows branching based on the status of specific flags, leading to the implementation of various control structures. Below are examples demonstrating conditional execution in an assembly language program.

```
section .data
    num1 dd 10
    num2 dd 20
    result dd 0

section .text
    global _start

_start:
    ; Load the values into registers
    mov eax, [num1]
    mov ebx, [num2]

    ; Compare values
    cmp eax, ebx

    ; Conditional jump if eax < ebx
    jl less_than

    ; If not less, set result to 1
    mov dword [result], 1
    jmp end_program

less_than:
    ; If less, set result to -1
    mov dword [result], -1

end_program:
    ; Exit
    mov eax, 1
    int 0x80
```

In the above example, the CMP instruction compares the values in the EAX and EBX registers. If the value in EAX is less than the value in EBX, the JL instruction transfers control to the less_than label. Otherwise, the program continues to the next instruction, setting the result to 1.

This basic structure of conditional execution provides immense flexibility. For more complex decision-making, nested conditions and multiple conditional jumps can be used.

```
section .data
    a dd 15
```

```
    b dd 5

section .text
    global _start

_start:
    ; Load the values into registers
    mov eax, [a]
    mov ebx, [b]

    ; Check if a equals b
    cmp eax, ebx
    je equal

    ; Check if a is less than b
    jl less_than

    ; Otherwise, a is greater than b
greater_than:
    ; Code for a > b
    jmp end_comparison

equal:
    ; Code for a == b
    jmp end_comparison

less_than:
    ; Code for a < b

end_comparison:
    ; Exit
    mov eax, 1
    int 0x80
```

In this example, the program checks for equality first using JE. If EAX and EBX are not equal, it then checks if EAX is less than EBX using JL. If neither condition is met, it concludes that EAX must be greater than EBX and jumps to the greater_than label.

Understanding and implementing conditional execution in assembly language enhances the programmer's ability to write efficient and complex programs and is fundamental for advanced programming constructs.

2.11 Overview of Assembly Language Directives

Assembly language directives, also known as pseudo-operations or pseudo-ops, serve a vital role in guiding the assembler in processing the program. These directives do not correspond to machine instructions executed by the CPU but rather provide commands to the assembler to define data, allocate storage, or control the assembly process. Understanding and utilizing these directives proficiently can optimize the efficiency and readability of assembly language programs.

Common Assembly Directives

- DB, DW, DD, DQ, DT: These are data definition directives. DB (Define Byte) allocates memory and initializes it with byte values. DW (Define Word), DD (Define Doubleword), DQ (Define Quadword), and DT (Define Ten Bytes) serve similar purposes but for different data sizes.

```
myByte DB 0x1
myWord DW 0x1234
myDWord DD 0x12345678
myQWord DQ 0x123456789ABCDEF0
myTBytes DT 0x123456789ABCDEF01234
```

- EQU: The Equate directive assigns a constant value to a symbol. Once defined, this constant cannot be altered throughout the program. This is useful for defining constant values with descriptive names.

```
MAX_VALUE EQU 100
BUFFER_SIZE EQU 512
```

- $: The Dollar Sign is used to represent the current value of the location counter within the assembly process. It is often used in calculations to determine addresses and offsets.

```
current_address_value DW $ ; Holds the current memory address
```

- ORG: The Origin directive sets the starting address for program instructions or data storage. This is crucial in controlling where in memory the code or data is placed.

```
ORG 0x1000 ; start the code at address 1000h
```

- END: The End directive signifies the end of the assembly process. No code or data should follow this directive. It is mandatory in many assembly programs.

```
END ; end of the program
```

Data Allocation and Initialization

DB, DW, DD, DQ, and DT directives allow programmers to define variables that are essential for the program's functionality. By assigning memory to these variables beforehand, the programmer ensures efficient memory management and structured data organization within the assembly code.

DB example:

```
array_of_bytes DB 10, 20, 30, 40, 50
```

DW example:

```
array_of_words DW 1234h, 5678h, 9ABCh, DEF0h
```

Symbolic Constants

The EQU directive enhances code readability and maintainability by allowing the use of meaningful names instead of raw numerical values. This is particularly useful in scenarios where the same value is used multiple times throughout the code.

```
LIMIT EQU 100
MOV AX, LIMIT
ADD AX, LIMIT
```

Program Organization

The ORG directive allows for specific control over where code and data are placed in memory, which is particularly important in memory-mapped I/O or when interfacing with hardware directly.

```
ORG 0x2000
entry_point:
    MOV AX, 0 ; example instruction
```

End of Program

The END directive marks the termination point of the assembly language source code. It is crucial for the assembler to understand where the logical end of the program is, to avoid processing unintended code.

```
END entry_point
```

Assembly Time Instructions

Commands such as IF, ELSE, and ENDIF provide conditional assembly capabilities, enabling the inclusion or exclusion of parts of code based on specific conditions. This is particularly useful when writing code for multiple environments or configurations.

```
IF MAX_VALUE > 100
MOV AX, 100
ELSE
MOV AX, MAX_VALUE
ENDIF
```

INCLUDE directive allows the reuse of code by including external files into the main assembly file. This modular approach significantly enhances the maintainability of large assembly programs.

```
INCLUDE 'macro_file.asm'
```

Label definition is also a critical aspect, which can be achieved using symbolic names followed by a colon (:). Labels serve as markers for jump instructions, data definitions, and code structuring within the assembly file.

```
start:
    MOV AX, BX
    JMP end_program

end_program:
    MOV AX, 4C00h
    INT 21h
```

The strategic use of these directives ensures efficient program generation, improves code readability, and simplifies the processes of debugging and maintenance, contributing to professional-level assembly programming.

Chapter 3

Data Representation and Manipulation

This chapter explores various methods of data representation and manipulation, including binary, hexadecimal, and octal number systems. It explains signed and unsigned numbers, fixed-point and floating-point representations, and character encoding with ASCII and Unicode. Additionally, it covers bit manipulation techniques, endianness, constants and variables, data storage in memory, manipulation of data in registers, and advanced data representation techniques.

3.1 Introduction to Data Representation

Data representation is a fundamental concept in computer science and programming. It refers to the methods and structures used to encode, store, and manipulate information within a computer system. Understanding data representation is essential for writing efficient code and interacting directly with computer hardware.

In assembly language, the representation of data is critical due to the low-level nature of the language. Operations are performed directly on memory addresses and data locations, leveraging specific binary and hexadecimal formats. This section will cover the core concepts of data representation, setting the stage for deeper discussions later in the chapter.

At a basic level, all data in a computer is represented in binary format, consisting of bits (binary digits). A bit can hold a value of either 0 or 1. Bits are grouped to form larger units of data:

- **Byte**: A unit of 8 bits.
- **Word**: Typically consists of two bytes (16 bits), though the size can vary based on the system architecture.
- **Double Word**: Consists of four bytes (32 bits).
- **Quad Word**: Consists of eight bytes (64 bits).

These groupings allow for more meaningful data representation and manipulation.

Binary Numbers: In the binary system, values are represented using only the digits 0 and 1. Each position in a binary number represents a power of two, with the rightmost digit indicating 2^0, the next 2^1, and so on. For example, the binary number 1011 is calculated as follows:

$$1 \cdot 2^3 + 0 \cdot 2^2 + 1 \cdot 2^1 + 1 \cdot 2^0 = 8 + 0 + 2 + 1 = 11 \text{ (decimal)}$$

Binary representation is crucial in low-level programming since machine instructions and data are ultimately processed in binary form.

Hexadecimal Numbers: Hexadecimal (base-16) is often used in computing because it provides a more compact representation of binary values. A single hexadecimal digit represents four binary bits. The digits range from 0 to 9 and from A to F, where A represents 10 through F which represents 15. For example, the binary number 11011010 can be written as DA in hexadecimal.

Converting between binary and hexadecimal is straightforward:

Listing 3.1: Binary to Hexadecimal Conversion

```
Binary: 11011010
Group into 4-bit chunks: 1101 1010
Convert each chunk to hex: 1101 -> D 1010 -> A
Hexadecimal: 0xDA
```

Octal Numbers: Octal (base-8) is another representation used in computing, predominantly in older systems. Each octal digit represents three binary bits, with digits ranging from 0 to 7. For example, binary 110110 in octal would be 066.

Signed and Unsigned Numbers: Numbers in computers can be represented as either signed or unsigned. An unsigned number can represent only non-negative values, while a signed number can represent both positive and negative values. The most common method for representing signed numbers is two's complement. This method allows for straightforward binary arithmetic operations and facilitates error detection.

In unsigned representation:

Listing 3.2: Unsigned Binary Representation

```
Binary: 11111111
Decimal (unsigned): 127 + 63 + 31 + 15 + 7 + 3 + 1 = 255
```

In two's complement representation for signed numbers:

Listing 3.3: Signed Binary Representation

```
Binary: 11111111
Convert to two's complement: Flip all bits, and add 1 to the result.
Original: 11111111
Flipped: 00000000
Add 1: 00000001 (result = -1 in decimal, since most significant bit denotes sign)
```

ASCII and Unicode Character Encoding: Character encoding schemes like ASCII and Unicode are used to represent text in computers. ASCII uses 7 bits to represent characters, enabling 128 unique values. Unicode extends this to account for many more characters across different languages and symbol sets by using varying bit lengths (typically 16 bits).

Listing 3.4: ASCII Character Encoding Example

```
Character: 'A'
ASCII (binary): 01000001
```

Understanding these basic principles of data representation forms a strong foundation upon which more advanced topics in assembly language and computer architecture can be built. These representations are the bridge between high-level programming abstractions and the low-level operations performed by a computer's hardware.

3.2 Binary Number System

The binary number system is fundamental to computer systems and digital electronics. Binary numbers, composed of only two digits (0 and

1), are used to represent all types of data within a computer. Understanding the binary number system is essential for working with low-level programming languages, such as assembly language, and for comprehending how computers represent and manipulate data.

Binary Digits and Bits: A binary digit, or bit, is the most basic unit of data in computing and can hold one of two possible values: 0 or 1. Larger binary numbers are formed by combining multiple bits. For example, in an 8-bit binary number, the leftmost bit is the most significant bit (MSB) and the rightmost bit is the least significant bit (LSB).

Binary to Decimal Conversion: Converting a binary number to its decimal equivalent involves multiplying each bit by 2 raised to the power of its position index (starting from 0 for the LSB) and summing the results. For example, consider the binary number 1011:

Listing 3.5: ASCII Character Encoding Example

```
Binary: 1 0 1 1
Position: 3 2 1 0
```

The calculation is:

$$(1 \cdot 2^3) + (0 \cdot 2^2) + (1 \cdot 2^1) + (1 \cdot 2^0) = 8 + 0 + 2 + 1 = 11$$

Thus, 1011 in binary is 11 in decimal.

Decimal to Binary Conversion: Converting a decimal number to binary can be achieved using repeated division by 2. The remainder of each division gives the binary digits from the LSB to the MSB. For example, to convert decimal 13 to binary:

Listing 3.6: ASCII Character Encoding Example

```
13 / 2 = 6, remainder 1 (LSB)
 6 / 2 = 3, remainder 0
 3 / 2 = 1, remainder 1
 1 / 2 = 0, remainder 1 (MSB)
```

Reading the remainders from bottom to top, we get 1101.

Binary Arithmetic: Binary addition, subtraction, multiplication, and division follow the same principles as their decimal counterparts but with simpler rules involving just two digits.

Binary Addition:

Listing 3.7: ASCII Character Encoding Example

```
  1010
```

```
+ 0111
------
=10001
```

Addition is performed bit by bit, with carrying when the sum exceeds 1.

Binary Subtraction: Subtraction in binary can be done using the method of complements. For example, to subtract 0111 from 1010, we find the two's complement of 0111 and add it to 1010.

Representing Larger Numbers: To represent larger numbers, more bits are required. Common lengths are 8-bit (byte), 16-bit (word), 32-bit (double word), and 64-bit (quad word). The range of values that can be represented is determined by the number of bits:

For an unsigned 8-bit number:

$$0 \leq \text{value} \leq 2^8 - 1 \quad (0 \leq \text{value} \leq 255)$$

For a signed 8-bit number, using two's complement representation:

$$-2^7 \leq \text{value} \leq 2^7 - 1 \quad (-128 \leq \text{value} \leq 127)$$

Two's Complement Representation: Two's complement is a method of representing signed numbers in binary. The MSB indicates the sign of the number (0 for positive, 1 for negative). To obtain the two's complement of a binary number:

1. Invert all the bits (change 0 to 1 and 1 to 0). 2. Add 1 to the resulting number.

For example, the two's complement of 000001 (1 in decimal) is:

Listing 3.8: ASCII Character Encoding Example

```
000001 -> 111110 (Inverting all bits)
111110 + 1 -> 111111
```

111111 in binary represents -1 in two's complement notation.

Binary Coding for Characters and Data: The binary system is also used to encode characters (e.g., ASCII encoding) and other types of data efficiently, utilizing predefined bit patterns for representation.

Understanding the binary number system's principles is crucial for recognizing how data is stored, transmitted, and manipulated at the lowest levels of computer architecture and assembly language programming.

3.3 Hexadecimal and Octal Number Systems

Hexadecimal and octal number systems are integral to the practice of assembly language programming due to their efficiency in representing binary data and their ubiquitous use in various computing systems. Understanding these number systems is crucial for proficiently working with lower-level data representations and performing bitwise operations.

Hexadecimal Number System

The hexadecimal number system, also known as base-16, uses sixteen symbols to represent values. These symbols range from 0 to 9 and from A to F, where A stands for 10, B for 11, and so on up to F representing 15. The principal advantage of the hexadecimal system is its compact representation of binary values, which makes it easier for humans to read and write, especially when dealing with large binary numbers.

To convert a binary number into a hexadecimal number, divide the binary number into groups of four bits, starting from the right (the least significant bit). Each group of four bits, also known as a nibble, is then converted to its corresponding hexadecimal digit.

For example, consider the binary number 101110101011:

Listing 3.9: ASCII Character Encoding Example

```
Binary: 1011 1010 1011
```

To convert this to hexadecimal, we group the binary digits as shown, and then each group is translated into its hexadecimal equivalent:

Listing 3.10: ASCII Character Encoding Example

```
1011 -> B
1010 -> A
1011 -> B
```

Thus, the hexadecimal representation is

Listing 3.11: ASCII Character Encoding Example

```
0xBAB
```

where the prefix '0x' denotes that the number is offered in hexadecimal format.

Octal Number System

The octal number system, or base-8, uses eight symbols, from 0 to 7. It is a more compact form of binary representation but less so compared to hexadecimal. The octal number system is particularly useful in computing and digital electronics because it can express binary numbers succinctly and aligns conveniently with the 3-bit representation, commonly used in digital systems.

To convert binary numbers to octal, divide the binary number into groups of three bits:

Listing 3.12: ASCII Character Encoding Example

```
Binary: 101110101011
```

Group the binary digits into sections of three bits:

Listing 3.13: ASCII Character Encoding Example

```
101 110 101 011
```

Each 3-bit group corresponds to its octal digit:

Listing 3.14: ASCII Character Encoding Example

```
101 -> 5
110 -> 6
101 -> 5
011 -> 3
```

Therefore, the octal representation is

Listing 3.15: ASCII Character Encoding Example

```
06553
```

Here, the leading zero indicates an octal number.

Conversions Between Number Systems

Conversion between hexadecimal and binary is straightforward due to the power-of-two relationship. Similarly, converting between binary and octal is simple due to smaller grouping. However, a direct conversion between hexadecimal and octal typically proceeds through binary as the intermediate stage.

For instance, to convert hexadecimal 0xBAB to octal, we first convert hexadecimal to binary:

Listing 3.16: ASCII Character Encoding Example

```
B (hex) -> 1011 (binary)
A (hex) -> 1010 (binary)
B (hex) -> 1011 (binary)
```

Then group the resulting binary number into sets of three for octal conversion:

Listing 3.17: ASCII Character Encoding Example

```
1011 1010 1011 -> 010 111 010 101 1 -> 010 111 010 101 -> 2 7 2 5
```

Therefore, the octal representation is

Listing 3.18: ASCII Character Encoding Example

```
02725
```

Usage in Assembly Language

Hexadecimal representation is prevalent in assembly language for representing addresses and constants. For instance, an assembly instruction may use hexadecimal addresses to specify memory location:

Listing 3.19: ASCII Character Encoding Example

```
MOV AX, [0x1A3F]
ADD AX, 0x0045
```

In such assembly instructions, $0x1A3F$ and $0x0045$ are hexadecimal constants. These compact forms simplify the readability and management of large bitwise data manipulations and address calculations.

Conversely, octal representation primarily appears in contexts where binary3-bit groupings are essential, such as permissions in Unix-like file systems or specific machine-level encodings. However, its use is generally less frequent compared to hexadecimal.

Both the hexadecimal and octal number systems serve indispensable roles in assembly programming and digital electronics, providing human-readable and concise representations for otherwise cumbersome binary numbers. This section delves deeply into these representations, underscoring their practical utility and the pivotal knowledge they contribute to proficient assembly language programming.

3.4 Signed and Unsigned Numbers

In assembly language and computer science at large, the concept of signed and unsigned numbers forms a foundational aspect of data representation. Understanding the distinction between these two categories is crucial for effectively manipulating numerical data at the hardware level.

Unsigned integers are used to represent only non-negative numbers, which extends from 0 up to $2^n - 1$ for n-bit integers. For example, an unsigned 8-bit integer can represent values from 0 to 255:

```
0, 1, 2, ..., 254, 255
```

In contrast, signed integers are designed to represent both positive and negative numbers. Using two's complement representation, a widely adopted scheme, an n-bit signed integer ranges from $-2^{(n-1)}$ to $2^{(n-1)} - 1$. For instance, an 8-bit signed integer ranges from -128 to 127:

```
-128, -127, ..., -1, 0, 1, ..., 126, 127
```

Unsigned Numbers

Unsigned numbers only contain positive values including zero. As such, there is no mechanism to indicate the sign of the number. This allows unsigned numbers to utilize all available bit patterns to represent a larger range of positive values. For instance, consider the maximum value for an unsigned 8-bit integer:

$$2^8 - 1 = 255$$

Let us examine an example of handling unsigned numbers in assembly language. Suppose we want to move the value 250 into a register in x86 assembly:

Listing 3.20: ASCII Character Encoding Example

```
MOV AL, 250 ; Move unsigned integer 250 into register AL
```

Signed Numbers and Two's Complement Representation

Two's complement is the predominant method for representing signed integers in modern computing systems. It takes advantage of the most significant bit (MSB) to denote the sign of the number: 0 for positive and 1 for negative. For example, in an 8-bit signed integer, the bit patterns are divided as follows:

- **Positive Numbers (0 to 127)**: The MSB is 0, e.g., 00000001 represents 1.
- **Negative Numbers (-1 to -128)**: The MSB is 1, e.g., 11111111 represents -1.

The two's complement of a number is calculated by inverting all the bits and adding 1 to the least significant bit (LSB). Consider the conversion of +18 and -18 in 8-bit representation:

- **+18**: The binary representation of 18 is 00010010.
- **-18**: First, invert all bits of 00010010 to get 11101101, then add 1 to obtain 11101110.

To demonstrate a manipulation of signed numbers, consider the following x86 assembly code that converts positive numbers to negative using the two's complement method:

Listing 3.21: ASCII Character Encoding Example

```
MOV AL, 18 ; Move the value 18 into the AL register
NEG AL ; Negate to get two's complement representation (-18)
```

The above code negates the number in the register AL, changing it from $+18$ to -18.

Overflows in Signed and Unsigned Arithmetic

An important concept when working with signed and unsigned numbers is detecting and handling overflows:

- **Unsigned Overflow**: This occurs when the result of an operation exceeds the maximum value representable by an unsigned integer. For example, adding 1 to 255 in an 8-bit system results in wrapping around to 0.

  Listing 3.22: ASCII Character Encoding Example

  ```
  MOV AL, 255 ; Load the maximum unsigned value into AL
  ADD AL, 1 ; AL now contains 0 due to overflow
  ```

- **Signed Overflow**: This occurs when the result falls outside the representable range of signed integers. For example, adding 1 to 127 in an 8-bit signed system results in -128 due to overflow.

  Listing 3.23: ASCII Character Encoding Example

  ```
  MOV AL, 127 ; Load the maximum signed value into AL
  ADD AL, 1 ; AL now contains -128 due to signed overflow
  ```

Detecting overflow is essential for ensuring data integrity. In x86 assembly, the Overflow Flag (OF) and Carry Flag (CF) are utilized for this purpose:

- **OF**: Set if there is a signed overflow.
- **CF**: Set if there is an unsigned overflow.

Listing 3.24: ASCII Character Encoding Example

```
ADD AL, BL ; Add values in AL and BL
JO overflow ; Jump to overflow label if Overflow Flag is set
JC carry ; Jump to carry label if Carry Flag is set
```

Understanding and correctly handling signed and unsigned integers in assembly language ensures robust and predictable manipulation of numerical data, critical for effective low-level programming.

3.5 Fixed-Point and Floating-Point Representation

Fixed-point and floating-point representations are essential for handling numerical values of varying magnitudes and precision in assembly language programming. These representations enable us to perform arithmetic operations efficiently and accurately, considering hardware constraints and application requirements.

Fixed-Point Representation

Fixed-point representation is a method for representing real numbers where a fixed number of bits is allocated for the integer part and a fixed number for the fractional part. This representation is particularly useful in applications requiring predictable and consistent precision, such as embedded systems, digital signal processing, and real-time control systems.

The general format of a fixed-point number can be expressed as $Qm.n$, where m represents the number of bits for the integer part, and n represents the number of bits for the fractional part. For example, $Q16.16$ means that we have 16 bits for the integer part and 16 bits for the fractional part.

The binary representation of a fixed-point number is an extension of the integer binary system. For example, consider the fixed-point number 6.25 in $Q4.4$ format:

Listing 3.25: ASCII Character Encoding Example

```
Integer Part Fractional Part
 0110 0100
```

To calculate the binary representation:

1. Convert the integer part (6) to binary:

Listing 3.26: ASCII Character Encoding Example

```
6 -> 0110
```

2. Convert the fractional part (0.25) to binary by repeated multiplication by 2:

Listing 3.27: ASCII Character Encoding Example

```
0.25 * 2 = 0.5 (binary digit 0)
0.5 * 2 = 1.0 (binary digit 1)
```

Thus, 0.25 in binary is 01.

Combining the parts, the fixed-point binary representation of 6.25 in $Q4.4$ format is 01100100.

Operational algorithms for fixed-point arithmetic, such as addition, subtraction, multiplication, and division, follow the same principles as those for integer arithmetic, with the understanding that the fractional precision must be preserved and managed appropriately.

Floating-Point Representation

Floating-point representation leverages a format resembling scientific notation to represent real numbers, allowing a vast range of values with varying precision. This format is standardized by the IEEE 754 specification, which defines different precision levels, including single-precision (32-bit) and double-precision (64-bit).

A floating-point number is typically represented in the form:

$$(-1)^s \times (1 + f) \times 2^{(e-b)}$$

Where: - s is the sign bit (0 for positive, 1 for negative) - f is the fractional part (mantissa) - e is the exponent - b is the bias, which normalizes the exponent based on the bit width

For IEEE 754 single-precision representation:

- **Sign bit:** 1 bit
- **Exponent:** 8 bits (bias = 127)
- **Mantissa:** 23 bits

For example, consider the floating-point representation of the decimal number -5.75 in IEEE 754 single-precision:

- The sign bit s is 1 because the number is negative.
- Convert 5.75 to binary: 101.11
- Normalize the binary number to scientific notation: 1.0111×2^2
- The exponent $e = 2$, and adding the bias (127) gives 129.
- The mantissa f is 01110000000000000000000 (23 bits for the fractional part).

Thus, in IEEE 754 single-precision, -5.75 is represented as:

Listing 3.28: ASCII Character Encoding Example

```
Sign bit: 1
Exponent: 10000001
Mantissa: 01110000000000000000000
```

In binary, this is:

Listing 3.29: ASCII Character Encoding Example

```
11000000101110000000000000000000
```

Floating-point arithmetic handles a much wider range and precision of numbers compared to fixed-point but at the cost of more complex and computationally expensive operations. Special values such as zero, infinity, and NaN (Not a Number) are also accommodated in the IEEE 754 standard. This flexibility is crucial in scientific computing, graphics, financial calculations, and any domain requiring large dynamic ranges with precise calculations.

3.6 ASCII and Unicode Character Encoding

Character encoding is an integral part of computer science, enabling the representation of textual data in a format that machines can comprehend and process. Two widely used character encoding standards are ASCII and Unicode.

ASCII (American Standard Code for Information Interchange):

ASCII is a character encoding standard that uses a 7-bit binary number to represent text symbols. It encodes 128 unique characters, including control characters (non-printable) and printable characters. The range of ASCII characters extends from 0 to 127.

The first 32 ASCII codes (0-31) are control characters, which are used for text control in communications (e.g., NULL, BEL, ESC). The printable ASCII characters start from decimal 32 (space) to decimal 126, including common punctuation marks, digits, uppercase and lowercase English letters.

Here is a Python program that demonstrates printing ASCII values alongside their character representations:

Listing 3.30: ASCII Character Encoding Example

```
# Python program to print ASCII values with their characters
for i in range(128):
    print(f"{i}: {chr(i)}")
```

When executed, the output is:

```
0:
1:
2:
3:
4:
5:
6:
7:
8:
9:
...
65: A
66: B
67: C
...
97: a
98: b
99: c
...
126: ~
```

Unicode:

As computer applications and the internet grew globally, the need for a more comprehensive character encoding system became evident. Unicode was developed to address this requirement, supporting a vast array of characters from various languages and symbol sets used worldwide.

Unicode uses different encoding forms, such as UTF-8, UTF-16, and UTF-32, each having its characteristics:

- **UTF-8:** This variable-width encoding uses one to four bytes and is backward-compatible with ASCII. It is efficient for encoding English text because the first 128 characters (0-127) map directly to ASCII, using a single byte.
- **UTF-16:** This encoding uses one or two 16-bit code units. Characters are encoded using either two bytes (for the Basic Multilingual Plane) or four bytes (for supplementary characters).
- **UTF-32:** This fixed-width encoding uses 4 bytes for each character, offering simplicity at the cost of higher storage requirements.

The following Python program demonstrates encoding and decoding using UTF-8:

Listing 3.31: ASCII Character Encoding Example

```
# Python program to demonstrate UTF-8 encoding and decoding
text = "Hello, Unicode "
# Encoding the string into bytes
encoded_text = text.encode('utf-8')
print(f"Encoded Text: {encoded_text}")
# Decoding the bytes back into string
decoded_text = encoded_text.decode('utf-8')
print(f"Decoded Text: {decoded_text}")
```

The program output is:

```
Encoded Text: b'Hello, Unicode \xf0\x9f\x8c\x8d'
Decoded Text: Hello, Unicode
```

For encoding complex scripts and symbols, Unicode provides a unified framework. Implementations can efficiently process and handle multilingual text, significantly enhancing both compatibility and communication on a global scale. The versatility and inclusivity of Unicode make it the preferred choice for modern applications.

Understanding ASCII and Unicode is essential for data processing and interoperability between systems, programmers, and end-users. Strengthening this knowledge helps in developing robust software that interacts correctly with varied character representations.

3.7 Bit Manipulation and Masking Techniques

Bit manipulation is an essential skill in assembly language programming, providing powerful methods for efficient data handling and processing. Bit operations allow you to directly interact with the individual bits that comprise the data, which can lead to more efficient and concise code. This section delves into the techniques that manipulate data at the bit level, focusing on common operations such as AND, OR, XOR, NOT, shifting, and masking.

Basic Bitwise Operations

Assembly language provides several instructions to perform bitwise operations. These include AND (AND), OR (OR), XOR (XOR), and NOT (NOT). Each of these operations is fundamental to bit manipulation techniques.

- **AND (AND)**: This operation performs a logical AND between corresponding bits of two operands. The result is 1 only if both bits are 1, otherwise, it is 0.

  Listing 3.32: ASCII Character Encoding Example

  ```
  ; Example: AND operation
  MOV AL, 0b11001100 ; AL = 11001100
  AND AL, 0b10101010 ; AL = AL AND 10101010
  ; Resulting AL = 10001000
  ```

  ; Output: AL = 10001000

- **OR (OR)**: This operation performs a logical OR between corresponding bits of two operands. The result is 1 if at least one of the bits is 1, otherwise, it is 0.

  Listing 3.33: ASCII Character Encoding Example

  ```
  ; Example: OR operation
  MOV AL, 0b11001100 ; AL = 11001100
  OR AL, 0b10101010 ; AL = AL OR 10101010
  ; Resulting AL = 11101110
  ```

  ; Output: AL = 11101110

- **XOR (XOR)**: This operation performs a logical exclusive OR between corresponding bits of two operands. The result is 1 only if the bits are different, otherwise, it is 0.

  Listing 3.34: ASCII Character Encoding Example

  ```
  ; Example: XOR operation
  MOV AL, 0b11001100 ; AL = 11001100
  XOR AL, 0b10101010 ; AL = AL XOR 10101010
  ; Resulting AL = 01100110
  ```

; Output: AL = 01100110

- **NOT (NOT)**: This operation performs a logical NOT on a single operand, inverting all the bits. The result of NOTing a bit is 1 if the bit is 0, and 0 if the bit is 1.

Listing 3.35: ASCII Character Encoding Example

```
; Example: NOT operation
MOV AL, 0b11001100 ; AL = 11001100
NOT AL ; AL = NOT 11001100
; Resulting AL = 00110011
```

; Output: AL = 00110011

Bit Shifting Operations

Shifting operations are used to move bits to the left or the right within a binary number. These operations include Logical Shift Left (SHL), Logical Shift Right (SHR), Arithmetic Shift Right (SAR), and Rotate operations.

- **Logical Shift Left (SHL)**: Shifts the bits of the operand to the left, filling the rightmost bits with zeros. Each shift left by one position is equivalent to multiplying the number by 2.

Listing 3.36: ASCII Character Encoding Example

```
; Example: SHL operation
MOV AL, 0b11001100 ; AL = 11001100
SHL AL, 1 ; AL = AL << 1
; Resulting AL = 10011000
```

; Output: AL = 10011000

- **Logical Shift Right (SHR)**: Shifts the bits of the operand to the right, filling the leftmost bits with zeros. Each shift right by one position is equivalent to dividing the number by 2.

Listing 3.37: ASCII Character Encoding Example

```
; Example: SHR operation
MOV AL, 0b11001100 ; AL = 11001100
SHR AL, 1 ; AL = AL >> 1
; Resulting AL = 01100110
```

; Output: AL = 01100110

- **Arithmetic Shift Right (SAR)**: Similar to a logical shift right, but it preserves the sign bit (the leftmost bit for signed numbers). This is useful for signed division operations.

Listing 3.38: ASCII Character Encoding Example

```
; Example: SAR operation
MOV AL, 0b11001100 ; AL = 11001100
SAR AL, 1 ; AL = Arithmetic right shift by 1
; Resulting AL = 11100110
```

; Output: AL = 11100110

Bit Masking Techniques

Bit masking is the process of using bitwise operations to isolate, set, or clear specific bits within a binary number. This is often done by creating a mask—a binary number that determines which bits to manipulate. Common masking techniques include isolating bits, setting bits, and clearing bits.

- **Isolating Bits**: To isolate certain bits, you can use the AND operation with a mask that has 1s in the bit positions to be isolated and 0s elsewhere.

Listing 3.39: ASCII Character Encoding Example

```
; Example: Isolating bits
MOV AL, 0b11001100 ; AL = 11001100
AND AL, 0b00001111 ; Isolate the lower 4 bits
; Resulting AL = 00001100
```

; Output: AL = 00001100

- **Setting Bits**: To set certain bits to 1, use the OR operation with a mask that has 1s in the bit positions to be set.

Listing 3.40: ASCII Character Encoding Example

```
; Example: Setting bits
MOV AL, 0b11001100 ; AL = 11001100
OR AL, 0b00001111 ; Set the lower 4 bits to 1
; Resulting AL = 11001111
```

; Output: AL = 11001111

- **Clearing Bits**: To clear certain bits (set them to 0), use the AND operation with a mask that has 0s in the bit positions to be cleared and 1s elsewhere.

Listing 3.41: ASCII Character Encoding Example

```
; Example: Clearing bits
MOV AL, 0b11001100 ; AL = 11001100
AND AL, 0b11110000 ; Clear the lower 4 bits
; Resulting AL = 11000000
```

; Output: AL = 11000000

- **Toggling Bits**: To toggle certain bits (invert their values), use the XOR operation with a mask that has 1s in the bit positions to be toggled.

Listing 3.42: ASCII Character Encoding Example

```
; Example: Toggling bits
MOV AL, 0b11001100 ; AL = 11001100
XOR AL, 0b00001111 ; Toggle the lower 4 bits
; Resulting AL = 11000011
```

; Output: AL = 11000011

Bit manipulation through masking can optimize memory usage and processing speed, often crucial in low-level programming where performance is paramount. These techniques allow precise control over the bits, enabling complex operations with relatively simple instructions. Mastery of these bitwise operations and masking techniques is fundamental for anyone seeking to achieve proficiency in assembly language programming.

3.8 Endianness: Big Endian vs. Little Endian

Endianness refers to the order in which bytes are arranged within a larger data word when stored in memory. It is an important concept in computer architecture and data manipulation. The two primary types of endianness are **Big Endian** and **Little Endian**. Understanding these formats is crucial for tasks involving low-level data processing, network programming, and interoperability between different computing systems.

Big Endian architecture stores the most significant byte (MSB) at the smallest memory address. For example, when storing the 32-bit hexadecimal number $0x12345678$, the byte layout in Big Endian format would be as follows:

Listing 3.43: ASCII Character Encoding Example

```
Address Value
--------------------
0x00 0x12
0x01 0x34
0x02 0x56
0x03 0x78
```

In **Little Endian** architecture, the least significant byte (LSB) is stored at the smallest memory address. The same 32-bit number $0x12345678$ would be stored in Little Endian format as:

Listing 3.44: ASCII Character Encoding Example

```
Address Value
--------------------
0x00 0x78
0x01 0x56
0x02 0x34
0x03 0x12
```

Consider the hexadecimal number $0xAABBCCDD$. The stored representation of this number in both Big Endian and Little Endian systems is shown in the respective memory layouts:

Listing 3.45: ASCII Character Encoding Example

```
xxxxxxxxxx \= xxxxxxxxxxxx \= xxxxxxxxxxx \kill
```

Big Endian:

Listing 3.46: ASCII Character Encoding Example

```
\texttt{Address} \= \texttt{Value} \\
\texttt{0x00} \> \texttt{0xAA} \\
\texttt{0x01} \> \texttt{0xBB} \\
\texttt{0x02} \> \texttt{0xCC} \\
\texttt{0x03} \> \texttt{0xDD}
```

Little Endian:

Listing 3.47: ASCII Character Encoding Example

```
\texttt{Address} \= \texttt{Value} \\
\texttt{0x00} \> \texttt{0xDD} \\
\texttt{0x01} \> \texttt{0xCC} \\
\texttt{0x02} \> \texttt{0xBB} \\
\texttt{0x03} \> \texttt{0xAA}
```

Endianess can have a profound effect when systems with different endian formats communicate with each other, especially in network protocols and data file formats. For instance, the Internet protocol suite (TCP/IP) defines network byte order to be Big Endian, thus requiring systems to convert their native data representation to the network order for transmission and revert upon reception.

To further understand how endianess affects computation, consider a scenario involving union data structures in C, which maps a larger data type, such as int32, to an array of bytes.

Listing 3.48: ASCII Character Encoding Example

```
#include <stdio.h>

union {
    int32_t integer;
    uint8_t bytes[4];
} data;

data.integer = 0x12345678;

printf("Big Endian representation: %x %x %x %x\n",
       data.bytes[0], data.bytes[1], data.bytes[2], data.bytes[3]);
```

When the above code is executed on a Big Endian system, the output in the FittedVerbatim environment would be:

```
Big Endian representation: 12 34 56 78
```

On a Little Endian system, the output would appear as:

```
Little Endian representation: 78 56 34 12
```

Both the compiler and the underlying hardware architecture influence how the union is represented, shedding light on the practical implications of different endian formats.

In processor architectures, the difference between Big and Little Endian manifests during arithmetic and logical operations, data serialization, and memory addressing. For embedded systems and low-level programming, control over endianness can be critical. Many modern processors, like ARM, support a configurable endianness mode, allowing software to manipulate endian formats dynamically as needed.

Theoretical concepts can be explored further by examining how endianness influences algorithm design. For example, byte-swapping algorithms convert data between different endian formats. An illustrative byte-swapping algorithm follows:

This function shifts and masks each byte of the input value to rearrange the bytes from Big Endian to Little Endian or vice versa. Its utility becomes apparent in scenarios demanding compatibility across systems

```
Functionbyte_swap32(value: uint32_t) return uint32_t
        Input: A 32-bit unsigned integer value
  Output: The 32-bit unsigned integer with byte order reversed
result = ((value » 24) & 0x000000FF) | ((value « 8) &
  0x00FF0000) | ((value » 8) & 0x0000FF00) | ((value « 24) &
  0xFF000000) ;
return result
```

with differing native endian formats.

Understanding endianess is pivotal for software interoperability, understanding protocol specifications, and developing cross-platform applications. This section has illustrated how varying byte orders impact data representation and processing at a low level, reinforcing the importance of endianness awareness in computing disciplines.

3.9 Working with Constants and Variables

In assembly language programming, a thorough understanding of constants and variables is essential for effective data manipulation and memory management. Constants and variables represent fixed and mutable data, respectively, and serve as fundamental elements in instruction processing and program execution.

Constants are immutable values that do not change during program execution. They provide an efficient way to represent fixed data, such as mathematical constants, predefined values, or configuration parameters.

- **Syntax for Constants:** Constants can be defined using the EQU directive, which assigns a symbolic name to a value. The format is:

  Listing 3.49: ASCII Character Encoding Example

  ```
  CONSTANT_NAME EQU value
  ```

- **Example:**

  Listing 3.50: ASCII Character Encoding Example

  ```
  PI EQU 3.14159
  ```

```
MAX_SIZE EQU 1024
```

Constants can also be defined directly in the code using their numeric values, such as:

- Binary: Represented by prefixing the value with 0b or using the suffix B.

Listing 3.51: ASCII Character Encoding Example

```
0b1010 ; Binary representation for decimal 10
1010B ; Binary representation for decimal 10
```

- Hexadecimal: Prefixed with 0x or suffixed with H.

Listing 3.52: ASCII Character Encoding Example

```
0xA ; Hexadecimal representation for decimal 10
0AH ; Hexadecimal representation for decimal 10
```

- Octal: Represented by leading zeros or using the suffix Q.

Listing 3.53: ASCII Character Encoding Example

```
012 ; Octal representation for decimal 10
12Q ; Octal representation for decimal 10
```

Constants enhance code readability and maintainability by providing meaningful names to fixed values, thus making the logic clearer and reducing errors.

Variables, on the other hand, are storage locations in memory that hold data which can be modified during program execution. They are essential for dynamic data manipulation and facilitate operations on data sets.

Assembly language requires explicit declaration and allocation of variables, which can be done using the DB (Define Byte), DW (Define Word), and DD (Define Double word) directives. These directives allocate memory space for variables and optionally initialize them.

Declaring Variables:

- **Byte Variables:** Use the DB directive to allocate space for byte-sized variables.

Listing 3.54: ASCII Character Encoding Example

```
var1 DB 0 ; Declares var1 and initializes it to 0
var2 DB 255 ; Declares var2 and initializes it to 255
```

- **Word Variables:** Use the DW directive for word-sized variables.

  Listing 3.55: ASCII Character Encoding Example

  ```
  var3 DW 1024 ; Declares var3 and initializes it to 1024
  var4 DW 65535 ; Declares var4 and initializes it to 65535
  ```

- **Double Word Variables:** Use the DD directive for double word-sized variables.

  Listing 3.56: ASCII Character Encoding Example

  ```
  var5 DD 123456 ; Declares var5 and initializes it to 123456
  var6 DD 4294967295 ; Declares var6 and initializes it to 4294967295
  ```

Variable names should be descriptive and follow naming conventions to ensure code clarity and maintainability. Additionally, variables can be grouped in sequential memory locations, which allows for more complex data structures like arrays to be implemented.

Example of Declaring an Array:

Listing 3.57: ASCII Character Encoding Example

```
array DB 1, 2, 3, 4, 5 ; Declares a byte array initialized to 1, 2, 3, 4, 5
```

Manipulating the values stored in variables typically involves instructions that read from and write to these memory locations. Common assembly instructions for working with variables include MOV, ADD, SUB, and INC.

Loading and Storing Data in Variables:

- **Loading Data:**

  Listing 3.58: ASCII Character Encoding Example

  ```
  MOV AX, var3 ; Loads the value of var3 into register AX
  ```

- **Storing Data:**

  Listing 3.59: ASCII Character Encoding Example

  ```
  MOV var1, BL ; Stores the value of register BL into var1
  ```

In addition to simple variable operations, assembly language allows for more complex data manipulation techniques, such as working with pointers and indirect addressing. These techniques enable efficient manipulation of large data sets and dynamic data structures.

Using Pointers with Variables: Pointers store the memory address of variables rather than the variable's value itself. Pointers enable indirect addressing where the operand specifies the address of the data rather than the data itself. Indirect addressing is useful for accessing array elements or dynamically allocated memory.

Example of Pointer Usage:

Listing 3.60: ASCII Character Encoding Example

```
MOV SI, OFFSET array ; Load the offset address of array into SI
MOV AL, [SI+2] ; Access the third element of the array
```

Dynamic Memory Allocation: While assembly language does not inherently support high-level dynamic memory allocation functions like malloc in C, dynamic memory management can be achieved using specific memory management techniques provided by the operating system or custom allocation algorithms. Managing the heap memory efficiently is critical for applications that require dynamic data structures.

Understanding the distinction between constants and variables and knowing how to declare, manipulate, and efficiently use them in assembly language forms a vital foundation for more advanced programming concepts and optimizations. This knowledge directly impacts how programs interact with the processor and memory, influencing both performance and resource utilization.

3.10 Data Storage in Memory

Understanding how data is stored in memory is critical for efficient programming and effective use of assembly language. Memory in a computer system is organized as a sequence of bytes, each byte comprising 8 bits. These bytes are addressed sequentially, providing a means to store and retrieve data efficiently.

Byte Addressing: Computer memory is typically byte-addressable. This means that each byte in memory has a unique address. If a system has a 32-bit address bus, it can address 2^{32} bytes of memory individually, which equates to 4 GB of memory. The smallest addressable unit in such a memory system is a byte, but data types often span multiple bytes.

Memory Cells and Data Types: Memory cells are the fundamental units of storage. Depending on the architecture, these cells can store various data types, such as integers, floating-point numbers, characters, and more complex structures. For instance, an integer might require 4 bytes (32 bits), whereas a character typically requires 1 byte (8 bits). The actual size and layout depend on the type declaration and the alignment rules of the architecture.

Memory Layout and Alignment: Memory alignment is the process of aligning data types to specific address boundaries. For performance reasons, it is often advantageous to align larger data types to addresses divisible by certain powers of 2. This helps the processor fetch data more efficiently. Misaligned data access can lead to additional cycles or even faults depending on the architecture.

Listing 3.61: ASCII Character Encoding Example

```
int main() {
    int a = 42;
    char b = 'A';
    float c = 3.14;
}
```

In this C program, the integer variable a might be stored starting at address 0x1000, occupying addresses 0x1000 to 0x1003. The character variable b could then be stored at 0x1004, and the float variable c could be stored starting at 0x1008 due to alignment requirements.

Endianness: Different computer architectures store multiple-byte data differently. This is known as endianness. Big-endian systems store the most significant byte at the smallest address, whereas little-endian systems store the least significant byte at the smallest address. Consider the following 32-bit integer, 0x12345678:

Big-endian representation:

```
Address:  0x1000 0x1001 0x1002 0x1003
Data:     0x12   0x34   0x56   0x78
```

Little-endian representation:

```
Address:  0x1000 0x1001 0x1002 0x1003
Data:     0x78   0x56   0x34   0x12
```

The Stack and the Heap: Memory is typically divided into several segments, including the stack and the heap. The stack supports function call management, including local variables and control flow information, while the heap is used for dynamically allocated memory. The stack grows downward, from higher to lower memory addresses, whereas the heap grows upward, from lower to higher addresses.

Registers and Memory Access: Accessing data in registers is significantly faster than accessing it in main memory, as registers reside within the CPU. However, due to limited register availability, most programs store data in memory and use registers for temporary storage and operations.

Listing 3.62: ASCII Character Encoding Example

```
MOV EAX, [0x1000] ; Move data from memory address 0x1000 to register EAX
MOV [0x1004], EAX ; Move data from register EAX to memory address 0x1004
```

Memory Latency and Performance: Memory latency refers to the delay between initiating a request for data and the start of the data transfer. Techniques such as caching, where frequently accessed data is stored closer to the CPU, can mitigate latency issues. Each cache level (L1, L2, L3) progressively reduces access time at the cost of increased complexity and space requirements.

Caching Mechanisms: Caches are smaller, faster memory locations that store copies of frequently accessed data to reduce latency. Modern CPUs employ multiple levels of caches (L1, L2, and often L3), each providing different trade-offs between speed, size, and complexity.

Efficient use of memory involves understanding the nuances of memory access patterns, alignment, and the capabilities of the underlying hardware.

3.11 Manipulating Data in Registers

In assembly language programming, one of the core functionalities is the manipulation of data in registers. Registers are small, fast storage locations within a CPU that hold instructions, storage addresses, or any kind of data such as integers and floating points. These operations are fundamental for performance and efficiency, making it essential to understand how to read, write, and modify the data stored within these registers.

Data manipulation in registers involves several key operations: moving data, arithmetic operations, logical operations, and bit shifting operations. Each of these operations will be detailed below.

Moving Data: The MOV instruction is fundamental for transferring data between registers or between registers and memory. The general syntax for the MOV instruction is:

Listing 3.63: ASCII Character Encoding Example

```
MOV destination, source
```

Where destination is the register or memory location where the data will be moved to, and source is the register or memory location from where the data is sourced. For example,

Listing 3.64: ASCII Character Encoding Example

```
MOV AX, BX
MOV AX, 1234h
```

In the first line, the contents of register BX are copied into register AX. In the second line, the immediate hexadecimal value 1234h is copied into register AX.

Arithmetic Operations: Registers are often used for arithmetic operations such as addition, subtraction, multiplication, and division. These operations modify the data in the registers directly. Examples include the ADD, SUB, MUL, and DIV instructions.

Addition:

Listing 3.65: ASCII Character Encoding Example

```
ADD AX, BX
```

This instruction adds the contents of register BX to the contents of register AX and stores the result in AX.

Subtraction:

Listing 3.66: ASCII Character Encoding Example

```
SUB AX, BX
```

This instruction subtracts the contents of register BX from the contents of register AX and stores the result in AX.

Multiplication:

Listing 3.67: ASCII Character Encoding Example

```
MUL BX
```

This instruction multiplies the contents of register AX by the contents of register BX. The result is stored in AX and DX.

Division:

Listing 3.68: ASCII Character Encoding Example

```
DIV BX
```

This instruction divides the contents of the AX by the contents of BX. The quotient is stored in AX, and the remainder is stored in DX.

Logical Operations: Logical operations such as AND, OR, XOR, and NOT are used to manipulate individual bits within the register. These operations are fundamental for bitwise manipulation and control.

AND:

Listing 3.69: ASCII Character Encoding Example

```
AND AX, 0Fh
```

This instruction performs a bitwise AND operation between the contents of register AX and the hexadecimal value 0Fh.

OR:

Listing 3.70: ASCII Character Encoding Example

```
OR AX, 0F0h
```

This instruction performs a bitwise OR operation between the contents of register AX and the hexadecimal value 0F0h.

XOR:

Listing 3.71: ASCII Character Encoding Example

```
XOR AX, 0FFh
```

This instruction performs a bitwise XOR operation between the contents of register AX and the hexadecimal value 0FFh.

NOT:

Listing 3.72: ASCII Character Encoding Example

```
NOT AX
```

This instruction performs a bitwise NOT operation on the contents of register AX, flipping all bits within the register.

Bit Shifting: Bit shifting operations move the bits in a register left or right. These operations can be used for various purposes, including bit manipulation and arithmetic operations. The main instructions include SHL, SHR, SAL, and SAR.

Shift Left Logical (SHL):

Listing 3.73: ASCII Character Encoding Example

```
SHL AX, 1
```

This instruction shifts all bits in register AX to the left by 1 position. The empty bit positions on the right are filled with zeros.

Shift Right Logical (SHR):

Listing 3.74: ASCII Character Encoding Example

```
SHR AX, 1
```

This instruction shifts all bits in register AX to the right by 1 position. The empty bit positions on the left are filled with zeros.

Shift Arithmetic Left (SAL):

Listing 3.75: ASCII Character Encoding Example

```
SAL AX, 1
```

This instruction is identical to SHL and shifts bits to the left while filling the rightmost bit with zero.

Shift Right Arithmetic (SAR):

Listing 3.76: ASCII Character Encoding Example

```
SAR AX, 1
```

This instruction shifts all bits in register AX to the right by 1 position, but the leftmost bit retains its original value, useful for signed numbers.

Understanding these operations and how to exploit them enables efficient data manipulation at the register level. These low-level manipulations are crucial for optimizing performance by minimizing memory access and ensuring that the CPU operates with maximum efficiency. Mastery of register operations is a foundational skill in assembly language programming, providing the tools necessary for precise control over data handling and logical process execution.

3.12 Advanced Data Representation Techniques

Advanced data representation techniques go beyond the traditional methods of handling binary, hexadecimal, and octal number systems. This section delves into complex forms of data representation that are essential in various computational contexts. These techniques are crucial for optimizing memory usage, enhancing computing efficiency, and providing accurate numerical representations in diverse applications.

Packed BCD Representation: The packed Binary-Coded Decimal (BCD) format is a method of encoding decimal numbers where each digit is represented by a fixed number of binary bits, typically four. This technique is particularly advantageous when dealing with decimal digits in contexts where precise arithmetic operations are required, such as in financial calculations.

Listing 3.77: ASCII Character Encoding Example

```
; Packed BCD representation example
section .data
    packed_bcd db 0x56 ; Represents the decimal number 56 as packed BCD
section .text
    ; Instructions processing packed BCD values
    -- snip --
```

In the example above, the decimal number 56 is encoded as 0x56 in packed BCD format. Each nibble (half-byte) contains a decimal digit, making arithmetic straightforward while ensuring accuracy.

Gray Code: Gray code, or reflected binary code, is a binary numeral system where two successive values differ in only one bit. This property reduces the chance of errors during the transition between two states and is valuable in applications like digital encoders and error correction.

Listing 3.78: ASCII Character Encoding Example

```
# Python example of converting binary to Gray code
def binary_to_gray(n):
    return n ^ (n >> 1)

binary_number = 0b1010 # Binary for decimal 10
gray_code = binary_to_gray(binary_number)
print(bin(gray_code)) # Output: 0b1111
```

Gray code conversion ensures minimal bit errors during transitions, thus enhancing stability in digital systems where precise state changes are crucial.

Floating-Point Representation: When performing calculations requiring a wide range of values, floating-point representation offers a powerful way to represent numbers. The IEEE 754 standard defines the format for floating-point arithmetic, including single precision (32 bits) and double precision (64 bits).

Listing 3.79: ASCII Character Encoding Example

```
# Python example of IEEE 754 floating-point conversion
import struct

# Convert float to binary representation according to IEEE 754
def float_to_bin(num):
    packed = struct.pack('>f', num)
    return ''.join(f'{byte:08b}' for byte in packed)

float_number = 3.14
binary_repr = float_to_bin(float_number)
print(binary_repr) # Example output: 01000000010010001111010111000011
```

Understanding the underlying binary format of floating-point numbers is essential for activities such as low-level debugging and performance optimization.

Arbitrary-Precision Arithmetic: Standard floating-point representations can be insufficient for applications requiring extremely high precision. Arbitrary-precision arithmetic libraries support computations with an arbitrary number of digits, overcoming the limitations of fixed-precision types.

Listing 3.80: ASCII Character Encoding Example

```
# Python example of arbitrary-precision arithmetic using the 'decimal' module
from decimal import Decimal, getcontext

# Set precision level
getcontext().prec = 50

# Arbitrary-precision floating-point calculations
num1 = Decimal('1.12345678901234567890123456789')
num2 = Decimal('2.98765432109876543210987654321')
result = num1 * num2
print(result) # Output: 3.3565005304881065102197638669070976012291536897509
```

Arbitrary-precision arithmetic is paramount in fields such as cryptography and computational mathematics, ensuring exact calculations are maintained.

Data Compression Techniques: Data compression reduces the size of data while maintaining its integrity. Techniques such as Huffman coding, run-length encoding, and dictionary-based methods like Lempel-Ziv-Welch (LZW) are pivotal in optimizing storage and transmission efficiency.

Listing 3.81: ASCII Character Encoding Example

```
import heapq
from collections import defaultdict

# Huffman Coding for Data Compression Example
class HuffmanCoding:
    def __init__(self, data):
        self.data = data
        self.heap = []
        self.codes = {}
        self.reverse_mapping = {}

    def make_frequency_dict(self):
        frequency = defaultdict(int)
        for char in self.data:
            frequency[char] += 1
        return frequency

    def make_heap(self, frequency):
        for key in frequency:
            heapq.heappush(self.heap, (frequency[key], key))

    # Implementation of the Huffman encoding algorithm...

data = "example for Huffman encoding"
huffman = HuffmanCoding(data)
frequency = huffman.make_frequency_dict()
huffman.make_heap(frequency)
# Additional steps to build the Huffman Tree and generate codes
```

Data compression is integral to modern computing environments, significantly reducing the bandwidth and storage requirements.

Matrix Representation of Data: In numerous scientific computations and machine learning models, data is represented as matrices. Advanced matrix representations and operations, such as sparse matrices and singular value decomposition (SVD), are critical for efficiently handling large datasets.

Listing 3.82: ASCII Character Encoding Example

```
import numpy as np
from scipy.sparse import csr_matrix

# Example dense matrix
dense_matrix = np.array([[0, 0, 1], [4, 0, 0], [0, 3, 0]])

# Convert to sparse matrix format
sparse_matrix = csr_matrix(dense_matrix)

# Perform operations on sparse matrix
sparse_matrix_sum = sparse_matrix.sum()
print(sparse_matrix_sum) # Output: 8
```

Sparse matrices optimize memory and computational resources by storing only non-zero elements, which is essential for scalable machine learning and scientific computations.

Adopting these advanced data representation techniques enhances computational efficiency, improves data accuracy, and enables effective problem-solving in complex scenarios. By integrating these representations, we can address specific challenges and optimize performance in various domains.

Chapter 4

Control Flow in Assembly Language

This chapter addresses the mechanisms of control flow within assembly language programs. It covers unconditional and conditional jumps, loop constructs, and the use of labels. The implementation of if-else structures and switch-case statements is discussed, along with procedure calls, returns, and handling interrupts and exceptions. Additionally, it provides strategies for managing control flow in large programs and optimizing it for performance, enriched with practical examples.

4.1 Introduction to Control Flow

Control flow is a fundamental concept in assembly language programming that dictates the order in which instructions are executed within a program. Effective management of control flow allows a program to make decisions, repeat certain tasks, and execute specific sections of code based on conditional or unconditional criteria. This section elucidates the basic constructs utilized to manage control flow, which are pivotal in developing complex and efficient programs in assembly language.

Assembly language provides various mechanisms to control the flow of execution, including unconditional jumps, conditional jumps, loop constructs, and the utilization of labels. These constructs enable the programmer to direct the execution path of the program explicitly and are the building blocks for implementing high-level constructs like if-else structures and switch-case statements.

The most basic control flow instruction is the JMP command, which allows for an unconditional jump to a specified label or address. This means the processor will continue execution from the target location without any condition evaluations. Here is how a simple JMP instruction is used:

Listing 4.1: ASCII Character Encoding Example

```
JMP TARGET_LABEL
; Continue execution at the address marked by TARGET_LABEL
```

For more complex decision-making, conditional jumps are employed. These instructions evaluate the state of certain flags within the processor's status register and decide whether to continue to the next sequential instruction or to jump to a specified label. Common conditional jumps include:

- JE (Jump if Equal)
- JNE (Jump if Not Equal)
- JG (Jump if Greater)
- JL (Jump if Less)

For example, the JE instruction checks the Zero Flag (ZF) and jumps if the ZF is set (indicating that the previous comparison was equal):

Listing 4.2: ASCII Character Encoding Example

```
CMP EAX, EBX
JE EQUAL_LABEL
; Continue execution at EQUAL_LABEL if EAX is equal to EBX
```

Loops facilitate repeating a block of code multiple times. The LOOP instruction, combined with a counter register (typically ECX), decrements the counter each iteration and jumps to a specified label if the counter has not yet reached zero:

Listing 4.3: ASCII Character Encoding Example

```
MOV ECX, 10
START_LOOP:
; Code to be repeated
```

```
LOOP START_LOOP
; Repeat the loop 10 times
```

In addition to LOOP, assembly language features other loop constructs such as LOOPE (Loop While Equal) and LOOPNE (Loop While Not Equal), which combine looping with conditional checks.

Labels serve as reference points within the code, aiding in control flow management. They mark addresses in the code to which control instructions can jump. A label is defined by a string followed by a colon:

Listing 4.4: ASCII Character Encoding Example

```
START:
MOV EBX, 0
; Start of a code block
```

Labels are used with both unconditional and conditional jumps, providing clarity and organization to the code structure.

By utilizing these constructs effectively, programmers can implement high-level control structures found in other languages directly within assembly. For example, if-else structures and switch-case constructs are built using a combination of conditional jumps and labels. Procedure calls and returns, handled by CALL and RET instructions, enable modularity and reuse of code by allowing functions to be defined and invoked.

Handling interrupts and exceptions also involves control flow manipulation. Interrupts are used to handle external or internal events that require immediate attention, while exceptions deal with exceptional conditions or errors during program execution. These mechanisms ensure robust behavior and response to various scenarios during program execution.

Proper management of control flow is crucial in large programs where maintaining readability, minimizing complexity, and optimizing performance become paramount. As we advance through subsequent sections, we will delve deeper into these control flow constructs, exploring their usage, implications, and strategies for optimal implementation in assembly programming.

4.2 Unconditional Jumps: JMP

The JMP instruction in assembly language is utilized for implementing an unconditional jump, allowing the control flow to continue from a non-sequential instruction within the program. This command transfers the execution to the specified address label without considering any conditions. It is a fundamental element in control flow, enabling the redirection to different parts of code based on the program's requirements.

The syntax for the JMP instruction is:

Listing 4.5: ASCII Character Encoding Example

```
JMP destination
```

Here, destination represents the label or address to which the program counter (PC) should jump.

Example of JMP instruction

Consider a simple scenario where we want to jump to a label called TARGET. The assembling code might look like this:

Listing 4.6: ASCII Character Encoding Example

```
section .text
    mov eax, 1 ; Initialize eax register
    jmp TARGET ; Unconditional jump to TARGET
    mov ebx, 2 ; This line is not executed

TARGET:
    mov ecx, 3 ; Execution continues here
```

In this example, the instruction mov ebx, 2 will never be executed because the JMP statement transfers control directly to the TARGET label.

Memory Addressing

The JMP instruction can utilize different types of memory addressing modes:

- **Direct Jump**

  Listing 4.7: ASCII Character Encoding Example

  ```
  JMP label
  ```

  This jumps directly to the label.

- **Register Indirect Jump**

Listing 4.8: ASCII Character Encoding Example

```
JMP eax
```

The jump address is taken from the eax register.

- **Memory Indirect Jump**

Listing 4.9: ASCII Character Encoding Example

```
JMP [eax]
```

Here, the jump address is stored in memory, pointed to by the eax register.

Practical Use Case: Loop Implementation

Unconditional jumps can be essential in creating loops. Consider the following example where a loop counts down from 5 to 1:

Listing 4.10: ASCII Character Encoding Example

```
section .data
    count db 5 ; Initialize count to 5

section .text
_start:
    mov ecx, [count]
loop_start:
    cmp ecx, 0
    je loop_end
    ; Do some work
    dec ecx
    jmp loop_start

loop_end:
    ; Continue with the rest of the program
```

In this code, the loop utilizes the JMP instruction to repeatedly test and decrement the ecx register until it reaches zero. Upon reaching zero, the je loop_end statement jumps out of the loop.

Error and Exception Handling

Unconditional jumps are also crucial for error and exception handling in assembly language. Consider a scenario where a division operation might result in division by zero. The JMP command can redirect the flow to an error handler:

Listing 4.11: ASCII Character Encoding Example

```
section .text
_start:
    mov eax, 10
```

```
    mov ebx, 0
    cmp ebx, 0
    je error_handler ; Jump to error handler on division by zero

    div ebx ; This line will cause an exception if ebx is zero

continue_execution:
    ; Continue normal execution

error_handler:
    ; Handle the error: for instance, set eax to a default value
    mov eax, -1
    jmp continue_execution
```

In this example, the program checks if ebx is zero before executing a division. If ebx is zero, it jumps to the error_handler label, effectively handling the potential division by zero error.

The JMP instruction forms the backbone of more complex control flow constructs, making it essential to understand its nuances and applications. Understanding its functionality provides a solid foundation for manipulating control flow effectively in assembly language programming.

4.3 Conditional Jumps: JE, JNE, JG, JL, etc.

Conditional jumps in assembly language are fundamental to controlling the flow of execution based on certain conditions. These jumps allow programs to make decisions, facilitate branching, and implement traditional high-level language constructs such as if-else, while loops, and for loops. A conditional jump occurs by evaluating the result of a comparison or status of specific flags set by prior instructions.

The x86 assembly language offers a variety of conditional jump instructions, each tailored to specific conditions. The most commonly used conditional jumps include JE, JNE, JG, and JL. Understanding these instructions and their correct application is crucial for effective control flow management in assembly programming.

1. JE (Jump if Equal)/JZ (Jump if Zero):

   The JE instruction triggers a jump if the zero flag (ZF) is set, indicating that the result of the last comparison was equal.

   Listing 4.12: ASCII Character Encoding Example

   ```
   CMP AX, BX ; Compare AX and BX
   JE EQUAL_LABEL ; Jump to EQUAL_LABEL if AX == BX
   ```

2. JNE (Jump if Not Equal)/JNZ (Jump if Not Zero):

   The JNE instruction causes a jump if the zero flag (ZF) is not set, meaning the last comparison yielded an unequal result.

   Listing 4.13: ASCII Character Encoding Example

   ```
   CMP AX, DX ; Compare AX and DX
   JNE NOTEQUAL_LABEL ; Jump to NOTEQUAL_LABEL if AX != DX
   ```

3. JG (Jump if Greater):

   The JG instruction will jump if the sign flag (SF) is equal to the overflow flag (OF) and the zero flag (ZF) is clear, indicating the first operand is greater than the second for signed comparisons.

   Listing 4.14: ASCII Character Encoding Example

   ```
   CMP CX, BX ; Compare CX and BX
   JG GREATER_LABEL ; Jump to GREATER_LABEL if CX > BX
   ```

4. JL (Jump if Less):

   The JL instruction jumps when the sign flag (SF) is not equal to the overflow flag (OF), suggesting the first operand is less than the second for signed comparisons.

   Listing 4.15: ASCII Character Encoding Example

   ```
   CMP AX, CX ; Compare AX and CX
   JL LESS_LABEL ; Jump to LESS_LABEL if AX < CX
   ```

In addition to these basic conditional jumps, several other instructions exist to address various comparison needs, including for unsigned integers. These include JA (Jump if Above), JAE (Jump if Above or Equal), JB (Jump if Below), and JBE (Jump if Below or Equal).

Key to understanding these instructions is the status flags within the CPU's flags register:

- ZF (Zero Flag): Set if the result of an operation is zero.
- SF (Sign Flag): Reflects the sign of the result (0 for positive, 1 for negative).
- OF (Overflow Flag): Indicates whether an arithmetic overflow has occurred.
- CF (Carry Flag): Reflects an arithmetic carry or borrow out of the most significant bit.

Let's consider a complex example where multiple conditional jumps determine which label to jump to:

Listing 4.16: ASCII Character Encoding Example

```
CMP AX, BX ; Compare AX and BX

; If AX == BX, jump to EQUAL_LABEL
JE EQUAL_LABEL

; If AX > BX, jump to GREATER_LABEL
JG GREATER_LABEL

; If AX < BX, jump to LESS_LABEL
JL LESS_LABEL

; Continue to OTHER_LABEL if none of the above conditions are met
OTHER_LABEL:
; Code execution continues here

EQUAL_LABEL:
; Code for the case AX == BX
JMP CONTINUE

GREATER_LABEL:
; Code for the case AX > BX
JMP CONTINUE

LESS_LABEL:
; Code for the case AX < BX

CONTINUE:
; Further code execution
```

This example illustrates the practical application of conditional jumps to control the program flow based on comparisons. By understanding and implementing these conditional jumps adeptly, programmers can construct efficient and logical control structures within their assembly applications. Here is the revised LaTeX text of the section based on your provided content and the requested format adjustments:

"'latex

4.4 Loops and Iteration: LOOP, LOOPE, LOOPNE

Assembly language provides several control flow constructs to manage repetitive tasks and loops. The most commonly used looping instructions are LOOP, LOOPE, and LOOPNE. Their operation involves the use of the CX register, which is decremented automatically with each iteration. The behavior of these loops is determined based on the value of CX, and optionally, the state of the zero flag (ZF).

The LOOP Instruction

The LOOP instruction is the simplest and most frequently used looping construct. It decrements the CX register and transfers control to a target label if the CX register is not zero. The syntax is:

Listing 4.17: ASCII Character Encoding Example

```
LOOP target
```

An illustrative example of the LOOP instruction:

Listing 4.18: ASCII Character Encoding Example

```
MOV CX, 5 ; Initialize CX to 5
start_loop:
    ; Code to be repeated
    ; Example: incrementing AX by 1
    INC AX
    LOOP start_loop ; Decrement CX and jump to start_loop if CX != 0
```

If CX is greater than 0, the LOOP instruction decrements CX and jumps to the label start_loop. When CX is finally decremented to 0, the loop exits, and control falls through to the next instruction.

The LOOPE Instruction

The LOOPE (Loop While Equal) instruction operates by transferring control to a specified label as long as the CX register is not zero and the ZF is set (equal to 1). This instruction is useful in scenarios where you want to continue looping as long as both conditions are simultaneously satisfied. The syntax is:

Listing 4.19: ASCII Character Encoding Example

```
LOOPE target
```

An example of the LOOPE instruction:

Listing 4.20: ASCII Character Encoding Example

```
MOV CX, 5 ; Initialize CX to 5
CMP AX, BX ; Compare AX with BX
start_loope:
    ; Code to be repeated
    ; Example: decrementing BX
    DEC BX
    LOOPE start_loope ; Decrement CX, jump to start_loope if CX != 0 and ZF = 1
```

In this example, the loop will continue executing as long as CX is not zero and ZF is 1 (i.e., AX == BX). If either CX reaches 0 or ZF is cleared, the loop terminates.

The LOOPNE Instruction

The LOOPNE (Loop While Not Equal) instruction is similar to LOOPE, but it continues looping as long as CX is not zero and ZF is cleared (equal to 0). This is useful for checking inequality conditions. The syntax for LOOPNE is:

Listing 4.21: ASCII Character Encoding Example

```
LOOPNE target
```

An example of the LOOPNE instruction:

Listing 4.22: ASCII Character Encoding Example

```
MOV CX, 5 ; Initialize CX to 5
CMP AX, BX ; Compare AX with BX
start_loopne:
    ; Code to be repeated
    ; Example: incrementing BX
    INC BX
    LOOPNE start_loopne ; Decrement CX, jump to start_loopne if CX != 0 and ZF
        = 0
```

This loop will continue to execute as long as CX is not zero and ZF is 0 (i.e., AX != BX). If either condition fails, the loop exits.

Algorithmic Representation

To visualize these looping constructs algorithmically, consider the following pseudocode expressions for clarity:

Practical usage of these loop instructions is essential for efficient low-level programming. Proper initialization and conditions are critical to avoid infinite loops or early termination. By harnessing these constructs along with conditional jumps, a programmer can implement complex iterative logic efficiently in assembly language. "'

This corrected text addresses your reported LaTeX compilation error by changing 'algorithm2e' to 'algorithm', ensuring seamless integration into the broader document without requiring preamble adjustments.

4.5 Using Labels for Control Flow

Labels are fundamental elements in assembly language that guide the control flow of programs. They act as markers or landmarks allowing for the accurate navigation of the instruction sequence. By naming

```
Data: CX initialized, optional condition for ZF
Result: Repeated execution of loop body
if Instruction is LOOP then
    while CX != 0 do
        Execute loop body;
        CX = CX - 1;
    end
end
if Instruction is LOOPE then
    while CX != 0 and ZF = 1 do
        Execute loop body;
        CX = CX - 1;
    end
end
if Instruction is LOOPNE then
    while CX != 0 and ZF = 0 do
        Execute loop body;
        CX = CX - 1;
    end
end
```

a specific memory address or an instruction, labels enable branching mechanisms that are critical for implementing loops, conditional statements, procedure calls, and more.

A label is defined by appending a unique identifier, often followed by a colon, before the instruction or memory address it specifies. Consider the following example:

Listing 4.23: ASCII Character Encoding Example

```
start:
    mov eax, 5
    add eax, 2
    jmp end_program

loop:
    dec eax
    jne loop

end_program:
```

In this snippet, start, loop, and end_program serve as labels marking different sections of the code.

- start: Marks the beginning of the program or a major segment.
- loop: Designates the beginning of a loop structure.
- end_program: Indicates the end of the program sequence.

The jmp instruction, utilized for unconditional jumps, relies on labels to know the destination of the branch. For example, jmp end_program directs the control flow to the instruction immediately following the end_program label.

To implement loop constructs efficiently, labels are crucial. Here is a detailed examination using an iterative decrement counter with a loop:

Listing 4.24: ASCII Character Encoding Example

```
section .data
    counter db 10

section .text
    global _start

_start:
    mov al, [counter]

decrement_loop:
    dec al
    jnz decrement_loop
```

```
    ; Exit program
    mov eax, 60
    xor edi, edi
    syscall
```

In this iteration example: - counter is initialized with the value 10. - The loop labeled decrement_loop decrements the value in al register until it reaches zero. - The jnz (jump if not zero) instruction checks the zero flag. If al is not zero, the control flow jumps back to the decrement_loop label.

Using labels is also essential for implementing if-else structures:

Listing 4.25: ASCII Character Encoding Example

```
section .data
    num1 db 3
    num2 db 5

section .text
    global _start

_start:
    mov al, [num1]
    cmp al, [num2]
    jle less_than_equal

greater_than:
    ; Code for num1 > num2
    jmp end_if

less_than_equal:
    ; Code for num1 <= num2

end_if:

    ; Exit the program
    mov eax, 60
    xor edi, edi
    syscall
```

Here: - cmp al, [num2] compares al (which contains the value of num1) with num2. - The jle instruction causes a jump to the less_than_equal label if al is less than or equal to num2. - If al is greater than num2, control continues to the code labeled greater_than. - Regardless of the branch taken initially, both branches converge at the end_if label, ensuring a unified exit point.

Labels also facilitate procedure calls and returns. When calling a procedure, a label can indicate the start of the procedure, and another label at the return point ensures that control correctly resumes after the procedure:

Listing 4.26: ASCII Character Encoding Example

```
section .text
    global _start

_start:
    ; Some initial code
    call my_procedure
    ; Code after the procedure call

    ; Exit the program
    mov eax, 60
    xor edi, edi
    syscall

my_procedure:
    ; Procedure code
    ret
```

In this example: - The call instruction transfers control to the my_procedure label. - The ret instruction within my_procedure returns control to the instruction immediately following call my_procedure.

Interrupt handling also often depends on labels. When an interrupt is triggered, the interrupt service routine (ISR) label directs to special handling code, allowing for effective interrupt management.

The correct and strategic use of labels contributes significantly to maintaining organized and readable code structures, enabling complex control flow patterns in assembly language programming. Intelligent placement of labels ensures optimal execution paths and facilitates easier debugging and future code modifications.

4.6 Implementing If-Else Structures

In assembly language, implementing if-else structures requires a meticulous approach to the use of conditional jumps and labels. This section covers how to convert high-level language if-else constructs into their assembly language counterparts. Understanding this conversion is vital for mastering control flow in assembly, as it lacks direct high-level constructs and instead relies on low-level operations.

To begin, consider the typical if-else construct in a high-level language such as C:

Listing 4.27: ASCII Character Encoding Example

```
if (condition) {
    // Then block
} else {
```

```
    // Else block
}
```

In assembly language, this is translated using conditional jump instructions like JE (Jump if Equal), JNE (Jump if Not Equal), JG (Jump if Greater), and JL (Jump if Lesser), as well as the JMP (Unconditional Jump) instruction.

Consider the following specific example in C:

Listing 4.28: ASCII Character Encoding Example

```
if (eax == ebx) {
    // Then block
} else {
    // Else block
}
```

In assembly language, we must first compare the two registers eax and ebx using the CMP instruction, followed by a conditional jump instruction:

Listing 4.29: ASCII Character Encoding Example

```
CMP eax, ebx ; Compare eax and ebx
JE ThenBlock ; Jump to ThenBlock if eax == ebx
; Else block code
JMP EndIf ; Unconditional jump to EndIf
ThenBlock:
; Then block code
EndIf:
```

The CMP instruction sets the processor's flags based on the result of the comparison. The JE instruction, which stands for "Jump if Equal," checks the Zero Flag (ZF). If the two values are equal, the ZF is set, and the program jumps to the ThenBlock label. If they are not equal, the execution continues to the lines that follow the JE instruction, which represent the else block.

Here is an example demonstrating a more complex if-else structure, where we check multiple conditions:

Listing 4.30: ASCII Character Encoding Example

```
if (eax == ebx) {
    // Then block
} else if (ecx < edx) {
    // Else-If block
} else {
    // Else block
}
```

This requires nested comparisons and jumps:

Listing 4.31: ASCII Character Encoding Example

```
CMP eax, ebx ; Compare eax and ebx
JE ThenBlock ; Jump to ThenBlock if eax == ebx
CMP ecx, edx ; Compare ecx and edx
JL ElseIfBlock ; Jump to ElseIfBlock if ecx < edx
; Else block code
JMP EndIf ; Unconditional jump to EndIf
ElseIfBlock:
; Else-If block code
JMP EndIf ; Jump past the ThenBlock code
ThenBlock:
; Then block code
EndIf:
```

The use of JMP instructions ensures that once a block's execution is completed, the program does not inadvertently execute subsequent blocks. This structure efficiently directs the control flow to the correct block based on the comparison results, mimicking the behavior of high-level if-else constructs.

To further illustrate, consider conditional execution involving logical operators. For example, implementing if ((eax == ebx) && (ecx != edx)) {} requires handling both conditions:

Listing 4.32: ASCII Character Encoding Example

```
CMP eax, ebx ; Compare eax and ebx
JNE ElseBlock ; Jump to ElseBlock if eax != ebx
CMP ecx, edx ; Compare ecx and edx
JNE ThenBlock ; Jump to ThenBlock if ecx != edx
ElseBlock:
; Else block code
JMP EndIf ; Unconditional jump to EndIf
ThenBlock:
; Then block code
EndIf:
```

In this scenario, JNE (Jump if Not Equal) is used to ensure both conditions are satisfied. Failing to meet either condition results in a jump to the ElseBlock. This logical conjunction requires careful sequencing to align with the simplicity of assembly operations.

When managing more extensive code, labels must be clear and meaningful to maintain readability. Consistent use of labels such as ThenBlock, ElseBlock, and EndIf helps in tracing the control flow accurately.

Advanced control flow optimizations, such as reordering comparisons to minimize jumps or using processor-specific instructions for efficiency, can yield performance benefits in large programs. However, the fundamental translation of high-level if-else constructs into conditional jumps and labels remains a cornerstone of assembly language programming.

4.7 Switch-Case Implementation in Assembly

In high-level programming languages, the switch-case construct is used to select one of many blocks of code to execute based on the value of a variable. The equivalent construct in assembly language must be explicitly coded since assembly languages do not have a built-in switch-case construct. This involves using jump tables or series of conditional jumps. This section will explore both methods for implementing switch-case in assembly language.

The switch-case structure generally involves evaluating a variable and comparing it against multiple constant values. Depending on the result, a different part of the code is executed. Here's a high-level example in C for context:

Listing 4.33: ASCII Character Encoding Example

```
switch(value) {
    case 1:
        // Code for case 1
        break;
    case 2:
        // Code for case 2
        break;
    default:
        // Code for default case
}
```

Jump Table Implementation

One efficient way to implement the switch-case in assembly is through a jump table. A jump table is an array of addresses to which the program jumps based on the index calculated from the switch variable. This method reduces the number of comparisons and results in a more optimized execution path.

Here is an assembly example demonstrating the use of a jump table for a switch-case structure:

Listing 4.34: ASCII Character Encoding Example

```
section .data
    jump_table: dq case1, case2, default_case

section .text
    global _start

_start:
    mov rax, [value]
    cmp rax, 2
```

```
    ja default_case ; If value > 2, jump to default case
    jmp [jump_table + rax * 8] ; Each address is 8 bytes

case1:
    ; Code for case 1
    jmp end_switch

case2:
    ; Code for case 2
    jmp end_switch

default_case:
    ; Code for default case

end_switch:
    ; Continue with the rest of the program
```

In this example: - The value variable is loaded into the rax register. - A comparison is made to ensure the value is within the bounds of the jump table. - The jmp [jump_table + rax * 8] instruction uses the value as an index into the jump table and jumps to the corresponding case.

Sequential Conditional Jumps

Alternatively, implementing the switch-case could use a series of conditional jumps. This approach is straightforward but less efficient for a large number of cases because it executes sequential comparisons until it finds a match.

Here's how it can be coded in assembly:

Listing 4.35: ASCII Character Encoding Example

```
section .data
    ; Data section

section .text
    global _start

_start:
    mov rax, [value]
    cmp rax, 1
    je case1
    cmp rax, 2
    je case2

default_case:
    ; Code for default case
    jmp end_switch

case1:
    ; Code for case 1
    jmp end_switch

case2:
    ; Code for case 2

end_switch:
```

```
; Continue with the rest of the program
```

In this script: - The program evaluates the value in the rax register against each case using cmp and je instructions. - If none of the conditions match, it defaults to default_case.

The choice between using a jump table and sequential conditional jumps should be informed by considerations of readability, maintainability, and performance. Jump tables are generally more efficient but require careful management to ensure that values are within the valid range. Conditional jumps are simple but can lead to performance drawbacks with a large number of cases due to the linear search time complexity.

The described methods enable the realization of the switch-case construct's flexibility and functionality within the constraints and particularities of assembly language programming, offering insights into low-level control flow management.

4.8 Procedure Calls and Returns: CALL, RET

In assembly language programming, procedures, also known as subroutines or functions, are essential constructs that enable code modularity and reusability. Procedures allow for the encapsulation of repetitive tasks into discrete callable units, promoting clear and maintainable code. This section delves into the mechanics of procedure calls and returns, focusing on the CALL and RET instructions.

The CALL instruction is used to invoke a procedure, while the RET instruction is used to return control to the calling procedure. Let us start by examining the CALL instruction.

CALL ProcedureName

When the CALL instruction is executed, it performs the following steps:

- The address of the next instruction (i.e., the instruction following the CALL) is pushed onto the stack. This address is referred to as the return address.
- Control is transferred to the address specified by ProcedureName.

The RET instruction is used to return from a procedure. Its syntax is as follows:

RET

Upon the execution of RET, the following actions occur:

- The return address is popped from the stack.
- Control is transferred to the return address, resuming execution at the point immediately following the original CALL instruction.

Consider the following example for a procedure named Sum, which computes the sum of two integers:

Listing 4.36: ASCII Character Encoding Example

```
section .data
    num1 dd 5
    num2 dd 10
    result dd 0

section .text
    global _start

_start:
    CALL Sum
    ; Continue execution here after returning from Sum
    ; Exit program (OS specific code might be needed here)

Sum:
    mov eax, [num1] ; Load the first integer into eax
    add eax, [num2] ; Add the second integer to eax
    mov [result], eax ; Store the result
    RET ; Return to the calling procedure (_start)
```

In this example, the CALL instruction invokes the Sum procedure. Within Sum, the sum of num1 and num2 is computed and stored in the result variable. The RET instruction then returns control to the _start label, where execution continues.

Now, let's discuss the stack's role in managing procedure calls. Each CALL instruction causes the return address to be pushed onto the stack, and each RET instruction pops the return address from the stack. This LIFO (last in, first out) behavior ensures that the return addresses are managed correctly, allowing for nested and recursive procedure calls.

Consider a scenario with nested procedure calls:

Listing 4.37: ASCII Character Encoding Example

```
section .data
```

```
    num1 dd 5
    num2 dd 10
    result dd 0

section .text
    global _start

_start:
    CALL OuterProcedure

OuterProcedure:
    CALL InnerProcedure
    ; Additional code
    RET

InnerProcedure:
    ; Procedure code
    RET
```

In this example, _start calls OuterProcedure, which in turn calls InnerProcedure. The return address for the call to OuterProcedure is pushed first, followed by the return address for the call to InnerProcedure. Upon executing RET in InnerProcedure, control returns to OuterProcedure. A subsequent RET in OuterProcedure returns control to _start.

When dealing with recursive procedures, where a procedure calls itself, it is crucial to manage the stack appropriately. Each recursive CALL results in stacking return addresses, requiring a corresponding number of RET to unwind the stack properly.

To illustrate, consider a recursive implementation of the factorial function:

Listing 4.38: ASCII Character Encoding Example

```
section .data
    n dd 5
    result dd 0

section .text
    global _start

_start:
    CALL Factorial
    ; Exit program (OS specific code might be needed here)

Factorial:
    mov eax, [n]
    cmp eax, 1
    jle FactorialEnd
    dec eax
    push eax ; Save n-1 on the stack
    CALL Factorial ; Recursive call
    pop ebx ; Retrieve n-1 from stack
    mul ebx ; EAX = EAX * EBX
FactorialEnd:
    mov [result], eax
```

```
RET
```

In this recursive factorial calculation, the Factorial procedure calls itself until the base case (i.e., $n <= 1$) is reached. To maintain the correct state across recursive calls, the value of $n - 1$ is pushed onto the stack before the recursive call and popped off afterward. Each recursive call and return keeps the stack balanced, ensuring the correct calculation.

By understanding the mechanics of CALL and RET, assembly language programmers can effectively manage control flow with procedures. This knowledge is fundamental for writing modular, maintainable code. Keep in mind that meticulous handling of the stack is imperative, particularly in complex or recursive procedures, to ensure the integrity of control flow and to prevent stack corruption.

4.9 Handling Interrupts and Exceptions

Handling interrupts and exceptions is a critical aspect of control flow in assembly language programming. Interrupts are events that alter the flow of execution of a program, triggered either by hardware (external) or software (internal). Exceptions, on the other hand, are special types of interrupts generated by the CPU in response to errors or unusual conditions during program execution.

Interrupts can be broadly classified into the following categories:

- **Hardware Interrupts:** Generated by peripheral devices such as keyboards, mice, disk drives, etc.
- **Software Interrupts:** Invoked by executing a specific instruction in the program, often used to request services from the operating system.
- **Processor Exceptions:** Triggered by conditions such as divide-by-zero errors, invalid instructions, or page faults.

An interrupt mechanism involves the following key components:

- **Interrupt Vector Table (IVT):** A table holding the addresses of all the interrupt service routines (ISRs).
- **Interrupt Service Routine (ISR):** A function executed in response to a specific interrupt.

- **Interrupt Request (IRQ) Line:** Lines used by hardware devices to signal interrupts to the CPU.

When an interrupt is triggered, the CPU performs the following steps:

1. **Save the current state:** The CPU saves the current state of its registers, typically onto the stack.
2. **Determine the cause:** The CPU identifies the interrupt vector number, which determines the ISR to execute.
3. **Execute the ISR:** The CPU switches control to the ISR pointed to by the interrupt vector table.
4. **Restore the state:** Upon completion of the ISR, the CPU restores its previous state and resumes execution from where it was interrupted.

Below is a simple example demonstrating how software interrupts can be used in assembly language. This example utilizes the 'int' instruction to invoke a service routine provided by the BIOS or operating system.

Listing 4.39: ASCII Character Encoding Example

```
section .data
    msg db 'Hello, World!', 0 ; Message to be printed

section .text
    global _start

_start:
    ; Print the message using software interrupt
    mov edx, len ; Length of the message
    mov ecx, msg ; Message to be printed
    mov ebx, 1 ; File descriptor (stdout)
    mov eax, 4 ; System call number (sys_write)
    int 0x80 ; Call kernel

    ; Exit the program
    mov eax, 1 ; System call number (sys_exit)
    int 0x80 ; Call kernel

section .bss
len equ $ - msg ; Length of the message
```

In the code above, 'int 0x80' is the software interrupt used to invoke the kernel services in a Linux environment. The values in registers 'eax', 'ebx', 'ecx', and 'edx' are used to pass the parameters for the system call.

Exceptions are managed similarly to hardware interrupts. For example, a divide-by-zero exception triggers an ISR to handle the error. The code snippet below demonstrates how to handle a divide-by-zero exception using assembly language.

Listing 4.40: ASCII Character Encoding Example

```
section .text
    global _start

_start:
    ; Try dividing by zero
    mov eax, 10
    xor edx, edx ; Clear edx to ensure no remainder
    mov ecx, 0 ; Set ecx to zero for division
    div ecx ; This will cause a divide-by-zero exception

    ; Exit the program
    mov eax, 1
    xor ebx, ebx ; Return code 0
    int 0x80
```

In a protected mode environment such as that provided by modern operating systems, exceptions like divide-by-zero automatically trigger an ISR, which handles the exception according to predefined routines, usually terminating the affected process and reporting the error to the user.

Exception handling can also be implemented by defining custom ISRs for specific exception vectors. For instance, the Intel x86 architecture supports up to 256 interrupt vectors, where the first 32 are reserved for processor exceptions.

When designing software that aims to efficiently handle interrupts and exceptions, the following strategies are essential:

- Efficiently manage the Interrupt Vector Table ensuring minimal ISR execution time.
- Prioritize interrupts to allow critical events to be handled promptly.
- Employ nested interrupt handling techniques where higher priority interrupts can interrupt lower priority ISRs.
- Implement exception handling routines to safely manage and recover from errors or unexpected conditions.

Below is an example of setting up the Interrupt Descriptor Table (IDT) for x86 protected mode, a critical step for controlling hardware interrupts and exceptions.

Listing 4.41: ASCII Character Encoding Example

```
section .data
idt: ; Start of the IDT
    dw idt_end - idt - 1 ; Limit of IDT
    dd idt ; Base address of IDT

section .text
global load_idt

load_idt:
    lidt [idt] ; Load the IDT using lidt instruction

idt_end:
```

In this snippet, the 'lidt' instruction loads the IDT register with the address and limit of the Interrupt Descriptor Table, enabling the CPU to properly route interrupts and exceptions to the configured ISRs.

4.10 Managing Control Flow in Large Programs

When developing large programs in assembly language, effectively managing control flow becomes crucial to maintaining readability, scalability, and performance. To achieve this, we employ a combination of structured programming principles, modularity, and careful documentation. Below, we explore techniques and best practices essential for managing control flow in large assembly language programs.

Structuring Code Using Procedures: Procedures, also known as functions or subroutines, enable the division of a program into smaller, manageable sections, each responsible for a specific task. This modular approach simplifies control flow by reducing complexity and enhancing readability.

To define and call a procedure in x86 assembly language:

Listing 4.42: ASCII Character Encoding Example

```
section .data
    ; Variables and constants

section .text
    global _start

_start:
    ; Main program entry point
    ; Call the procedure
    call my_procedure

    ; Exit the program
    mov eax, 1 ; sys_exit
```

```
    xor ebx, ebx ; status 0
    int 0x80

; Procedure definition
my_procedure:
    ; Procedure code
    ; Return from procedure
    ret
```

my_procedure represents a reusable unit encapsulating specific functionality. The call instruction transfers control to the procedure, and execution continues with the ret instruction returning control to the point immediately following the call.

Leveraging Labels for Clarity: Labels act as markers within code, facilitating navigation and the implementation of control flow constructs such as loops and conditional branches. When managing numerous branches in large programs, name labels descriptively to enhance clarity.

Listing 4.43: ASCII Character Encoding Example

```
section .data
    ; Variables and constants

section .text
    global _start

_start:
    ; Example loop with descriptive labels
    mov ecx, 10 ; Loop counter

loop_start:
    cmp ecx, 0 ; Compare counter with 0
    je loop_end ; Exit loop if zero

    ; Loop body
    dec ecx ; Decrement counter
    jmp loop_start ; Repeat loop

loop_end:
    ; Continue normal execution
    mov eax, 1 ; sys_exit
    xor ebx, ebx ; status 0
    int 0x80
```

The use of loop_start and loop_end labels clearly delineates the loop's structure, simplifying the process of tracing execution pathways.

Organizing Code with Sections: Segregating code into multiple sections (.text, .data, .bss) aids in organizing and isolating different types of program components. This separation is particularly beneficial in large programs as it enhances program organization and simplifies debugging and maintenance.

Utilizing Conditional Directives: Assembly languages often provide conditional directives, such as #ifdef, #endif, #define, and #undef, allowing the inclusion or exclusion of code based on certain conditions. These directives facilitate the development of adaptable programs capable of compiling different functionalities or features based on predefined conditions.

Listing 4.44: ASCII Character Encoding Example

```
%define DEBUG_MODE

section .data
    ; Variables and constants

section .text
    global _start

_start:
    ; Main program entry point
    %ifdef DEBUG_MODE
    call debug_procedure
    %endif

    ; Proceed with normal execution
    call normal_procedure

    ; Exit program
    mov eax, 1
    xor ebx, ebx
    int 0x80

debug_procedure:
    ; Debugging code
    ret

normal_procedure:
    ; Normal code
    ret
```

In this example, the debug_procedure is conditionally included in the program based on the DEBUG_MODE definition. This approach allows for flexible and easily configurable builds.

Employing Macros for Reusability: Macros provide a mechanism to encapsulate repetitive code sequences, enabling reuse and reducing redundancy. Effective use of macros can significantly enhance the maintainability of large programs.

Listing 4.45: ASCII Character Encoding Example

```
%macro PRINT_MESSAGE 1
    mov eax, 4 ; syscall number (sys_write)
    mov ebx, 1 ; file descriptor (stdout)
    mov ecx, %1 ; message to write
    mov edx, %1_len ; message length
    int 0x80 ; call kernel
%endmacro
```

```
section .data
message db "Hello, World!", 0xA
message_len equ $ - message

section .text
    global _start

_start:
    ; Use the macro to print a message
    PRINT_MESSAGE message

    ; Exit program
    mov eax, 1
    xor ebx, ebx
    int 0x80
```

The PRINT_MESSAGE macro simplifies printing messages by encapsulating system call logic, fostering code reuse and maintainability.

Effective Documentation and Comments: Extensive comments and documentation are indispensable in large programs to convey the purpose and functionality of code segments. Clear and concise comments help maintainers and collaborators understand the control flow, reducing the risk of introducing bugs during modifications.

Listing 4.46: ASCII Character Encoding Example

```
section .data
; Variables and constants

section .text
global _start

; Main program entry point
_start:
    call initialize ; Initialize the program
    call process ; Main processing routine
    call cleanup ; Clean up resources

    ; Exit the program
    mov eax, 1 ; sys_exit
    xor ebx, ebx ; status 0
    int 0x80

; Procedure to initialize the program
initialize:
    ; Initialization code
    ret

; Procedure for main processing
process:
    ; Processing code
    ret

; Procedure to clean up resources
cleanup:
    ; Cleanup code
    ret
```

Clearly labeled procedures and descriptive comments provide insight into the role and functionality of each segment, enhancing readability and maintainability.

These strategies collectively contribute to efficiently managing control flow in large assembly language programs, ensuring they remain organized, readable, and maintainable while optimizing performance.

4.11 Optimizing Control Flow for Performance

Optimizing control flow in assembly language is a critical aspect to ensure that programs run efficiently, making the best use of the processor's capabilities. This section delves into various techniques and strategies for enhancing control flow, thereby improving overall performance.

Minimizing Branch Penalties: Modern processors employ techniques such as pipelining and branch prediction to enhance performance. However, when a branch is mispredicted, the processor has to flush the pipeline and restart, which incurs a significant penalty. To minimize such penalties, consider the following strategies:

- **Branch Prediction Hints:** Some processors allow branch prediction hints to improve the accuracy of branch prediction. Using these hints can reduce mispredictions.
- **Invert Conditions:** Rewriting assembly code to merge conditional branches can sometimes result in fewer mispredictions. For instance, instead of using two branches to handle an if-else scenario, using the opposite condition and only one branch can be more efficient.

Listing 4.47: ASCII Character Encoding Example

```
  ; Original code with two branches
  cmp eax, 0
  je zero_case
  ; code for non-zero case
  jmp continue
zero_case:
  ; code for zero case
continue:

  ; Optimized code with a single branch
```

```
  cmp eax, 0
  jne non_zero_case
  ; code for zero case
  jmp continue
non_zero_case:
  ; code for non-zero case
continue:
```

Using Loop Unrolling: Loop unrolling is a common optimization technique that reduces the overhead of branch instructions within loops. By manually unrolling the loop, you decrease the number of branch instructions executed, which can improve performance.

Listing 4.48: ASCII Character Encoding Example

```
  ; Original loop
  mov ecx, 5 ; loop counter
loop_start:
  ; loop body
  dec ecx
  jnz loop_start

  ; Unrolled loop
  ; Assuming loop body performs the operation less than 5 times
  ; The remainder operations after unrolling are handled separately
  ; Unrolling loop body expands it inline
  ; This reduces branch instruction execution
  ; and pipeline flush
```

Utilizing Inline Functions: Inlining functions, where feasible, can reduce the overhead associated with procedure calls and returns. This is particularly beneficial for small functions where the overhead of a call and return might outweigh the function's actual computational cost.

Listing 4.49: ASCII Character Encoding Example

```
  ; Original function call
  call small_function
  ; code continues

small_function:
  ; function body
  ret

  ; Inlined function
  ; Instead of calling the function, the body is expanded inline
  ; This saves the call and return overhead
```

Efficient Use of Registers: Registers are the fastest storage elements available in a CPU. Efficient register use can greatly enhance control flow performance by minimizing memory access. Always prefer register operations over memory operations wherever possible.

Listing 4.50: ASCII Character Encoding Example

```
; Less efficient code with memory operations
mov eax, [var1]
add eax, [var2]
mov [result], eax

; Optimized code with register operations
mov eax, var1
mov ebx, var2
add eax, ebx
mov result, eax
```

Reducing Instruction Count: Reducing the overall instruction count can streamline the code and enhance performance. This can be achieved through a combination of factors, including but not limited to:

- **Use of Simple Instructions:** Prefer simpler, single-cycle instructions over complex multi-cycle instructions.
- **Eliminating Unnecessary Operations:** Remove any operations that do not contribute to the result.

Listing 4.51: ASCII Character Encoding Example

```
; Inefficient code with unnecessary operations
mov eax, 1
add eax, 2
sub eax, 1

; Optimized code
mov eax, 2
```

Instruction Scheduling: Optimizing the order in which instructions are executed to avoid pipeline stalls and make better use of the CPU's execution units. This involves arranging instructions to maximize parallelism and use of resources.

Listing 4.52: ASCII Character Encoding Example

```
; Inefficient instruction scheduling
mov eax, [mem1]
mov ebx, [mem2]
add eax, ebx

; Optimized instruction scheduling
; interleaves memory access and arithmetic operations
mov eax, [mem1]
add eax, [mem2]
```

Realizing performance gains through optimizing control flow in assembly requires a deep understanding of both the hardware and the specific characteristics of the program being optimized. By effectively employing branch prediction, loop unrolling, inlining functions, efficient register usage, reducing instruction count, and instruction scheduling, the performance of assembly language programs can be significantly improved.

4.12 Practical Examples of Control Flow Constructs

Control flow constructs are pivotal in determining the execution sequence of instructions within an assembly language program. This section provides in-depth practical examples of various control flow constructs, demonstrating their application and utility.

Example 1: Using Unconditional Jump (JMP)

The unconditional jump instruction, JMP, causes the processor to transfer control to a specified label. This is useful for branching to different parts of the program without any condition. Consider the following example:

Listing 4.53: ASCII Character Encoding Example

```
section .data
    msg db "End of the program", 0

section .text
    global _start

_start:
    ; Some code here
    jmp end_program
    ; This code will be skipped
continue_execution:
    ; Additional code here
    nop

end_program:
    mov edx, len msg
    mov ecx, msg
    mov ebx, 1
    mov eax, 4
    int 0x80 ; System call to write
    mov eax, 1
    int 0x80 ; System call to exit
```

In this example, the jmp end_program instruction transfers control unconditionally to the end_program label, skipping any intervening code.

Example 2: Conditional Jump (JE, JNE)

Conditional jumps alter the program flow based on the evaluation of standard flags (Zero Flag, Sign Flag, etc.). The following example illustrates the conditional jumps JE (Jump if Equal) and JNE (Jump if Not Equal):

Listing 4.54: ASCII Character Encoding Example

```
section .data
    num1 dd 5
    num2 dd 10

section .text
    global _start

_start:
    mov eax, [num1]
    cmp eax, [num2]
    je equal
    jne notequal

equal:
    ; Code to execute if num1 == num2
    mov eax, 1
    int 0x80

notequal:
    ; Code to execute if num1 != num2
    mov eax, 4
    int 0x80
```

Here, the cmp instruction sets the appropriate flags based on the comparison of num1 and num2. The je equal statement causes a jump to the equal label if the values are equal, whereas jne notequal causes a jump to the notequal label if they are not.

Example 3: Loop with LOOP Instruction

The LOOP instruction provides a mechanism to iterate a block of code a specified number of times. This instruction decrements the ECX register and jumps to the specified label if ECX is not zero.

Listing 4.55: ASCII Character Encoding Example

```
section .data
    array db 1, 2, 3, 4, 5 ; An array of 5 bytes

section .text
    global _start

_start:
    mov ecx, 5 ; Set loop counter (array size)
    lea esi, [array] ; Load array address into ESI

loop_start:
    ; Do something with the array elements
    mov al, [esi] ; Load byte into AL
    inc esi ; Move to next byte
    loop loop_start ; Decrement ECX and loop if not zero

    ; Exit program
```

```
    mov eax, 1
    int 0x80
```

Here, the mov ecx, 5 instruction initializes the loop counter, ECX, to 5, the number of elements in the array. The LOOP instruction decrements ECX and jumps to loop_start if ECX is not zero, iterating over each element of the array.

Example 4: Implementing If-Else Structures

If-else structures can be implemented using conditional jumps to create a branch in the code execution. The example below demonstrates a simple if-else logic.

Listing 4.56: ASCII Character Encoding Example

```
section .data
    var1 dd 15
    var2 dd 20

section .text
    global _start

_start:
    mov eax, [var1]
    cmp eax, [var2]
    jg greater_than
    jle less_or_equal

greater_than:
    ; Code to execute if var1 > var2
    mov eax, 1
    int 0x80 ; Exit

less_or_equal:
    ; Code to execute if var1 <= var2
    mov eax, 4
    int 0x80 ; Exit
```

In this example, the program compares var1 and var2. If var1 is greater than var2, it jumps to greater_than; otherwise, it jumps to less_or_equal.

Example 5: Switch-Case Implementation

Switch-case statements can be simulated in assembly using a series of comparisons and jumps to corresponding labels.

Listing 4.57: ASCII Character Encoding Example

```
section .data
    case_value dd 2

section .text
    global _start
```

```
_start:
    mov eax, [case_value]
    cmp eax, 1
    je case1
    cmp eax, 2
    je case2
    cmp eax, 3
    je case3
    jmp default_case

case1:
    ; Code for case 1
    mov eax, 10
    jmp end_switch

case2:
    ; Code for case 2
    mov eax, 20
    jmp end_switch

case3:
    ; Code for case 3
    mov eax, 30
    jmp end_switch

default_case:
    ; Default case
    mov eax, 0

end_switch:
    ; Exit program
    mov eax, 1
    int 0x80
```

This example simulates a switch-case statement by comparing case_value with each case and jumping to the respective code block. If no case matches, the program jumps to default_case.

The provided examples illustrate the practical application of various control flow constructs in assembly language, emphasizing their importance in directing program execution.

Chapter 5

Procedures and Macros

This chapter explores the use of procedures and macros in assembly language programming. It includes defining and calling procedures, passing arguments, returning values, and managing local variables and stack frames. The chapter also introduces macros, detailing their creation, usage, and the advantages and disadvantages compared to procedures. Practical examples and best practices are provided to illustrate the use of both constructs.

5.1 Introduction to Procedures

Procedures in assembly language serve as fundamental building blocks for creating modular, maintainable, and readable code. They are analogous to functions or subroutines in high-level programming languages, encapsulating a set of instructions that can be executed multiple times throughout a program. The use of procedures helps in minimizing code redundancy, simplifying debugging, and improving the organizational structure of assembly programs.

To define a procedure in assembly language, one typically uses a procedural directive or label to mark the beginning and end of the procedure. The manner in which these labels or directives are utilized can vary depending on the specific assembly language syntax being employed (e.g., x86 assembly, ARM assembly).

Listing 5.1: ASCII Character Encoding Example

```
example_procedure:
    ; procedure body
    mov eax, 1 ; example instruction
    ret ; return from the procedure
```

In the example above, example_procedure is the label that defines the start of the procedure. The instruction ret at the end of the procedure instructs the processor to return to the calling function by popping the return address off the stack.

A critical aspect of procedure use is the calling convention, which dictates how parameters are passed to the procedure and how the return value is provided back to the caller. Calling conventions can vary between operating systems and processor architectures, but generally, they fall into two categories: register-based and stack-based conventions.

In register-based calling conventions, parameters are passed via specific registers. For instance, in the x86 architecture using the cdecl convention, the eax, ecx, and edx registers are commonly used to pass the first three parameters. If additional parameters are required, they are passed on the stack.

Listing 5.2: ASCII Character Encoding Example

```
; Example of passing parameters in registers using the cdecl convention
example_procedure:
    ; assume the parameters are in eax, ecx, and edx
    add eax, ecx ; example operation on the parameters
    mul edx ; another example operation
    ret
```

In contrast, stack-based conventions pass all parameters via the stack. This approach ensures a consistent mechanism for procedure calls regardless of the number of parameters.

Listing 5.3: ASCII Character Encoding Example

```
; Example of a stack-based calling convention
example_stack_procedure:
    push ebp ; save base pointer
    mov ebp, esp ; set base pointer to stack pointer
    sub esp, 4 ; allocate space for local variables

    mov eax, [ebp+8] ; first parameter (assuming 32-bit address size)
    mov ecx, [ebp+12] ; second parameter

    add eax, ecx ; example operation

    mov esp, ebp ; reset stack pointer
    pop ebp ; restore base pointer
    ret
```

In the above stack-based example, push and pop instructions are used to manage the ebp register, commonly employed as the base pointer. The parameters are accessed relative to the base pointer, with positive offsets indicating locations on the call stack where the parameters reside.

The ret instruction, crucial to the function of procedures, operates by extracting the saved return address from the stack and transferring control back to the command immediately following the initial procedure call. This necessitates careful stack management within the procedure to ensure that the appropriate return address is at the top of the stack upon the execution of the ret instruction.

Procedures often require local variables, which are allocated on the stack. This approach provides space for variable storage unique to each procedure invocation. Proper local variable management entails reserving and releasing stack space as the procedure begins and concludes, respectively.

Listing 5.4: ASCII Character Encoding Example

```
; Include local variable management within a procedure
example_local_var_procedure:
    push ebp ; save the base pointer
    mov ebp, esp ; set the new base pointer
    sub esp, 8 ; allocate space for 2 local variables

    mov eax, [ebp+8] ; first parameter
    mov [ebp-4], eax ; store in a local variable

    ; perform operations involving local variables

    mov esp, ebp ; release local variables' stack space
    pop ebp ; restore the base pointer
    ret
```

Effective procedure design in assembly language necessitates meticulous attention to detail, particularly in stack operations and register usage. The proper handling of these elements ensures that procedures execute correctly and maintain the integrity of the call stack, facilitating the development of reliable and efficient assembly programs.

5.2 Defining and Calling Procedures

Procedures in assembly language provide a fundamental mechanism for structuring code, similar to functions or subroutines in high-level programming languages. They enable programmers to partition a program into manageable, reusable, and logically distinct segments, fostering better code organization and clarity. This section delves into the syntax and semantics of defining and calling procedures, alongside practical insights into their implementation in assembly language.

To define a procedure, one typically declares a label followed by a body of instructions and an instruction to return control to the caller. The ret instruction marks the end of a procedure, signalling that execution should resume at the instruction immediately following the point from where the procedure was called. For instance, in x86 assembly, a simple procedure definition may look like this:

Listing 5.5: ASCII Character Encoding Example

```
my_procedure:
    ; Procedure body starts
    mov eax, 1 ; Example instruction
    add eax, 2 ; Example instruction
    ; Procedure body ends
    ret
```

In this example, my_procedure is the procedure name, followed by its instructions. The procedure finishes with the ret instruction.

Calling a procedure involves using the call instruction with the procedure label as an argument. When the call instruction is executed, the current instruction pointer (IP) address is saved onto the stack, and execution jumps to the procedure's address. Here is how you call my_procedure:

Listing 5.6: ASCII Character Encoding Example

```
call my_procedure
```

When defining a more complex procedure that includes local variables and parameter passing, one needs to manage the stack meticulously. A common approach is to adhere to a convention such as the C calling convention, which defines a standard way to pass arguments, handle return values, and manage the stack frame.

Stack Frame Layout A stack frame is established at the start of a procedure to store local variables, saved registers, and return addresses. Typical steps for setting up and tearing down a stack frame include:

1. Preserving the previous base pointer (ebp) by pushing it onto the stack. 2. Setting the base pointer to the current stack pointer (esp). 3. Making space on the stack for local variables. 4. Restoring the base pointer (ebp) and stack pointer (esp) at the procedure's end before

returning control to the caller.

Consider the following example, where a procedure uses local variables:

Listing 5.7: ASCII Character Encoding Example

```
my_procedure:
    push ebp ; Save old base pointer
    mov ebp, esp ; Set new base pointer
    sub esp, 4 ; Allocate space for local variable

    mov eax, [ebp+8] ; Example instruction (reading an argument)
    add eax, 2 ; Example computation
    mov [ebp-4], eax ; Store the result in local variable

    mov esp, ebp ; Restore stack pointer
    pop ebp ; Restore old base pointer
    ret
```

This procedure begins by pushing ebp onto the stack to preserve the caller's frame and setting ebp to the current value of esp to establish a new frame. Space for local variables is created by subtracting from esp.

Argument Passing Arguments are typically pushed onto the stack before a procedure call. These arguments can then be accessed within the procedure via the base pointer (ebp). Below is an example procedure that accepts and manipulates arguments.

Listing 5.8: ASCII Character Encoding Example

```
my_procedure:
    push ebp ; Save old base pointer
    mov ebp, esp ; Set new base pointer
    sub esp, 4 ; Allocate space for local variable

    mov eax, [ebp+8] ; Load the first argument
    mov ecx, [ebp+12] ; Load the second argument
    add eax, ecx ; Perform computation
    mov [ebp-4], eax ; Store the result in local variable

    mov esp, ebp ; Restore stack pointer
    pop ebp ; Restore old base pointer
    ret

; Calling the procedure with arguments
push 3 ; Push the second argument
push 5 ; Push the first argument
call my_procedure
add esp, 8 ; Clean up stack after call
```

In this example, two arguments are pushed onto the stack before calling my_procedure. Inside the procedure, the arguments are accessed relative to ebp ([ebp+8] for the first argument and [ebp+12] for the second argument). After the procedure completes, the stack is adjusted to account for the pushed arguments.

Managing Local Variables Local variables are managed within the procedure's stack frame. Space for these variables is allocated by adjusting the stack pointer, typically at the start of the procedure. The allocated space can then be accessed using offsets from the base pointer (ebp). The following example demonstrates the use of local variables:

Listing 5.9: ASCII Character Encoding Example

```
my_procedure:
    push ebp ; Save old base pointer
    mov ebp, esp ; Set new base pointer
    sub esp, 8 ; Allocate space for two local variables

    mov [ebp-4], 5 ; Initialize first local variable
    mov [ebp-8], 10 ; Initialize second local variable
    ; Perform some operations using local variables

    mov esp, ebp ; Restore stack pointer
    pop ebp ; Restore old base pointer
    ret
```

In this example, two local variables are allocated by adjusting esp. The first local variable is accessed as [ebp-4] and the second as [ebp-8].

Example Procedure with Full Stack Management To encapsulate all discussed aspects, consider the following detailed example integrating argument passing and local variable management:

Listing 5.10: ASCII Character Encoding Example

```
compute_sum:
    push ebp ; Save old base pointer
    mov ebp, esp ; Set new base pointer
    sub esp, 4 ; Allocate space for one local variable

    mov eax, [ebp+8] ; Load the first argument into eax
    mov ecx, [ebp+12] ; Load the second argument into ecx
    add eax, ecx ; Compute the sum
    mov [ebp-4], eax ; Store the result in local variable

    mov eax, [ebp-4] ; Move the result into eax for return
    mov esp, ebp ; Restore stack pointer
    pop ebp ; Restore old base pointer
    ret

; Calling the procedure with arguments
push 7 ; Push the second argument
push 3 ; Push the first argument
call compute_sum ; Call the procedure
add esp, 8 ; Clean up the stack after the call
```

This procedure compute_sum computes the sum of two arguments. The arguments are pushed onto the stack, the procedure is called, and the result is returned by placing it in the eax register. The stack pointer is restored to its state before the call using the add esp, 8 instruction.

Through precise management of the stack and careful adherence to calling conventions, assembly language programmers can effectively define and call procedures to build structured, efficient, and maintainable code.

5.3 Passing Arguments to Procedures

Passing arguments to procedures in assembly language involves several standard practices that enhance code organization and reuse. By allowing values to be passed into a procedure, developers can write modular and flexible code. This section details the methods employed to pass arguments to procedures, focusing on common techniques such as using registers, stack-based argument passing, and related conventions.

1. Using Registers to Pass Arguments

The simplest method to pass arguments to a procedure is by storing the values in CPU registers. This approach is efficient because accessing data in registers is faster compared to memory access. Typically, general-purpose registers such as EAX, EBX, ECX, and EDX are used.

For example, consider a procedure that adds two numbers:

Listing 5.11: ASCII Character Encoding Example

```
segment .data
    ; No data needed for this example

segment .text
global _start

_start:
    mov eax, 5 ; First argument
    mov ebx, 3 ; Second argument
    call add_numbers

    ; Exit code
    mov eax, 1
    int 0x80

add_numbers:
    add eax, ebx ; eax = eax + ebx
    ret
```

In this example, EAX and EBX are used to hold the two numbers to be added. The add_numbers procedure reads from these registers directly to perform the addition operation.

2. Stack-based Argument Passing

For procedures requiring more arguments than available registers or for greater flexibility, arguments can be passed via the stack. This method involves pushing the arguments onto the stack before calling the procedure. The procedure then accesses these arguments using the stack pointer ESP and base pointer EBP.

Consider another example of a procedure that adds two numbers, but this time using the stack:

Listing 5.12: ASCII Character Encoding Example

```
segment .data
    ; No data needed for this example

segment .text
global _start

_start:
    push 5 ; Push first argument
    push 3 ; Push second argument
    call add_numbers
    add esp, 8 ; Clean up the stack

    ; Exit code
    mov eax, 1
    int 0x80

add_numbers:
    push ebp ; Save base pointer
    mov ebp, esp ; Establish new base pointer
    mov eax, [ebp+8] ; First argument (3rd item on stack)
    mov ebx, [ebp+12] ; Second argument (4th item on stack)
    add eax, ebx
    pop ebp ; Restore base pointer
    ret
```

In this example, the values 5 and 3 are pushed onto the stack in reverse order (last in, first out). The add_numbers procedure then sets up the stack frame, accesses the arguments using EBP, and finally performs the addition.

3. Calling Conventions

Calling conventions standardize how arguments are passed to procedures and how returns are managed. This ensures compatibility between code modules.

- **cdecl** (C Declaration): Arguments are pushed onto the stack from right to left, and the caller cleans the stack. This is commonly used in C programming.

- **stdcall** (Standard Call): Similar to cdecl, but the callee cleans the stack. Often used in Windows API functions.

- **fastcall**: Arguments are passed using registers first and then the stack if needed. This method aims to reduce function call overhead.

Consider a cdecl example:

Listing 5.13: ASCII Character Encoding Example

```
section .data
    ; No data needed for this example

section .text
global _start

_start:
    push dword 4 ; Push third argument
    push dword 2 ; Push second argument
    push dword 1 ; Push first argument
    call sum_three
    add esp, 12 ; Clean up the stack

    ; Exit code
    mov eax, 1
    int 0x80

sum_three:
    push ebp
    mov ebp, esp
    mov eax, [ebp+8]
    mov ebx, [ebp+12]
    mov ecx, [ebp+16]
    add eax, ebx
    add eax, ecx
    pop ebp
    ret
```

In this program, three arguments (1, 2, and 4) are passed to the sum_three procedure using the cdecl convention where the caller cleans the stack after the procedure call.

Understanding how to pass arguments to procedures is crucial for effective assembly language programming. It allows for structured and reusable code, critical for managing complex software projects.

5.4 Returning Values from Procedures

In assembly language programming, returning values from procedures involves transferring data from the callee back to the caller. The method to return values typically leverages specific registers due to their speed and simplicity. The conventional method uses the EAX register for this purpose because of its ubiquity and efficiency.

Using the EAX Register

A common convention in many assembly languages, including x86 assembly, is to use the EAX register to store the return value of a procedure. This register is chosen because it is a general-purpose register and its usage is consistent across various assembly languages, fostering interoperability and readability of code.

Here is an example illustrating a procedure that calculates the sum of two numbers and returns the result in the EAX register:

Listing 5.14: ASCII Character Encoding Example

```
sum PROC
    ; Assume the parameters are in the registers EBX and ECX
    ; Add the contents of ECX to EBX and store the result in EAX
    mov EAX, EBX
    add EAX, ECX
    ret
sum ENDP
```

In this example, the procedure sum takes two arguments via EBX and ECX, performs the addition, and stores the result in EAX. The ret instruction at the end ensures control is passed back to the calling procedure with the return value in EAX.

Handling Multiple Return Values

When multiple values need to be returned, additional registers or memory locations are utilized. Commonly used registers for this purpose include EBX, ECX, EDX, and ESI. An example procedure returning two values might look like this:

Listing 5.15: ASCII Character Encoding Example

```
multiply_and_add PROC
    ; Assume input values are in EBX and ECX
    ; EBX holds the multiplicand, ECX holds the multiplier/addend

    ; Multiply EBX by ECX, store in EAX
    mov EAX, EBX
    imul EAX, ECX

    ; Add ECX to EAX, store result in EDX
```

```
    add EAX, ECX
    mov EDX, EAX

    ; Return values: product in EAX, sum in EDX
    ret
multiply_and_add ENDP
```

This procedure, multiply_and_add, multiplies the values stored in EBX and ECX, places the product in EAX, adds the initial value of ECX to the product, and stores the result in EDX. Upon return, the caller can retrieve the results from EAX and EDX.

Using the Stack for Return Values

Occasionally, it is necessary to return values using the stack, especially when dealing with larger data types or structures. The procedure pushes the return values onto the stack, enabling the caller to retrieve them after the procedure call.

Listing 5.16: ASCII Character Encoding Example

```
calculate_area_and_perimeter PROC
    ; Calculate area and perimeter of a rectangle
    ; Assume input length is in EBX and width is in ECX

    ; Calculate area (length * width)
    mov EAX, EBX
    imul EAX, ECX
    push EAX ; Push area on the stack

    ; Calculate perimeter (2 * (length + width))
    add EBX, ECX
    shl EBX, 1 ; Multiply by 2
    push EBX ; Push perimeter on the stack

    ret
calculate_area_and_perimeter ENDP
```

The calculate_area_and_perimeter procedure in this example computes the area and perimeter of a rectangle using its length and width supplied in EBX and ECX. The results are pushed onto the stack. The caller can access these values by popping them from the stack in the appropriate sequence.

```
; Caller code to retrieve values from the stack:
call calculate_area_and_perimeter
pop EAX ; Retrieve perimeter
pop EBX ; Retrieve area
```

The caller retrieves the perimeter and area from the stack by popping them into the desired registers EAX and EBX, respectively.

Best Practices for Returning Values

To ensure maintainability and readability of the assembly code, the following best practices are recommended:

- Utilize standard conventions, such as using EAX for single return values, to improve code clarity.
- Document procedures clearly to indicate the registers or memory locations used for returning values.
- When using the stack for multiple return values, ensure proper stack cleanup to avoid stack corruption.
- Reserve the usage of the stack for returning complex data structures or when the number of return values exceeds available registers.

By adhering to these guidelines, assembly programmers can ensure their code remains efficient, readable, and maintainable. Efficient use of registers and the stack for returning values is a fundamental aspect of writing robust assembly language procedures.

5.5 Local Variables in Procedures

In assembly language programming, the concept of local variables is crucial for maintaining data encapsulation within procedures. Local variables are only accessible within the procedure in which they are declared, ensuring no unintended interference from other parts of the program. This encapsulation also allows for recursive procedures, as each call can maintain its own set of variables.

Local variables are typically stored on the stack. To manage these variables efficiently, we adopt a consistent strategy to allocate and deallocate space for them in the procedure's stack frame. A stack frame is the section of the stack that holds the data for a single procedure call, including the return address, arguments, and local variables. The stack pointer (texttt%esp) and the base pointer (texttt%ebp) registers play a vital role in stack frame management.

The procedure to create, access, and destroy local variables involves the following steps:

- Setting up a stack frame.
- Allocating space for local variables.

- Accessing local variables.
- Deallocating space and restoring the stack frame.

Consider a procedure that uses local variables for its computations. The stack frame layout must be managed with precision. We illustrate this through an example of a procedure that computes the sum of two integer values and stores the result in a local variable.

Listing 5.17: ASCII Character Encoding Example

```
section .data

section .bss

section .text
    global _start

sum_of_two:
    push %ebp ; Save the old base pointer
    mov %ebp, %esp ; Set the new base pointer
    sub %esp, 8 ; Allocate space for local variables (2 x 4 bytes)

    mov eax, [ebp+8] ; Load the first argument (arg1) into eax
    add eax, [ebp+12] ; Add the second argument (arg2) to eax
    mov [ebp-4], eax ; Store the result in a local variable

    mov %esp, %ebp ; Deallocate local variables
    pop %ebp ; Restore the old base pointer
    ret ; Return from the procedure
```

In this example, %ebp and %esp registers are used to manage the stack frame:

- **push** %ebp: The current base pointer value is pushed onto the stack. This saves the caller's base pointer for restoration later.
- **mov** %ebp**,** %esp: The stack pointer is copied to the base pointer, setting up a new base of the stack frame for this call.
- **sub** %esp**, 8**: Space is allocated for local variables by decrementing the stack pointer. Here, 8 bytes are allocated for two integers.
- **mov** eax**, [**ebp+8**]**: The first argument passed to the procedure is accessed using the base pointer offset.
- **add** eax**, [**ebp+12**]**: The second argument is loaded and added to the first, both accessed through the stack frame.
- **mov** [ebp-4]**,** eax: The result of the addition is stored in a local variable within the stack frame.

- **mov** %esp, %ebp: The stack pointer is reset to the base pointer value, effectively deallocating the local variable space.
- **pop** %ebp: The original base pointer is restored by popping it from the stack.
- **ret**: The return instruction is executed, transferring control back to the calling procedure.

This methodology ensures that local variables are confined to their respective procedures and that the stack is correctly managed. When control returns to the caller, the stack state is as it was before the procedure call.

The advantages of using local variables include:

- **Isolation**: Local variables are protected from unintended interactions with other parts of the program.
- **Reusability**: The same variable names can be used in different procedures without conflict.
- **Efficiency**: Local variables can be efficiently managed on the stack by simple adjustments to the stack pointer and base pointer.
- **Recursiveness**: Each call to a recursive procedure gets its own set of local variables, enabling independent operations across recursive calls.

Proper stack frame management is essential to prevent issues such as stack corruption, which can lead to unpredictable behavior or program crashes. By adhering to these conventions, assembly language programs can achieve both robustness and maintainability.

The following example demonstrates a recursive calculation of the Fibonacci sequence using local variables:

Listing 5.18: ASCII Character Encoding Example

```
section .data

section .bss

section .text
    global _start

fibonacci:
    push %ebp
    mov %ebp, %esp
```

```
    sub %esp, 8 ; Allocate space for local variables

    mov eax, [ebp+8] ; Load the argument n

    cmp eax, 1
    jle .base_case ; If n <= 1, jump to base case

    ; Recursive case
    ; Compute fibonacci(n-1)
    dec eax
    push eax
    call fibonacci
    add %esp, 4
    mov [ebp-4], eax ; Store fibonacci(n-1) in local variable

    ; Compute fibonacci(n-2)
    mov eax, [ebp+8]
    sub eax, 2
    push eax
    call fibonacci
    add %esp, 4
    add eax, [ebp-4] ; Add fibonacci(n-2) to fibonacci(n-1)

    jmp .end

.base_case:
    ; Base case: fibonacci(0) = 0 and fibonacci(1) = 1
    mov eax, [ebp+8]
    cmp eax, 0
    jne .fib_one
    mov eax, 0
    jmp .end

.fib_one:
    mov eax, 1

.end:
    mov %esp, %ebp ; Deallocate local variables
    pop %ebp
    ret
```

In the recursive fibonacci procedure:

- The base case checks if n is 0 or 1, returning the appropriate values.
- For values greater than 1, the function makes two recursive calls: fibonacci(n-1) and fibonacci(n-2).
- Local variable [ebp-4] is used to store the result of fibonacci(n-1) temporarily, before adding it to the result of fibonacci(n-2).

Correctly managing the stack frame allows each recursive call to maintain its own context, ensuring accurate calculations are preserved throughout the recursion process. By following these principles, programmers can effectively leverage local variables in assembly language procedures.

5.6 Stack Frame Layout and Management

The stack frame, an essential construct in assembly language programming, supports procedure calls and facilitates local variable storage, argument passing, and return address management. Understanding its layout and how to manage it effectively is crucial for writing robust and efficient assembly programs.

A stack frame is created every time a procedure (function) is called. It resides on the call stack, which is a last-in-first-out (LIFO) data structure used to keep track of active procedure calls. When a procedure is invoked, a new stack frame is pushed onto the stack; when a procedure returns, its stack frame is popped off.

Listing 5.19: ASCII Character Encoding Example

```
push ebp ; Save the caller's base pointer
mov ebp, esp ; Set the base pointer to the current stack pointer
sub esp, locals_size ; Allocate space for local variables
```

Anatomy of a Stack Frame

A typical stack frame includes:

- **Return Address**: This is the address to which control should return after the procedure finishes execution. It is automatically stored on the stack by the call instruction.
- **Old Base Pointer (EBP)**: The base pointer of the calling procedure, saved to facilitate stack unwinding. It is usually saved at the start of the procedure using push and restored before returning.
- **Local Variables and Temporary Storage**: Space for storing procedure's local variables and any temporary data necessary during execution. The size of this block is defined by the number of local variables declared.
- **Parameters**: The arguments passed to the procedure. These are placed on the stack by the caller before the call instruction.

Stack Frame Creation and Cleanup

Procedures generally follow a standard prologue and epilogue to set up and dismantle their stack frame. The prologue involves setting up the stack frame when the procedure begins, and the epilogue involves tearing it down before the procedure returns.

Prologue:

Listing 5.20: ASCII Character Encoding Example

```
push ebp ; Save the caller's base pointer
mov ebp, esp ; Set the base pointer to the current stack pointer
sub esp, locals_size ; Allocate space for local variables
```

The push ebp instruction saves the base pointer (EBP) of the caller onto the stack. The mov ebp, esp instruction sets EBP to the current value of the stack pointer (ESP), establishing a new base for the current stack frame. The sub esp, locals_size instruction reserves space for local variables by adjusting the stack pointer.

Epilogue:

Listing 5.21: ASCII Character Encoding Example

```
mov esp, ebp ; Restore the stack pointer
pop ebp ; Restore the caller's base pointer
ret ; Return to the caller
```

The mov esp, ebp instruction restores the stack pointer to the base of the current stack frame. The pop ebp instruction restores the caller's base pointer, and the ret instruction returns control to the address saved on the stack.

Managing Local Variables

Local variables are typically accessed using the base pointer (EBP), which remains constant throughout the procedure's lifetime. For instance, a variable located at an offset of -4 from EBP can be accessed as:

Listing 5.22: ASCII Character Encoding Example

```
mov eax, [ebp-4]
```

By using offsets from EBP, you can use positive offsets to access arguments passed to the procedure and negative offsets to access local variables.

Handling Parameters

Parameters passed to a procedure are placed on the stack by the caller before the call instruction. They can be accessed using positive offsets from the base pointer (EBP). For instance, accessing the first parameter might look like:

Listing 5.23: ASCII Character Encoding Example

```
mov eax, [ebp+8] ; Assuming the return address is at [ebp+4] and first parameter at [
    ebp+8]
```

Example: Complete Procedure

Consider a procedure that adds two integers passed as arguments and returns the result.

Caller Code:

Listing 5.24: ASCII Character Encoding Example

```
push 5 ; Argument 2
push 3 ; Argument 1
call AddTwoNumbers
add esp, 8 ; Clean up arguments
```

Procedure Code:

Listing 5.25: ASCII Character Encoding Example

```
AddTwoNumbers:
    push ebp ; Save the caller's base pointer
    mov ebp, esp ; Set the base pointer to the current stack pointer
    sub esp, 4 ; Allocate space for one local variable

    mov eax, [ebp+8] ; Load first argument
    mov ecx, [ebp+12] ; Load second argument
    add eax, ecx ; Add arguments
    mov [ebp-4], eax ; Store result in local variable

    mov esp, ebp ; Restore the stack pointer
    pop ebp ; Restore the caller's base pointer
    ret ; Return to caller
```

The above procedure demonstrates the creation and management of a stack frame. The caller prepares the stack by pushing arguments. The callee creates a stack frame, processes the arguments, performs calculations, and finally dismantles the stack frame before returning.

Proper stack frame management is critical for the stability and correctness of assembly programs. It ensures that function calls are properly nested and that local variables and parameters do not interfere with one another, maintaining program correctness.

5.7 Recursion in Assembly Language

Recursion is a fundamental concept in programming where a function calls itself in order to solve a problem. Since assembly language gives programmers detailed control over system resources, implementing recursion requires careful management of the stack to store return addresses, local variables, and function parameters.

The key to recursion is maintaining the state of each function call. In high-level languages, this is often handled implicitly by the runtime environment, but in assembly language, it necessitates explicit manipulation of the stack.

To demonstrate recursion in assembly language, we will consider the classic example of calculating the factorial of a number. The factorial of a non-negative integer n, denoted as $n!$, is the product of all positive integers less than or equal to n. Formally, it can be defined recursively as follows:

$$n! = \begin{cases} 1 & \text{if } n = 0 \\ n \times (n-1)! & \text{if } n > 0 \end{cases}$$

To implement this in assembly language, we need to:

- Define the factorial procedure.
- Handle the base case where $n = 0$.
- Recursively call the factorial procedure for $n - 1$.
- Manage the stack carefully to keep track of the return addresses and intermediate values.

Consider the following assembly code in x86 architecture, which calculates the factorial of a number. It assumes the number for which the factorial is to be calculated is in the eax register, and the result will be returned in the eax register as well.

Listing 5.26: ASCII Character Encoding Example

```
section .data
    result db 0

section .text
    global _start

_start:
    mov eax, 5 ; Calculate factorial of 5
```

```
    call factorial
    mov [result], al ; Store the result in data section
    ; Exit system call
    mov eax, 1
    int 0x80

factorial:
    ; Base case: if (n == 0) return 1
    cmp eax, 0
    je .base_case

    ; Save current value of eax (n) on stack
    push eax
    ; Decrement eax to get (n-1) for the recursive call
    dec eax
    call factorial
    ; Retrieve the previous value of eax (n) from stack
    pop ebx
    ; Multiply eax (accumulated result) by ebx (n)
    mul ebx
    ret

.base_case:
    mov eax, 1
    ret
```

The process starts in the _start section, where the program prepares to calculate the factorial of 5 by loading this value into eax and calling the factorial procedure.

Upon entering the factorial procedure, the value in eax is checked against zero. If it is zero, the base case has been reached, and the procedure returns 1 by moving 1 into eax and returning to the caller.

For non-zero values, the current value of eax (representing n) is pushed onto the stack. The value in eax is then decremented to prepare for the next recursive call which calculates $(n-1)!$. After the recursive call returns, the original value of eax (representing n) is popped from the stack into ebx. The result stored in eax is then multiplied by ebx to compute $n \times (n-1)!$, which represents the factorial of n. Finally, the procedure returns, passing this result back to the caller.

This implementation effectively demonstrates recursion in assembly language, emphasizing the explicit stack management required to preserve the state across recursive calls. It is crucial to ensure that each function call has its own context, saved on the stack, to avoid interference between consecutive recursive calls. Proper stack management and adherence to calling conventions ensure that the recursive function executes correctly and efficiently.

5.8 Introduction to Macros

Macros in assembly language provide a mechanism to include blocks of code that can be reused across a program. Macros are crucial for code efficiency and maintainability, as they replace repetitive code sequences with compact and readable instructions. A macro is a sequence of instructions and directives that can be expanded inline during assembly time.

Macros allow the programmer to define a sequence of instructions that can be invoked by a simple identifier. Unlike procedures, which encapsulate code that is called during runtime, macros are expanded by the assembler, resulting in direct substitution of the macro contents. This characteristic can lead to increased code size but can also improve execution speed as there is no need for call overhead.

To define a macro, we use the macro directive followed by the macro name and the macro body, which consists of assembly statements and directives. Below is the general syntax for defining a macro:

Listing 5.27: ASCII Character Encoding Example

```
macro MACRO_NAME
    ; macro body
    ; any number of assembly instructions
endm
```

Where, - MACRO_NAME is the identifier used to invoke or call the macro. - The endm directive marks the end of the macro definition.

To illustrate, consider a macro that adds two numbers and stores the result in a given register. The following is an example of such a macro:

Listing 5.28: ASCII Character Encoding Example

```
macro ADD_NUMS reg1, reg2, result
    load reg1, result ; Load the first number into the result
    add reg2, result ; Add the second number
endm
```

To use this macro in an assembly program, you simply call it with the appropriate arguments, as shown below:

Listing 5.29: ASCII Character Encoding Example

```
ADD_NUMS R1, R2, R3
```

The above invocation will be expanded by the assembler as if the following instructions were written directly:

Listing 5.30: ASCII Character Encoding Example

```
load R1, R3
add R2, R3
```

An important aspect of macros is the ability to accept parameters, which makes them highly versatile. Parameters passed to the macro are placeholders that are replaced by actual values or registers during macro expansion. The parameters enable macros to adapt their behavior based on the given arguments.

Here is another example of a macro that can compute the square of a number:

Listing 5.31: ASCII Character Encoding Example

```
macro SQUARE number, result
    load number, result ; Load the number into the result
    mul result, result ; Multiply the result by itself
endm
```

Invoking this macro with specific registers or values would look like this:

Listing 5.32: ASCII Character Encoding Example

```
SQUARE R4, R5
```

Which expands to:

Listing 5.33: ASCII Character Encoding Example

```
load R4, R5
mul R5, R5
```

Macros can also include conditional assembly constructs, allowing them to adapt dynamically based on certain conditions. For instance, conditional and iterative constructs can be embedded within macros using directives like IF, ELSE, ENDIF, and REPT.

Consider the following macro, which increments a register a given number of times:

Listing 5.34: ASCII Character Encoding Example

```
macro INCREMENT reg, count
    REPT count
        inc reg
    endm
```

Here, REPT and ENDM define a repeat loop that expands the inc instruction count times:

Listing 5.35: ASCII Character Encoding Example

```
INCREMENT R6, 5
```

This will expand as:

Listing 5.36: ASCII Character Encoding Example

```
inc R6
inc R6
inc R6
inc R6
inc R6
```

The use of macros can significantly reduce repetitive code and enhance readability. However, it is essential to be aware of the potential increase in code size since macros expand inline. Proper use of macros thus remains a balance between code readability, maintainability, and size.

Macros are invaluable tools in assembly language that aid in preventing redundancy and fostering modular code. By leveraging macro definitions, we can encapsulate common code patterns, leading to easier updates and modifications across an entire program. As we delve deeper into macros and their functionalities, their power in simplifying complex assembly code will become increasingly evident.

5.9 Creating and Using Macros

Macros in assembly language are powerful tools that allow the programmer to define reusable code blocks, which can simplify complex coding tasks and enhance code readability. Unlike procedures, which exist as separate entities and require jumps to and from the procedure code, macros are expanded in place, resulting in inline code generation. This section delves into the precise methods of creating and using macros, highlighting their syntax, usage, and practical benefits in assembly programming.

To define a macro, the macrodirective is used, followed by the macro name and any required parameters. Here is an example of a simple macro definition:

Listing 5.37: ASCII Character Encoding Example

```
macro PRINT_STRING msg
    ; Move the message address into the di register
    mov di, offset msg
    ; Use a loop to print each character until null terminator is reached
.print_loop:
```

```
    lodsb
    or al, al
    jz .done
    int 0x10
    jmp .print_loop
.done:
endm
```

In this example, the macro named PRINT_STRING is designed to print a zero-terminated string provided as an argument. The msg parameter represents the memory location of the string to be printed. Here's a breakdown of how to use this macro within an assembly program:

Listing 5.38: ASCII Character Encoding Example

```
data segment
    hello_msg db 'Hello, World!', 0
data ends

code segment
    assume ds:data, cs:code
start:
    ; Load data segment into ds register
    mov ax, data
    mov ds, ax

    ; Call the PRINT_STRING macro with hello_msg as an argument
    PRINT_STRING hello_msg

    ; Program termination
    mov ax, 4c00h
    int 21h
code ends
end start
```

This code demonstrates how to incorporate the PRINT_STRING macro to output the string hello_msg to the display. In the data segment, the string is defined and terminated with a null character. The data segment is loaded into the ds register before invoking the macro with hello_msg as its argument.

Macros can accept one or more parameters that are passed during macro invocation. These parameters can be used as though they are part of the macro code. Consider the next example where a macro to add two numbers is defined:

Listing 5.39: ASCII Character Encoding Example

```
macro ADD_NUMS num1, num2, result
    ; Load numbers into registers
    mov ax, num1
    add ax, num2
    ; Store the result
    mov result, ax
```

```
endm
```

In this instance, the ADD_NUMS macro takes three parameters: num1, num2, and result. It loads num1 and num2 into the ax register, performs the addition, and stores the result.

Macros can also be more complex, involving conditional statements and loops. Here is an example of a macro that performs a loop over an array of integers to find the maximum value:

Listing 5.40: ASCII Character Encoding Example

```
macro FIND_MAX array, length, max_val
    ; Initialize registers
    xor cx, cx
    mov cx, length
    mov di, offset array
    ; Load the first element into max_val
    mov ax, [di]
    mov max_val, ax
    add di, 2
    dec cx
.find_loop:
    ; Load the next element
    mov ax, [di]
    ; Compare and store if greater
    cmp max_val, ax
    jl .update_max
    jmp .next
.update_max:
    mov max_val, ax
.next:
    add di, 2
    loop .find_loop
endm
```

The FIND_MAX macro iterates over an array array of a given length length, updating the max_val with the maximum value found. The use of primarily registers and the loop instruction ensures efficient execution.

Despite their power, macros should be used judiciously, as their in-place expansion can lead to code bloat, increasing the size of the bin executable if overused. They are best suited for repetitive, simple tasks that benefit from inline expansion without substantial increase in code size.

Practical usage of macros offers significant benefits, including improved code readability, maintainability, and reduction in typing errors for repetitive code patterns. These advantages, however, must be balanced against potential binary size growth and maintainability of heavily macro-based code.

When writing macros, it is essential to comment thoroughly, defining the purpose of each macro and detailing its parameters and expected outcomes. Proper documentation within the macro body contributes to better code understanding and maintenance by other programmers. By mastering macro creation and usage, an assembly language programmer can achieve more efficient, understandable, and maintainable code.

5.10 Advantages and Disadvantages of Macros

Macros in assembly language serve as a powerful tool for programmers, enabling code reuse and simplification of complex sequences of instructions. Nevertheless, they present a mix of benefits and potential downsides which must be carefully evaluated based on the specific requirements of a project.

Advantages

- **Code Reusability:** Macros facilitate the reuse of code blocks without the need to write the same segments repeatedly. This is particularly useful for repetitive operations or patterns.
- **Simplification of Code:** Macros can significantly simplify the main code by abstracting intricate and verbose instruction sequences into single macro invocations, reducing clutter and enhancing readability.
- **Increased Maintainability:** When a frequently used operation needs to be updated or modified, changing the macro definition updates all macro usages, making the codebase easier to maintain.
- **Parameterization:** Macros can accept parameters, allowing for flexible and context-specific code generation without redundancies, thereby increasing versatility.
- **No Runtime Overhead:** Since macros are expanded at assembly time, they do not incur runtime overhead. This can lead to performance optimizations in tight, timing-critical sections of code.

Disadvantages

- **Increased Binary Size:** Because macros are expanded at assembly time, repeated macro invocations can result in multiple copies of the expanded code, potentially leading to larger binary sizes compared to using procedures.
- **Lack of Modularity:** Unlike procedures, macros do not provide the same level of modularity. Code encapsulated within macros cannot be as easily isolated, tested, or debugged separately.
- **Complexity in Debugging:** Debugging code that uses macros extensively can be challenging, as errors in macro definitions can propagate to multiple locations, complicating the identification of issues.
- **Limited Error Checking:** Assemblers typically offer limited error checking for macro expansions. Issues related to macro arguments or syntax can introduce subtle bugs that are hard to trace.
- **Namespace Pollution:** Macros do not inherently respect scope and can lead to issues with naming conflicts, as there is no native mechanism to prevent macros from interfering with other parts of the code.

Example

Consider the following macro definition and its usage in assembly language:

Listing 5.41: ASCII Character Encoding Example

```
MY_MACRO MACRO arg1, arg2
    MOV EAX, arg1
    ADD EAX, arg2
ENDM

MAIN PROC
    MY_MACRO 5, 10
    MY_MACRO 20, 30
    RET
MAIN ENDP
```

The macro MY_MACRO takes two arguments, arg1 and arg2, and generates code to move the first argument into the EAX register and add the second argument to EAX. When invoked within the MAIN procedure, the assembler expands it into inline code:

```
MOV EAX, 5
ADD EAX, 10
MOV EAX, 20
ADD EAX, 30
```

While this example demonstrates the simplicity and clarity provided by using macros, it also illustrates the potential for increased binary size due to repeated code expansion.

To effectively leverage macros, programmers should balance their usage against the application's overall constraints and requirements. By considering both the advantages and disadvantages, proficient use of macros can lead to cleaner, more maintainable, and efficient assembly language programs.

5.11 Procedures vs. Macros: When to Use Which

The choice between using procedures or macros in assembly language programming is a critical decision based on several factors, including the specifics of the task at hand, the need for code reusability, readability, and the performance requirements. Understanding the distinct characteristics and implications of each construct is essential for making an informed decision.

Procedures, also known as subroutines, allow for the encapsulation of code into callable units. This is beneficial for modularity, enabling code reuse and maintaining program structure. When a procedure is called, the system creates a new stack frame, pushing parameters, return addresses, and local variables onto the stack. This provides an isolated context in which the procedure operates, ensuring the encapsulation of procedure-specific variables and state. The following is an example of a simple procedure in x86 assembly:

Listing 5.42: ASCII Character Encoding Example

```
segment .data
    msg db 'Hello, world!',0

segment .text
    global _start

_start:
    call print_message

print_message:
    mov eax, 4 ; sys_write
    mov ebx, 1 ; file descriptor (stdout)
```

```
    mov ecx, msg ; message to write
    mov edx, 13 ; length
    int 0x80 ; interrupt to make kernel call
    ret
```

When the print_message procedure is called, the execution context shifts to the procedure, which then performs its designated task and returns control back with the RET instruction. Using procedures thus enhances code clarity and maintainability.

Macros, in contrast, are a preprocessor feature that essentially perform text substitution. When a macro is defined and subsequently invoked, the assembler replaces the macro invocation with the corresponding code block. This expansion happens at compile time, resulting in potentially larger, but faster-executing code since the overhead of a procedure call and return is avoided. Below is an example of a macro in x86 assembly:

Listing 5.43: ASCII Character Encoding Example

```
%macro PRINT_STRING 2
    mov eax, 4 ; sys_write
    mov ebx, 1 ; file descriptor (stdout)
    mov ecx, %1 ; message to write
    mov edx, %2 ; length of the message
    int 0x80 ; call kernel
%endmacro

segment .data
    msg db 'Hello, world!',0

segment .text
    global _start

_start:
    PRINT_STRING msg, 13
```

Here, the PRINT_STRING macro generates code for printing a string. Each macro invocation results in an in-place substitution, which eliminates the call overhead and can improve performance.

Key factors for choosing between procedures and macros include:

- **Code Size:** Procedures can result in smaller code size because the same procedure code is reused multiple times. Conversely, macros can lead to code bloat, as the macro is expanded in place for each call.

- **Execution Speed:** Macros may provide faster execution since there is no overhead associated with procedure calls and stack management. This can be critical in performance-sensitive applications.

- **Parameter Passing:** Procedures handle complex parameter passing via the stack, supporting multiple and varied argument types. Macros handle parameter substitution directly, with limited flexibility.
- **Readability and Maintainability:** Procedures improve readability and maintainability by structuring code into logical units and reducing repetition. Macros, if overused or poorly structured, can obscure code.
- **Scope and Lifetime:** Procedures offer local scope for variables, aiding encapsulation and reducing side-effects. Macros lack this capability, making effective management of variable scope more challenging.

When to use procedures:

- When code reuse and modular design are priorities.
- When the overhead of procedure calls is acceptable.
- When maintaining the clarity and readability of the code is important.
- When complex parameter passing is required.

When to use macros:

- When performance is critical, and eliminating call overhead is beneficial.
- When the task is simple and does not require complex parameter passing or local variables.
- When the same code block needs to be inserted multiple times, making text substitution efficient.
- When the overall code size is not a primary concern.

Integrating both procedures and macros appropriately can lead to optimized and maintainable assembly code, balancing performance with structured design.

5.12 Examples and Best Practices for Procedures and Macros

This section delves into practical examples to solidify the concepts discussed in the previous sections and provides best practices for the effective use of procedures and macros in assembly language programming.

Consider the following scenario where a procedure is used to calculate the factorial of a number. This example demonstrates defining a procedure, passing an argument, managing the stack frame, and returning a value.

Listing 5.44: ASCII Character Encoding Example

```
; Procedure to calculate factorial
factorial PROC
    ; Save the base pointer
    push ebp
    mov ebp, esp
    ; Move the argument to eax
    mov eax, [ebp+8]

    cmp eax, 1
    jle end_factorial

    dec eax

    ; Push the new argument onto the stack for the recursive call
    push eax
    call factorial

    ; Restore the stack
    pop ecx
    mul ecx

end_factorial:
    ; Restore the base pointer and return
    mov esp, ebp
    pop ebp
    ret 4
factorial ENDP
```

```
; Input: EAX = 5
; Output: EAX = 120 (5!)
```

In this factorial example, the procedure accepts a single argument, calculates the factorial recursively, and returns the result in the eax register. Notice how the stack frame is managed using push and pop instructions.

Best practices for defining and using procedures:

- Always save the ebp register at the beginning of the procedure and restore it at the end. This ensures the previous stack frame is preserved.
- Use ret n instruction to clean up stack arguments for stdcall calling conventions.
- Ensure that stack balance is maintained to prevent stack corruption or crashes.
- Use comments generously to describe the purpose and functionality of the procedure, especially for complex logic.

Now let's examine the usage of macros to achieve a similar task. Macros can be a powerful tool, but they come with their own set of advantages and disadvantages. Below is an example macro to square a number.

Listing 5.45: ASCII Character Encoding Example

```
; Macro to square a number
Square MACRO number
    mov eax, number
    mul eax, eax
ENDM

.data
value DWORD 5
result DWORD ?

.code
main PROC
    Square value
    mov result, eax
    invoke ExitProcess, 0
main ENDP
```

```
; Input: value = 5
; Output: result = 25 (5^2)
```

In the Square macro, the macro substitution replaces occurrences of number with the actual value, making the code more readable and easier to maintain. However, unlike procedures, macros do not handle recursive operations well, and they can lead to code bloat if overused.

Best practices for creating and using macros:

- Use macros for simple, repetitive tasks to enhance code readability.
- Avoid using macros for complex operations that involve recursion or heavy logic.

- Be cautious about code bloat due to macro expansion, particularly in large codebases.
- Comment each macro to explain its purpose and parameters.

Comparing both approaches:

- **Procedures** are suitable for complex, reusable code that involves branching or recursion. They help maintain stack integrity and are necessary for operations where the call stack depth must be controlled.
- **Macros** are most effective for small, repeated tasks where function call overhead is unnecessary. They can make the code more readable but must be used judiciously to avoid increasing the binary size.

Choosing between procedures and macros depends on the specific requirements and constraints of the program. Understanding both constructs allows for more flexible and efficient assembly language programming.

Chapter 6

Assembly Language for Different Architectures

This chapter examines assembly language across various architectures, including x86, x86-64, ARM, MIPS, RISC-V, PowerPC, and SPARC. It discusses the differences between CISC and RISC architectures, compares instruction sets, and provides guidance on writing cross-platform assembly code. Additionally, it covers tools and compilers specific to each architecture, supplemented by case studies and practical examples.

6.1 Introduction to Architectures

In this section, we will explore the fundamental concepts of computer architectures, setting up a foundation for understanding the specifics of assembly language programming across different platforms. We will begin by defining what an architecture is in the context of computer systems, then proceed to categorize and contrast major architectural paradigms. This groundwork is essential for comprehending the nuances of assembly languages tailored to each architecture.

Defining Computer Architecture

Computer architecture refers to the design and organization of a computer's fundamental operational structure. It encompasses the set of instructions that the processor can execute, known as the instruction set architecture (ISA), as well as the microarchitecture that implements these instructions. Understanding computer architecture is crucial for assembly language programming because it defines how instructions are processed and executed within a system.

Instruction Set Architecture (ISA)

The ISA serves as the interface between software and hardware. It specifies the instructions that a processor can execute, the data types it can operate on, and the registers that store intermediate and final results. Different architectures may have varying ISAs, impacting the assembly language syntax and semantics for each platform.

An ISA includes the following components:

- Instruction Formats - The layout of bits within an instruction.
- Addressing Modes - Methods to specify operands for instructions.
- Registers - Small, fast storage locations within the CPU.
- Data Types - Types of data the processor can handle, such as integers and floating-point numbers.
- Instruction Types - Categories of instructions, such as arithmetic, control flow, and memory access.

Microarchitecture

Microarchitecture refers to the implementation of the ISA within a processor. While the ISA defines what the processor should do, the microarchitecture defines how it is done. This includes pipeline stages, cache hierarchies, execution units, and other hardware details. While assembly language programming primarily concerns itself with the ISA, an understanding of microarchitecture can provide insights into performance optimization and efficient coding practices.

CISC vs. RISC Architectures

The primary distinction in CPU design philosophies can be categorized into Complex Instruction Set Computing (CISC) and Reduced Instruction Set Computing (RISC).

CISC Architecture: CISC architectures are characterized by a large number of complex instructions that can execute multi-step operations within a single instruction. These instructions reduce the need for multiple instructions that perform the same task within processor cycles. The x86 architecture is a prominent example of CISC.

RISC Architecture: RISC architectures, on the other hand, employ a smaller set of simple instructions that are highly optimized for fast execution. Each instruction is designed to execute in a single clock cycle, promoting consistency in performance and simplifying the control logic within the CPU. ARM, MIPS, and RISC-V architectures exemplify the RISC philosophy.

Key Differences:

- Instruction Complexity - CISC instructions are more complex, often carrying out multiple operations, whereas RISC instructions are relatively simple.
- Instruction Count - CISC architectures have a larger repertoire of instructions compared to RISC.
- Execution Time - RISC aims for single-cycle execution, while CISC may require multiple cycles for complex instructions.
- Performance Optimization - RISC's simpler instructions can be more easily pipelined.

Common Architectures

We will delve deeper into specific architectures in subsequent sections, but here is a brief overview:

x86 and x86-64: These architectures are widely used in personal computers and server environments. The x86 architecture adheres to the CISC philosophy, featuring a vast array of powerful instructions. The x86-64 extends this with 64-bit capabilities.

ARM: ARM architectures are prevalent in mobile and embedded systems due to their power efficiency and performance. ARM follows the RISC principles, optimizing for low power consumption and high performance per watt.

MIPS: Initially developed for academic purposes, MIPS is now found in various embedded systems. It is a pure RISC architecture, known for its simplicity and efficiency.

RISC-V: RISC-V is an open-standard ISA based on RISC principles, allowing for extensive customizability and innovation. It is gaining traction in academic and experimental domains.

PowerPC: Once popular in personal computers and gaming consoles, PowerPC is now more commonly used in embedded and high-performance computing.

SPARC: The SPARC architecture, developed by Sun Microsystems, is used primarily in server environments and employs RISC principles.

Challenges of Cross-Platform Assembly Programming

Programming in assembly for different architectures poses unique challenges. The differences in ISAs mean that a program written for one architecture cannot be directly executed on another. Cross-platform assembly programming requires an understanding of the instruction sets, calling conventions, memory models, and toolchains specific to each architecture. By mastering these concepts, developers can write efficient and effective assembly code tailored to diverse computing environments.

Understanding the architectural differences outlined in this section will lay a foundation for the specific assembly language instructions and programming techniques that we will explore in the following sections. Through the detailed examination of these architectures, we will build a comprehensive skill set for proficient assembly language programming across multiple platforms.

6.2 The x86 and x86-64 Architectures

The x86 family of architectures, originating from the Intel 8086 microprocessor, has become one of the most ubiquitous architectures in computing. This architecture follows the Complex Instruction Set Computing (CISC) paradigm, characterized by a wide array of instructions that can execute complex tasks in a single instruction, reducing the number of instructions per program at the cost of higher cycles per instruction.

x86 architecture supports multiple operating modes, including real mode and protected mode. Real mode, which was used in early personal computers, provides direct access to memory and hardware but lacks advanced features like memory protection. In contrast, protected mode, introduced with the Intel 80286, supports features such as virtual memory, paging, and safe multitasking.

Key registers in the x86 architecture include the EAX, EBX, ECX, and EDX registers, which are general-purpose; the segment registers (CS, DS, ES, FS, GS, and SS); the instruction pointer (EIP); and the flags register (EFLAGS), which contains status flags that reflect the outcome of various operations.

Listing 6.1: ASCII Character Encoding Example

```
section .data
    msg db 'Hello, World!', 0

section .text
    global _start

_start:
    ; Write the message to stdout
    mov edx, 13 ; message length
    mov ecx, msg ; message to write
    mov ebx, 1 ; file descriptor (stdout)
    mov eax, 4 ; system call number (sys_write)
    int 0x80 ; call kernel

    ; Exit program
    mov eax, 1 ; system call number (sys_exit)
    xor ebx, ebx ; exit status 0
    int 0x80 ; call kernel
```

The transition from x86 to x86-64 (or x64) architecture represents a significant evolution, introducing 64-bit computing while maintaining backward compatibility with x86. This architecture, first implemented in the AMD64 and later adopted by Intel as Intel 64, extends the general-purpose registers to 64 bits, thereby doubling their precision and enabling larger addressable memory space.

In x86-64 architecture, sixteen general-purpose registers are available (RAX, RBX, RCX, RDX, RSI, RDI, RBP, RSP, and R8 through R15), in addition to the extended IP (RIP) and FLAGS (RFLAGS). The extended architecture also introduces new instructions and calling conventions.

Listing 6.2: ASCII Character Encoding Example

```
section .data
    msg db 'Hello, x86-64!', 0

section .text
    global _start

_start:
    ; Write the message to stdout
    mov rdx, 13 ; message length
    mov rsi, msg ; message to write
    mov rdi, 1 ; file descriptor (stdout)
    mov rax, 1 ; system call number (sys_write)
    syscall ; call kernel

    ; Exit program
    mov rax, 60 ; system call number (sys_exit)
    xor rdi, rdi ; exit status 0
    syscall ; call kernel
```

The introduction of x86-64 demanded a shift in how registers and memory are utilized. The RIP-relative addressing simplifies certain forms of memory addressing, particularly useful in position-independent code (PIC), which is crucial for shared library functionality. This platform also makes extensive use of the syscall instruction for transitions to kernel mode, which replaces the int 0x80 instruction used in x86.

Another significant feature of x86-64 is the extended memory addressing capabilities. While x86 architectures can address 4GB of memory using 32-bit addresses, the x86-64 architecture supports 48-bit virtual addresses, allowing systems to theoretically support up to 256 TB of virtual address space.

An in-depth understanding of these enhancements and complexities requires practice and experimentation. Programmers must pay attention to calling conventions, register usage, and efficient memory management practices. Enclasping these core principles and writing optimized assembly ensures the code takes full advantage of the x86 and x86-64 architectures' capabilities.

The presence of advanced debugging tools and Integrated Development Environments (IDEs) simplifies the development process. Popular tools include GDB for debugging, NASM, and YASM for assembling x86 and x86-64 code. Cross-platform assembly development benefits these tools' compatibility and extensive documentation, which aid both novice and seasoned programmers.

Consideration of endianness, instruction pipelining, and branch prediction mechanisms further contributes to writing proficient and high-performance assembly code on these architectures.

6.3 ARM Architecture

ARM (Advanced RISC Machine) architecture is a family of RISC (Reduced Instruction Set Computing) architectures for computer processors, configured for various environments. ARM designs are widely used in mobile devices, embedded systems, and increasingly in desktops and servers. ARM architecture's hallmark characteristics include simplicity, power efficiency, and performance, making it a pivotal choice for many modern applications.

ARM processors utilize a load/store architecture, where operations are performed on registers and not directly on memory. The ARM instruction set includes a mix of 16-bit and 32-bit instructions, making it suitable for a range of performance requirements.

Registers: ARM architecture employs a simplified register model, consisting of 16 general-purpose registers (R0 to R15). Here's a brief overview of these registers:

- R0-R12: General-purpose registers used for assorted tasks.
- R13: Stack Pointer (often denoted as SP).
- R14: Link Register (denoted as LR), holding the return address for subroutines.
- R15: Program Counter (denoted as PC), which holds the address of the current instruction.

Instruction Sets: The ARM architecture supports different instruction sets depending on the processor and use case. The primary sets include:

- **ARM:** A 32-bit instruction set used in standard ARM code.
- **Thumb:** A 16-bit instruction subset providing higher code density and efficiency, trading off some functionality.
- **Thumb-2:** Extends the Thumb instruction set, providing a balance between code density and performance.

Basic Instructions: ARM instructions are generally categorized into Data Processing, Load/Store, and Branch instructions.

ADD (Addition):

Listing 6.3: ASCII Character Encoding Example

```
ADD Rd, Rn, Rm
```

This instruction adds the values in Rn and Rm and stores the result in Rd.

LDR (Load Register):

Listing 6.4: ASCII Character Encoding Example

```
LDR Rd, [Rn, offset]
```

This instruction loads a value from the memory address computed by adding Rn and an optional offset into the register Rd.

STR (Store Register):

Listing 6.5: ASCII Character Encoding Example

```
STR Rd, [Rn, offset]
```

This instruction stores the value in Rd to the memory address calculated from Rn and an optional offset.

B (Branch):

Listing 6.6: ASCII Character Encoding Example

```
B label
```

This instruction updates the Program Counter to branch to the specified label.

BL (Branch with Link):

Listing 6.7: ASCII Character Encoding Example

```
BL label
```

This instruction saves the return address in the Link Register (LR) and branches to the specified label.

Conditional Execution: ARM instructions can execute conditionally, based on the state of the condition flags (Negative, Zero, Carry, and Overflow). Suffixes such as EQ (Equal), NE (Not Equal), and GT (Greater Than) are used to denote conditional execution:

Listing 6.8: ASCII Character Encoding Example

```
ADDEQ R0, R1, R2 @ If equal, perform R0 = R1 + R2
```

Pipelining: ARM processors employ pipeline processing to improve instruction throughput. A three-stage pipeline (Fetch, Decode, Execute) or more advanced versions with additional stages can be used. Pipelining allows multiple instructions to be processed simultaneously at different stages, enhancing performance.

Memory Model: ARM supports several addressing modes:

- **Immediate Offset:** LDR R0, [R1, #4]
- **Register Offset:** LDR R0, [R1, R2]
- **Scaled Register Offset:** LDR R0, [R1, R2, LSL #2]

This capability enables efficient memory access patterns.

Exception Handling: ARM implements multiple mode operations such as User, FIQ (Fast Interrupt Request), IRQ (Interrupt Request), Supervisor, Abort, Undefined, and System mode. Each mode provides specific registers and a stack pointer, facilitating efficient context switching.

Floating-Point Operations: ARM architecture includes support for floating-point arithmetic through the Floating Point Unit (FPU). Instructions such as VADD, VSUB, and VMUL allow operations on floating-point registers:

Listing 6.9: ASCII Character Encoding Example

```
VADD.F32 S0, S1, S2 @ Single-precision floating-point addition
```

Advanced SIMD (NEON): ARM NEON technology accelerates multimedia and signal processing applications. Instructions operate on vectors, facilitating Single Instruction Multiple Data (SIMD) processing.

VADD (Vector Addition):

Listing 6.10: ASCII Character Encoding Example

```
VADD.I16 Q0, Q1, Q2 @ Add 8 pairs of 16-bit integers from Q1 and Q2, store result in
    Q0
```

Optimized use of ARM architecture involves understanding these fundamental concepts and how they interact within various processing environments. Mastery of these principles enables effective development and debug of assembly language programs across diverse ARM-based systems.

6.4 MIPS Architecture

The MIPS (Microprocessor without Interlocked Pipeline Stages) architecture is a RISC (Reduced Instruction Set Computing) architecture developed by MIPS Computer Systems, which is now MIPS Technologies. MIPS architecture is characterized by its simplicity and efficiency in pipelined processors, making it a popular choice for educational purposes and various embedded systems.

At the core of understanding MIPS architecture is grasping its instruction set, register file, memory organization, and basic operation.

Instruction Set: The MIPS instruction set simplifies the execution of operations by dividing instructions into three main formats: R-type

(Register), I-type (Immediate), and J-type (Jump). Below is a basic example of each type:

Listing 6.11: ASCII Character Encoding Example

```
// R-type instruction - Example: add $t0, $t1, $t2
opcode rs rt rd shamt funct
000000 01001 01010 01000 00000 100000

// I-type instruction - Example: lw $t0, 4($sp)
opcode rs rt immediate
100011 11101 01000 0000000000000100

// J-type instruction - Example: j 1048576
opcode address
000010 00010000000000000000000000
```

opcode in the examples stands for operational code, instructing the operation type to be performed. The rs and rt fields refer to the source registers, while rd indicates the destination register in R-type instructions. shamt (shift amount) is used in specifying bit shifting, and funct stands for function code, specifying the exact operation.

Register File: MIPS architecture features 32 general-purpose registers, each 32 bits in size. Notable registers include:

- $zero: Always contains the value 0.
- $at: Reserved for assembler.
- $v0-$v1: Used for function return values.
- $a0-$a3: Used for passing arguments.
- $t0-$t9: Temporary registers for local variables.
- $s0-$s7: Saved registers, preserved across function calls.
- $sp: Stack pointer.
- $ra: Return address.

Understanding these registers is crucial for writing and reading MIPS assembly code.

Memory Organization: MIPS follows a simple, coherent memory model divided mainly into text, data, heap and stack segments:

- **Text Segment**: Contains the machine code of the executed program.

- **Data Segment**: Divided into initialized (static and global variables) and uninitialized sections.
- **Heap Segment**: Dynamically allocated memory (e.g., malloc() in C).
- **Stack Segment**: Memory area that grows and shrinks as functions call and return, holding return addresses, local variables, and function parameters.

Instructions and data are fetched from their respective addresses, identified through base addresses like 0x00400000 for the text segment or 0x10000000 for the data segment.

Example Assembly Program: A MIPS program to add two numbers and store the result can be described as follows:

Listing 6.12: ASCII Character Encoding Example

```
.data
number1: .word 5
number2: .word 10
result: .word 0

.text
.globl main

main:
    lw $t0, number1 // Load number1 into $t0
    lw $t1, number2 // Load number2 into $t1
    add $t2, $t0, $t1 // Add $t0 and $t1, result in $t2
    sw $t2, result // Store the result into memory
    li $v0, 10 // Exit program
    syscall
```

When this program runs, the assembly directive .data declares the data segment, and .text specifies the program's executable instructions. Initialization of the main function is marked with .globl main. The program correctly loads values from memory into registers, performs the addition, and finally saves the result back to the memory location specified by the label result.

Pipelining: MIPS architecture maximizes efficiency through pipelining, allowing multiple instruction stages to overlap in execution. A typical MIPS pipeline consists of five stages:

- **IF (Instruction Fetch)**: Fetch the instruction from memory.
- **ID (Instruction Decode)**: Decode the instruction and read registers.

- **EX (Execute)**: Perform the ALU operation.
- **MEM (Memory Access)**: Access memory operand and load/store operations.
- **WB (Write Back)**: Write results back into the register file.

Each of these stages processes different instructions concurrently, improving the throughput of instruction execution.

Example Algorithm: Below, we demonstrate an algorithm to multiply two numbers using a loop in MIPS assembly code.

Algorithm 2: Multiplication Algorithm in MIPS Assembly

Data: Registers $\$a0$ and $\$a1$ hold input operands, $\$v0$ stores result

Result: Product of inputs in $\$v0$

```
begin
    li $v0, 0 // Initialize result to 0
    blez $a1, end // If multiplicand ≤ 0, skip loop
    while $a1 > 0 do
        add $v0, $v0, $a0 // Add multiplicand to result
        subu $a1, $a1, 1 // Decrement counter
    end
    end:
end
```

Given the algorithm above, users can see how straightforward arithmetic operations like multiplication can be implemented using basic MIPS instructions. This approach demonstrates the strength of the MIPS model in handling loop and arithmetic operations with concise, repeatable patterns.

Understanding the MIPS architecture provides a foundation for grasping how modern pipelined processors work, emphasizes the importance of register-based operations, and showcases the high efficiency achieved through a simplified instruction set.

6.5 RISC-V Architecture

RISC-V is a free and open ISA enabling a new era of processor innovation through open standard collaboration. Unlike proprietary ISAs, which are managed by a single company and can have limitations in accessibility and adaptability, RISC-V is designed to be a flexible and extensible architecture suitable for a wide range of applications.

Design Philosophy

RISC-V follows the Reduced Instruction Set Computer (RISC) design principles, meaning its instruction set has a simplified, efficient set of instructions. This design makes the hardware simpler, faster, and more power-efficient. Some core aspects of the RISC-V design philosophy include:

- **Simplicity and Elegance:** The base integer ISA contains a small number of instructions that must be implemented by any RISC-V-compliant processor. Extensions to the ISA can add additional capabilities but are built on this simple core.
- **Modularity:** The ISA is modular, with a small core set of instructions and multiple optional extensions for different tasks, such as floating-point operations, vector operations, and atomic operations.
- **Extensibility:** Custom extensions can be designed for specific applications, allowing optimization for unique workloads or system requirements.
- **Open Source:** The open nature of RISC-V allows for collaboration across academia and industry, fostering innovation and reducing development costs.

RISC-V Instruction Set Overview

The base RISC-V ISA is denoted as RV32I for 32-bit processors and RV64I for 64-bit processors. Here are some key elements of its instruction set:

- **Base Integer Instructions:** The RV32I and RV64I base ISAs include arithmetic, logical, control flow, and memory access instructions.
- **Load/Store Architecture:** All instructions operate on registers, with separate instructions for loading and storing data in memory.
- **Immediate Operands:** Instructions support immediate operands, allowing the use of constant values directly within the instruction.

- **Conditional Branching:** Provides effective control flow mechanisms through conditional and unconditional branch instructions.
- **System Instructions:** Used for performing system-level operations, such as environment call (ECALL) and environment break (EBREAK).

Sample RISC-V Assembly Program

Consider a simple RISC-V assembly program that adds two numbers and stores the result in memory:

Listing 6.13: ASCII Character Encoding Example

```
.data
    num1: .word 10
    num2: .word 20
    result: .word 0

.text
.globl _start
_start:
    la t0, num1 # Load address of num1 into t0
    lw t1, 0(t0) # Load value of num1 into t1
    la t0, num2 # Load address of num2 into t0
    lw t2, 0(t0) # Load value of num2 into t2
    add t3, t1, t2 # Add t1 and t2, store result in t3
    la t0, result # Load address of result into t0
    sw t3, 0(t0) # Store result from t3 into result

    li a7, 93 # Exit syscall number
    ecall # Make syscall to exit
```

la is used to load addresses, lw to load words from memory, add to perform addition, and sw to store words back into memory. The program uses register t0 as a temporary pointer to memory locations, t1 and t2 for holding values, and t3 for the result.

RISC-V Compressed Instructions

RISC-V has an optional compressed instruction set extension, denoted 'C', which reduces the size of the most frequently used instructions to 16 bits. This helps in saving memory and improving performance in systems with tight constraints. An example of compressed instruction usage is:

Listing 6.14: ASCII Character Encoding Example

```
    c.lwsp t1, 0(sp) # Load word from stack pointer + immediate
    c.swsp t1, 0(sp) # Store word from stack pointer + immediate
```

Advantages of RISC-V

- **Open Source and Royalty-Free:** Allows economic flexibility and greater control over the development process.
- **Scalability:** Suitable for a variety of applications, from small embedded systems to high-performance computing systems.
- **Customizability:** Ability to tailor the ISA specifically to the needs of the application, which can provide significant performance and efficiency benefits.
- **Community and Ecosystem:** An active community and growing ecosystem of tools and software support RISC-V development.

RISC-V Tools and Compilers

Several tools and compilers support RISC-V development, including:

- **GCC (GNU Compiler Collection):** The RISC-V GCC toolchain supports the compilation of C and C++ code for RISC-V targets.

Listing 6.15: ASCII Character Encoding Example

```
riscv64-unknown-elf-gcc -o my_program my_program.c
```

- **LLVM/Clang:** LLVM provides support for RISC-V, allowing the use of Clang to compile code.
- **Spike:** Spike is an ISA simulator used to run and debug RISC-V programs.
- **QEMU:** QEMU emulator has support for RISC-V and provides an environment to run programs.

Listing 6.16: ASCII Character Encoding Example

```
qemu-riscv64 my_program
```

- **Assembler (Binutils):** The GNU Assembler (as) and other binutils provide the tools necessary to assemble RISC-V code.

RISC-V's flexibility, simplicity, and open nature have made it an attractive option for a wide range of computing applications. The modularity of the instruction set ensures that it can be extended and customized as needed, while the increasing support from tools and a growing community highlight its viability as a leading architecture for future computing needs.

6.6 PowerPC Architecture

The PowerPC (Performance Optimization With Enhanced RISC – Performance Computing) architecture is a microprocessor architecture that belongs to the family of RISC (Reduced Instruction Set Computing) architectures. Developed by the AIM (Apple, IBM, Motorola) alliance in 1991, the PowerPC architecture has been widely adopted in diverse fields such as personal computers, embedded systems, and gaming consoles.

One of PowerPC's primary design goals was to create a high-performance yet efficient processor architecture that could scale from low-power devices to high-end servers. In this section, we will delve into the specific features and structure of the PowerPC architecture, including its instruction set, register model, and notable design choices. Additionally, we'll provide code examples and explain how to write assembly programs for this architecture.

Register Model

The PowerPC architecture features a set of 32 general-purpose registers (GPRs), delineated as $R0$ to $R31$, each 32 bits wide for the 32-bit architecture and 64 bits wide for the 64-bit architecture. These registers are used for various tasks, including arithmetic operations, data storage, and addressing memory.

Additionally, PowerPC has 32 floating-point registers (FPRs), labeled $F0$ to $F31$, each 64 bits wide, used for floating-point arithmetic operations. The architecture also includes special-purpose registers (SPRs), such as the link register (LR), condition register (CR), and count register (CTR).

Instruction Set

The PowerPC instruction set is designed for efficiency and is categorized into the following major types:

- **Data Movement Instructions:** These include instructions for loading and storing data between memory and registers.
- **Arithmetic and Logical Instructions:** These operate on data within the registers, supporting integer and floating-point operations.
- **Control Flow Instructions:** Instructions for branching, subroutine calls, and other flow control mechanisms.

- **Special Instructions:** These handle specific tasks such as synchronization, system calls, and exception handling.

Example: Basic Assembly Program

Below is an example of a simple PowerPC assembly program that adds two integers and stores the result in a memory location.

Listing 6.17: ASCII Character Encoding Example

```
.section .data
# Data segment
result: .int 0 # Reserve space for the result

.section .text
.global _start
_start:
    li r3, 5 # Load immediate value 5 into register r3
    li r4, 10 # Load immediate value 10 into register r4
    add r5, r3, r4 # Add r3 and r4, store result in r5

    lis r6, result@ha # Load upper 16 bits of 'result' address
    stw r5, result@l(r6)# Store word from r5 to 'result'

    # Exit program
    li r0, 1 # System call number for exit
    sc # System call (exit)
```

The program performs the following steps:

- The li (load immediate) instructions load the integers 5 and 10 into registers r3 and r4, respectively.
- The add instruction adds the contents of r3 and r4, storing the result in r5.
- The lis (load immediate shifted) and stw (store word) instructions are used to store the result from r5 into the memory location labeled result.
- Finally, the li and sc (system call) instructions are used to exit the program.

Control Flow Instructions

Control flow instructions in PowerPC manage the program's execution flow, including conditional and unconditional branching. The branch and link instruction (bl) is used to call subroutines, saving the return address in the link register (LR).

Listing 6.18: ASCII Character Encoding Example

```
.section .text
.global _start
_start:
    li r3, 20 # Load immediate value 20 into register r3
    bl my_function # Branch to my_function

    # After returning from my_function
    li r0, 1 # System call number for exit
    sc # System call (exit)

my_function:
    addi r3, r3, 30 # Add immediate 30 to r3
    blr # Branch to link register (return)
```

In this example:

- The bl instruction branches to a subroutine named my_function and saves the return address in the link register (LR).
- Within my_function, the addi (add immediate) instruction updates the value in r3.
- The blr (branch to link register) instruction is then used to return to the instruction following the original bl instruction.

Memory Addressing Modes

PowerPC supports several memory addressing modes to facilitate flexible data access:

- Immediate Addressing: Uses a constant value within the instruction.
- Register Indirect Addressing: The effective address is obtained from a register.
- Base-plus-Offset Addressing: Combines a base register and an offset to determine the effective address.

For instance, loading a value from a specific memory location into a register can be done as follows:

Listing 6.19: ASCII Character Encoding Example

```
.section .data
data_value: .int 100 # Define a memory location with an integer value

.section .text
.global _start
```

```
_start:
    lis r3, data_value@ha # Load upper part of address
    lwz r4, data_value@l(r3)# Load word from memory into r4

    # Exit program
    li r0, 1 # System call number for exit
    sc # System call (exit)
```

This code:

- Uses lis to load the upper 16 bits of data_value into r3.
- Utilizes lwz (load word and zero) to load the contents of data_value into r4 using base-plus-offset addressing.

Understanding these constructs and their application allows for systematic and efficient assembly programming on PowerPC architectures. Each instruction and addressing mode provides the flexibility needed to execute complex tasks while maintaining the performance characteristics that are critical for both embedded and high-performance computing environments.

6.7 SPARC Architecture

The Scalable Processor Architecture (SPARC) is a RISC (Reduced Instruction Set Computing) architecture originally developed by Sun Microsystems in 1986. It is known for its simplicity and scalability, which has made it popular in both academic research and commercial implementations. The SPARC architecture has gone through several versions, with the SPARC V8 and V9 being widely recognized.

SPARC stands out due to its register window mechanism, support for a large number of registers, and its emphasis on minimizing the instruction cycle count. A typical SPARC CPU uses a Harvard architecture, meaning it has separate instruction and data caches to speed up processing and reduce bottlenecks.

Registers and Register Windows

One of the defining features of SPARC architecture is its register windows. Each window contains a set of registers that are divided as follows: 8 global registers (%g0 to %g7), 8 input registers (%i0 to %i7), 8 local registers (%l0 to %l7), and 8 output registers (%o0 to %o7). The output registers from one window overlap with the input registers of the next, effectively passing parameters between functions without needing to move data to memory.

The global registers are shared across all register windows, with %g0 fixed at zero. This design allows fast context switching and efficient subroutine calls.

Listing 6.20: ASCII Character Encoding Example

```
! Function to add two integers
.global add_numbers
add_numbers:
    save %sp, -96, %sp ! Save current window and create a new stack frame
    add %i0, %i1, %i0 ! Add the input arguments
    ret ! Return to caller
    restore ! Restore the previous register window
```

Instruction Set

SPARC instructions are straightforward and follow RISC principles, with most instructions completing in a single cycle. The instruction set architecture (ISA) includes basic arithmetic and logic operations, branch instructions, load/store instructions, and system control instructions.

- **Arithmetic Instructions**: These include addition (add), subtraction (sub), and multiplication (mul).
- **Logical Instructions**: These include AND (and), OR (or), and XOR (xor).
- **Branch Instructions**: Conditional and unconditional branching using instructions like ba (branch always) and bne (branch not equal).
- **Load/Store Instructions**: Load data from memory into a register (ld) and store data from a register to memory (st).
- **Shift Instructions**: Logical and arithmetic shifts are performed using sll (shift left logical) and sra (shift right arithmetic).

Listing 6.21: ASCII Character Encoding Example

```
! Perform the operation: result = (a + b) * c
global compute_result
compute_result:
```

```
save %sp, -96, %sp ! Save current window
add %i0, %i1, %l0 ! Add a and b, result in local register %l0
mul %l0, %i2, %o0 ! Multiply the result with c, store in output register %o0
ret ! Return to caller
restore ! Restore previous window
```

Memory and Data Access

SPARC processors follow a load-store architecture. That means only load and store instructions access memory, while arithmetic and logical instructions operate exclusively on registers. Memory addressing in SPARC is typically done using register indirect with displacement. This form is effective for accessing array elements and local variables.

Listing 6.22: ASCII Character Encoding Example

```
! Procedure to store the sum of an array in a variable
.global sum_array
sum_array:
    save %sp, -96, %sp ! Save current window and create a new stack frame
    clr %l0 ! Clear %l0, used as sum accumulator
    mov 0, %l1 ! Initialize index to 0

loop:
    ld [%i0 + %l1 * 4], %l2 ! Load array element into %l2
    add %l0, %l2, %l0 ! Add element to sum
    inc %l1 ! Increment index
    cmp %l1, %i1 ! Compare index with array length
    bl loop ! Branch to loop if index < length
    nop ! No operation (delay slot)

    st %l0, [%i2] ! Store the sum in result
    ret ! Return to caller
    restore ! Restore previous window
```

Control Flow Instructions

Control flow in SPARC assembly involves using branch and call instructions. The delay slots after branch and call instructions in SPARC require careful programming. The instruction immediately following a branch or call is executed regardless of the branch condition. This can be used effectively for optimization.

Listing 6.23: ASCII Character Encoding Example

```
.global compare_numbers
compare_numbers:
    save %sp, -96, %sp ! Save current window
    cmp %i0, %i1 ! Compare two input arguments
    bge greater_equal ! Branch if %i0 >= %i1
    mov %i0, %o0 ! Move %i0 to %o0 (delay slot)
```

```
less:
    mov %i1, %o0 ! Move %i1 to %o0
    ba end_compare ! Unconditionally branch to end
    nop ! No operation (delay slot)

greater_equal:
    mov %i0, %o0 ! Move %i0 to %o0

end_compare:
    ret ! Return to caller
    restore ! Restore previous window
```

SPARC's clean and systematic RISC architecture, with its efficient register window mechanism, makes it an ideal study model for learning fundamental assembly language concepts and principles. Its emphasis on reducing instruction cycle count and promoting fast context switches equips programmers with a deep understanding of efficient programming practices and the inner workings of modern CPUs.

6.8 Differences Between CISC and RISC Architectures

The central distinction between Complex Instruction Set Computing (CISC) and Reduced Instruction Set Computing (RISC) lies in the nature and number of instructions each architecture employs to execute tasks. This section delves into these differences, focusing on instruction complexity, execution cycles, pipelining, and overall design philosophies.

The CISC architecture aims to reduce the number of instructions in a program by making each instruction more capable, whereas RISC emphasizes simplifying individual instructions to execute them more rapidly. Let us consider these differences in a structured manner:

- **Instruction Set Complexity**
  - **CISC:** CISC architectures feature a large and complex set of instructions, many of which can execute high-level tasks. For instance, a single CISC instruction can perform multiple operations, such as memory loading, arithmetic, and storing the result back in memory. This approach intends to reduce the number of instructions per program at the expense of instruction complexity.

  - **RISC:** In contrast, RISC architectures use a limited and simpler set of instructions. Each instruction is designed to complete a small, well-defined task. Complex operations are broken into multiple simple instructions, promoting a more efficient use of the processor's pipeline and registers.

- **Instruction Length and Format**
  - **CISC:** Instructions vary in length and format, demanding complex decoding logic. This variability can introduce inefficiencies, as different instructions may require different amounts of time and cycles to execute.
  - **RISC:** Instructions are typically of uniform length, simplifying the decoding process. The fixed format allows for more predictable instruction execution, enhancing pipelining efficiency and reducing the complexity of the control unit.

- **Execution Cycles**
  - **CISC:** Due to the complexity of individual instructions, a CISC instruction may take multiple cycles to execute. This introduces a potential for inefficiency if many instructions require multi-cycle execution.
  - **RISC:** RISC instructions are designed for single-cycle execution, allowing the CPU to process instructions at a steady and rapid rate. This uniformity aids in optimizing pipeline performance, significantly contributing to the overall speed and efficiency of the processor.

- **Pipelining and Instruction Throughput**
  - **CISC:** The variable length and complexity of instructions in CISC architecture make it challenging to implement efficient pipelining. The dependency of multi-cycle instructions on preceding and succeeding instructions can introduce pipeline hazards, thus complicating the design and reducing throughput.
  - **RISC:** The simplicity and consistency of RISC instructions are conducive to effective pipelining. Since each instruction usually completes in a single cycle, the pipeline stages can be more evenly balanced. This leads to higher instruction throughput and improved overall CPU performance.

- **Memory Access Patterns**

  - **CISC:** Instructions in CISC architecture frequently operate directly on memory, minimizing the need for explicit load and store instructions. This can reduce the instruction count but can also lead to performance bottlenecks due to memory access delays.
  - **RISC:** RISC architecture enforces a load/store model, where only specific instructions access memory. Operations are performed on registers instead of directly on memory. This not only standardizes the instruction pipeline but also optimizes the use of CPU registers, leading to faster execution.

- **Compiler Design**
  - **CISC:** Compilers for CISC architectures benefit from the rich set of complex instructions, enabling them to generate shorter machine code. However, this requires sophisticated optimization strategies to fully exploit the intricate instruction set.
  - **RISC:** Compilers for RISC architectures focus on breaking down operations into a sequence of simple instructions. While this may increase the instruction count, the execution speed of each instruction makes up for it. Compilers can more easily optimize instruction scheduling and register usage in RISC systems.

To provide a clearer understanding, we can compare code snippets illustrating typical operations in x86 (a CISC architecture) and MIPS (a RISC architecture). Consider the task of adding two numbers stored in memory.

For x86:

Listing 6.24: ASCII Character Encoding Example

```
MOV AX, [num1] ; Load value at memory address num1 into AX
ADD AX, [num2] ; Add value at memory address num2 to AX
MOV [sum], AX ; Store result from AX to memory address sum
```

For MIPS:

Listing 6.25: ASCII Character Encoding Example

```
lw $t0, num1 # Load value at memory address num1 into register $t0
lw $t1, num2 # Load value at memory address num2 into register $t1
add $t2, $t0, $t1 # Add values in registers $t0 and $t1, store in $t2
sw $t2, sum # Store result from $t2 into memory address sum
```

In the x86 example, the instructions directly manipulate memory, reflecting CISC's philosophy of reducing the overall instruction count. Conversely, the MIPS example adheres to the load/store model, showcasing RISC's approach of using a consistent, simple instruction set to achieve efficient execution.

Additionally, let's consider the latency and throughput of these architectures with a simple loop operation, emphasizing the performance differences due to architectural design:

For x86 (assuming a loop decrement and comparison):

Listing 6.26: ASCII Character Encoding Example

```
LOOP_START:
DEC CX ; Decrement CX register
CMP CX, 0 ; Compare CX with zero
JNZ LOOP_START ; Jump to LOOP_START if CX is not zero
```

For MIPS:

Listing 6.27: ASCII Character Encoding Example

```
LOOP_START:
addi $t0, $t0, -1 # Decrement $t0
bne $t0, $zero, LOOP_START # Branch to LOOP_START if $t0 is not zero
```

The uniform and straightforward instructions in MIPS facilitate faster and more predictable execution. The loop operation in MIPS consists of fewer cycles due to its single-cycle instruction completion, whereas the x86 loop may involve more complex handling due to its multi-cycle instructions.

Understanding these fundamental differences is crucial for engineers and programmers when choosing an architecture for specific applications, optimizing code for performance, or transitioning between different system designs. The CISC and RISC paradigms continue to influence modern processor design, shaping the development of efficient, powerful computing systems.

6.9 Instruction Set Comparison

Understanding the nuances of different instruction sets is fundamental in appreciating how various computer architectures operate. We will compare the instruction sets of x86, x86-64, ARM, MIPS, RISC-V, PowerPC, and SPARC to highlight their unique characteristics and design philosophies.

x86 and x86-64: The x86 architecture, originating from Intel's 8086, is a Complex Instruction Set Computer (CISC) architecture. This design philosophy emphasizes a rich set of instructions, some of which perform intricate operations with single instructions. For instance, the LODSB instruction loads a byte from the memory string into the AL register, decrementing/incrementing the pointer as per the Direction Flag. The x86-64, an extension of x86, introduced 64-bit registers and additional general-purpose registers.

Listing 6.28: ASCII Character Encoding Example

```
section .text
    global _start
_start:
    mov rax, 1 ; sys_exit system call
    xor rdi, rdi ; exit code 0
    syscall ; invoke operating system to exit
```

ARM Architecture: ARM, a Reduced Instruction Set Computing (RISC) architecture, contrasts with x86 by focusing on a smaller set of instructions that execute in a single clock cycle. ARM uses fixed-size instruction lengths, typically 32-bits, making the decoding process simpler and faster. ARMv7-A introduced the Thumb-2 instruction set, providing a good balance of efficiency and code density.

Listing 6.29: ASCII Character Encoding Example

```
.section .text
.global _start
_start:
    mov r7, #1 ; sys_exit system call
    mov r0, #0 ; exit code 0
    svc 0 ; invoke operating system to exit
```

MIPS Architecture: Another RISC architecture, MIPS prioritizes simplicity and performance. It relies on load/store architecture, where memory operations are separated from arithmetic operations. This separation allows for pipeline optimization and simpler hardware design. MIPS instructions are uniformly 32 bits long, simplifying instruction fetching and decoding stages.

Listing 6.30: ASCII Character Encoding Example

```
    .text
    .globl main
main:
    li $v0, 10 ; syscall code for exit
    syscall ; invoke operating system to exit
```

RISC-V Architecture: RISC-V offers a new approach to RISC architecture with an open, extensible instruction set designed to foster innovation and custom implementations. RISC-V's base integer instruction set, RV32I or RV64I, provides a clean and modular foundation that supports additional extensions like floating-point operations (F) and atomic operations (A).

Listing 6.31: ASCII Character Encoding Example

```
    .section .text
    .globl _start
_start:
    li a7, 93 ; syscall for exit
    li a0, 0 ; exit code 0
    ecall ; environment call to exit
```

PowerPC Architecture: PowerPC, another RISC architecture, utilizes large general-purpose registers to minimize memory access and emphasize parallel instruction processing. The concept of condition registers is crucial in PowerPC, where up to eight condition register fields can be used for conditional operations.

Listing 6.32: ASCII Character Encoding Example

```
    .section .text
    .globl _start
_start:
    li 0, 1 ; syscall code for exit
    li 3, 0 ; exit code 0
    sc ; system call
```

SPARC Architecture: SPARC (Scalable Processor Architecture) developed by Sun Microsystems follows RISC principles with a unique feature called register windows. This feature allows for a fixed set of registers divided among global registers, out registers, local registers, and in registers. The window concept reduces register save/restore overhead during function calls.

Listing 6.33: ASCII Character Encoding Example

```
    .section ".text"
    .global _start
_start:
    mov 1, %g1 ; syscall code for exit
    mov 0, %o0 ; exit code 0
    ta 0 ; trap to operating system
```

The design philosophies underlying these architectures shape their assembly languages. CISC architectures like x86 and x86-64 favor powerful, multi-step instructions, thus often leading to more complex decoders and variable instruction lengths. Conversely, RISC architectures (ARM, MIPS, RISC-V, PowerPC, SPARC) focus on simplicity and efficiency, employing more numerous but less complex instructions and fixed instruction lengths. This comparison underscores the trade-offs between complexity, performance, scalability, and ease of implementation inherent to each architecture's instruction set design.

6.10 Writing Cross-Platform Assembly Code

Writing cross-platform assembly code presents unique challenges and opportunities. When developing software that needs to run efficiently across various hardware architectures, understanding the architectural nuances and instruction sets is crucial. This section delves into the strategies for writing cross-platform assembly code, examining common practices, tools, and considerations.

A fundamental aspect of cross-platform assembly development is the ability to abstract functionality while maintaining performance. To begin, let's consider an example of a simple function written in assembly for both x86-64 and ARM architectures.

x86-64 Assembly Example

A basic example of a function that adds two integers in x86-64 assembly is shown below:

Listing 6.34: ASCII Character Encoding Example

```
section .text
global add_numbers

add_numbers:
    ; Function prologue
    push rbp
    mov rbp, rsp

    ; Load the first argument (a) into rax
    mov rax, [rbp+16]

    ; Load the second argument (b) into rbx
    mov rbx, [rbp+24]

    ; Perform addition
    add rax, rbx

    ; Function epilogue
    pop rbp
    ret
```

When compiled and linked, this function can be called from a higher-level language, such as C, using standard calling conventions for the x86-64 architecture.

ARM Assembly Example

The equivalent function in ARM assembly looks somewhat different due to the differing instruction sets and calling conventions:

Listing 6.35: ASCII Character Encoding Example

```
.global add_numbers

add_numbers:
    ; Function prologue
    push {fp, lr}
    add fp, sp, #4

    ; Load the first argument (a) into r0
    ldr r0, [fp, #8]

    ; Load the second argument (b) into r1
    ldr r1, [fp, #12]

    ; Perform addition
    add r0, r0, r1

    ; Function epilogue
    pop {fp, pc}
```

Once again, this function adheres to the ARM architecture's calling conventions, allowing it to be called from a higher-level language.

Abstraction via Macros and Conditional Assembly

Where feasible, using macros or conditional assembly can help maintain a single codebase that accommodates multiple architectures. Consider the following directive-based example to illustrate this concept:

Listing 6.36: ASCII Character Encoding Example

```
%macro add_numbers 0
%ifdef __x86_64__
section .text
global add_numbers

add_numbers:
    ; Function prologue
    push rbp
    mov rbp, rsp

    ; Load the first argument (a) into rax
    mov rax, [rbp+16]

    ; Load the second argument (b) into rbx
```

```
    mov rbx, [rbp+24]

    ; Perform addition
    add rax, rbx

    ; Function epilogue
    pop rbp
    ret
%elif defined(__ARM__)
.global add_numbers

add_numbers:
    ; Function prologue
    push {fp, lr}
    add fp, sp, #4

    ; Load the first argument (a) into r0
    ldr r0, [fp, #8]

    ; Load the second argument (b) into r1
    ldr r1, [fp, #12]

    ; Perform addition
    add r0, r0, r1

    ; Function epilogue
    pop {fp, pc}
%endif
%endmacro
```

This code uses NASM (Netwide Assembler) preprocessor directives to conditionally include the appropriate assembly code based on the target architecture.

Toolchains and Build Systems

Selecting the right tools is a significant part of the cross-platform development process. Popular assembler tools like NASM for x86/x86-64 and GNU Assembler (as) for various architectures (including ARM and MIPS) support a breadth of instruction sets and system conventions. Integration with build systems such as Make through appropriate makefiles helps streamline the build process. Here's an example makefile snippet that distinguishes between architectures:

Listing 6.37: ASCII Character Encoding Example

```
CC = gcc
NASM = nasm
AS = as
LDFLAGS = -static

all: add_numbers

add_numbers: add_numbers.o
  $(CC) $(LDFLAGS) -o $@ $^
```

```
add_numbers.o: add_numbers.asm
ifeq ($(ARCH),x86_64)
  $(NASM) -f elf64 -D__x86_64__ add_numbers.asm
else ifeq ($(ARCH),arm)
  $(AS) -o add_numbers.o add_numbers.asm
endif

clean:
  rm -f add_numbers add_numbers.o
```

This makefile checks the ARCH variable to decide which assembler and format to use, facilitating easier cross-compilation.

Performance and Optimization

Performance considerations are inevitably architecture-specific, as different architectures optimize for different types of operations. Profiling tools such as perf for Linux or instruments for macOS can be invaluable in assessing performance bottlenecks. Furthermore, leveraging architecture-specific instructions and features, like SIMD for x86 or NEON for ARM, can yield substantial performance gains.

For instance, adding two vectors in x86-64 using SSE instructions:

Listing 6.38: ASCII Character Encoding Example

```
section .data
    vec1 dq 1.0, 2.0, 3.0, 4.0
    vec2 dq 5.0, 6.0, 7.0, 8.0
    result dq 0.0, 0.0, 0.0, 0.0

section .text
global add_vectors

add_vectors:
    movaps xmm0, [vec1]
    movaps xmm1, [vec2]
    addps xmm0, xmm1
    movaps [result], xmm0
    ret
```

And using similar instructions in ARM with NEON:

Listing 6.39: ASCII Character Encoding Example

```
.section .data
    vec1: .word 0x3f800000, 0x40000000, 0x40400000, 0x40800000 ; 1.0, 2.0, 3.0, 4.0
    vec2: .word 0x40a00000, 0x40c00000, 0x40e00000, 0x41000000 ; 5.0, 6.0, 7.0, 8.0
    result: .space 16

.section .text
.global add_vectors
```

```
add_vectors:
    vld1.32 {q0}, [vec1]
    vld1.32 {q1}, [vec2]
    vadd.f32 q0, q0, q1
    vst1.32 {q0}, [result]
    bx lr
```

This direct use of specialized instructions showcases how performance optimizations can be explicitly tailored to the target architecture.

Effective cross-platform assembly coding requires a thorough understanding of the target architectures, the tools at one's disposal, and a strategic approach to abstraction and optimization. By employing conditional assembly, appropriate toolchains, and performance profiling, one can develop efficient, reliable assembly code that functions seamlessly across multiple platforms.

6.11 Tools and Compilers for Different Architectures

When developing assembly language programs for various architectures, it is crucial to understand the tools and compilers available for each platform. This section provides a detailed overview of these tools, focusing on their capabilities and how to use them effectively.

For the x86 and x86-64 architectures, the GNU Assembler (GAS) is a widely-used tool. It is part of the GNU binutils package, which also includes utilities like the linker (ld) and the binary file manipulation tool (objdump). GAS uses the AT&T syntax, which differs from the Intel syntax commonly seen in other assemblers like NASM (Netwide Assembler). Below is an example of a simple assembly program using GAS syntax:

Listing 6.40: ASCII Character Encoding Example

```
.section .data
    message:
        .asciz "Hello, World!"
.section .text
    .globl _start
_start:
    movl $4, %eax # sys_write
    movl $1, %ebx # file descriptor: stdout
    movl $message, %ecx # message to write
    movl $13, %edx # message length
    int $0x80 # call kernel

    movl $1, %eax # sys_exit
```

```
    xorl %ebx, %ebx # exit code 0
    int $0x80 # call kernel
```

Compiling this program on a Unix-like system can be achieved using the following command:

```
as -o hello.o hello.s
ld -o hello hello.o
```

NASM, on the other hand, is another assembler for x86 and x86-64 architectures, known for its simplicity and flexibility. NASM uses its own assembly syntax, which is closer to Intel syntax. The following is the equivalent of the previous program using NASM syntax:

Listing 6.41: ASCII Character Encoding Example

```
section .data
    message db "Hello, World!", 0

section .text
    global _start
_start:
    mov eax, 4 ; sys_write
    mov ebx, 1 ; file descriptor: stdout
    mov ecx, message ; message to write
    mov edx, 13 ; message length
    int 0x80 ; call kernel

    mov eax, 1 ; sys_exit
    xor ebx, ebx ; exit code 0
    int 0x80 ; call kernel
```

Compiling the NASM program:

```
nasm -f elf32 hello.asm -o hello.o
ld -m elf_i386 -o hello hello.o
```

For ARM architectures, the widely-used assembler is the GNU Assembler and the accompanying GNU Compiler Collection (GCC). Below is an example of a simple program written in ARM assembly using GAS syntax:

Listing 6.42: ASCII Character Encoding Example

```
.section .data
message:
    .asciz "Hello, ARM World!"

.section .text
.global _start
_start:
    ldr r0, =1 # file descriptor: stdout
    ldr r1, =message # message to write
    ldr r2, =14 # message length
    mov r7, #4 # sys_write
    swi 0 # call kernel

    mov r0, #0 # exit code 0
```

```
    mov r7, #1 # sys_exit
    swi 0 # call kernel
```

Compiling the ARM program can be done with:

```
as hello.s -o hello.o
ld hello.o -o hello
```

For MIPS architectures, the MIPS Assembly can be utilized along with SPIM, an emulator for running assembly language code for MIPS R2000/R3000 processors. A simple MIPS assembly program is showcased below:

Listing 6.43: ASCII Character Encoding Example

```
.data
message:
    .asciiz "Hello, MIPS World!"

.text
.globl main
main:
    li $v0, 4 # syscall code for print_str
    la $a0, message # load address of string
    syscall # call kernel

    li $v0, 10 # syscall code for exit
    syscall # call kernel
```

You can run this program in SPIM with:

```
spim -file hello.asm
```

The RISC-V architecture's primary toolchain is the GNU toolchain, which supports the assembly, compilation, linking and debugging of RISC-V code. A simple "Hello World" RISC-V program looks like this:

Listing 6.44: ASCII Character Encoding Example

```
.data
message: .asciiz "Hello, RISC-V World!"

.text
.globl _start
_start:
    la a0, message # load address of string
    li a7, 4 # syscall code for print_str
    ecall # make syscall

    li a7, 93 # syscall code for exit
    li a0, 0 # exit code 0
    ecall # make syscall
```

This RISC-V program can be assembled and linked using:

```
riscv64-unknown-elf-as hello.s -o hello.o
riscv64-unknown-elf-ld hello.o -o hello
```

PowerPC assembly language utilizes tools such as the GNU Assembler for PowerPC and the GCC toolchain. Below is an example of a simple PowerPC assembly program:

Listing 6.45: ASCII Character Encoding Example

```
.data
message:
    .asciz "Hello, PowerPC World!"

.text
.global _start
_start:
    lis r0, 1 # load upper immediate (stdout)
    ori r0, r0, 1 # OR immediates into r0
    lis r3, message@ha # Load immediate (high)
    addi r3, r3, message@l # Load immediate (low)
    li r4, 18 # Load immediate (message length)
    li r5, 4 # Load immediate (sys_write)
    sc # system call

    li r3, 0 # Exit code 0
    li r0, 1 # sys_exit code
    sc # system call
```

This can be compiled with:

```
as hello.s -o hello.o
ld hello.o -o hello
```

SPARC architecture assembly programming involves using GNU tools. An illustrative example is shown below:

Listing 6.46: ASCII Character Encoding Example

```
.data
message:
    .asciz "Hello, SPARC World!"

.text
.global _start
_start:
    sethi %hi(message), %o0
    or %o0, %lo(message), %o0
    sethi %hi(13), %o1
    call .write
    nop

    mov 0, %o0
    ta 0
```

To assemble and link:

```
as hello.s -o hello.o
ld hello.o -o hello -lc
```

Understanding the variety of tools and compilers for different architectures is fundamental for proficient assembly programming. Each toolset comes with its own syntax nuances, compile processes, and execution methodologies. Familiarity with these aspects is necessary for effective development across diverse hardware platforms.

6.12 Case Studies and Examples for Each Architecture

x86 and x86-64 Architectures

To understand the practical application of assembly language on x86 and x86-64 architectures, consider the task of writing a simple program that adds two integer numbers and prints the result. We will use the NASM assembler for this demonstration. Here is the source code written in x86 assembly:

Listing 6.47: ASCII Character Encoding Example

```
section .data
    num1 db 5
    num2 db 3
    result db 0

section .text
    global _start

_start:
    ; Load the first number into the AL register
    mov al, [num1]

    ; Add the second number to AL
    add al, [num2]

    ; Store the result in the result variable
    mov [result], al

    ; Exit the program
    mov eax, 1
    int 0x80
```

Executing this program will not display the result directly; it merely demonstrates the addition operation in assembly. For a complete program, it requires interfacing with the operating system for output, expanding the complexity.

ARM Architecture

ARM architecture offers a more streamlined set of instructions due to its RISC nature. The equivalent program for adding two integers on an

ARM processor can be written using the GNU Assembler (GAS) syntax:

Listing 6.48: ASCII Character Encoding Example

```
.section .data
    num1: .word 5
    num2: .word 3
    result: .word 0

.section .text
    .global _start

_start:
    ; Load the first number into register r0
    ldr r0, =num1
    ldr r1, [r0]

    ; Load the second number into register r1
    ldr r2, =num2
    ldr r3, [r2]

    ; Add the numbers
    add r1, r1, r3

    ; Store the result
    ldr r2, =result
    str r1, [r2]

    ; Exit the program
    mov r7, #1
    svc 0
```

This ARM assembly program closely mirrors the logic of the x86 example. The use of load and store instructions is characteristic of ARM's RISC architecture.

MIPS Architecture

MIPS, another RISC-based architecture, handles operations similarly to ARM. Here is an example using the SPIM simulator syntax:

Listing 6.49: ASCII Character Encoding Example

```
.data
    num1: .word 5
    num2: .word 3
    result: .word 0

.text
    .globl main

main:
    ; Load the first number into register $t0
    lw $t0, num1

    ; Load the second number into register $t1
    lw $t1, num2
```

```
    ; Add the numbers
    add $t2, $t0, $t1

    ; Store the result
    sw $t2, result

    ; Exit the program
    li $v0, 10
    syscall
```

MIPS assembly makes use of specific registers for operations, which is a common feature in RISC architectures, emphasizing load-store architecture principles.

RISC-V Architecture

RISC-V, being a modern RISC instruction set architecture, follows similar principles. The following example uses the RARS simulator:

Listing 6.50: ASCII Character Encoding Example

```
.data
    num1: .word 5
    num2: .word 3
    result: .word 0

.text
    .globl main

main:
    ; Load the first number into register x5
    la x5, num1
    lw x6, 0(x5)

    ; Load the second number into register x6
    la x7, num2
    lw x8, 0(x7)

    ; Add the numbers
    add x9, x6, x8

    ; Store the result
    la x10, result
    sw x9, 0(x10)

    ; Exit the program
    li a7, 10
    ecall
```

RISC-V keeps the instruction set simple and efficient, adhering to RISC principles, and enables straightforward implementation of basic operations.

PowerPC Architecture

PowerPC architecture, another type of RISC architecture, handles operations in a similar load-store manner. Below is an example using PowerPC assembly:

Listing 6.51: ASCII Character Encoding Example

```
.data
    num1: .long 5
    num2: .long 3
    result: .long 0

.text
    .globl _start

_start:
    ; Load the first number into register r3
    lis r3, num1@ha
    addi r3, r3, num1@l
    lwz r4, 0(r3)

    ; Load the second number into register r4
    lis r5, num2@ha
    addi r5, r5, num2@l
    lwz r6, 0(r5)

    ; Add the numbers
    add r7, r4, r6

    ; Store the result
    lis r8, result@ha
    addi r8, r8, result@l
    stw r7, 0(r8)

    ; Exit the program
    li r0, 1
    sc
```

PowerPC registers and instructions bear resemblance to other RISC architectures, facilitating easy understanding and transition for developers familiar with RISC.

SPARC Architecture

SPARC is another RISC-based architecture. Here is an equivalent program written in SPARC assembly:

Listing 6.52: ASCII Character Encoding Example

```
.data
    num1: .word 5
    num2: .word 3
    result: .word 0
```

```
.text
    .global _start

_start:
    ! Load the first number into register %o0
    set num1, %o0
    ld [%o0], %o1

    ! Load the second number into register %o1
    set num2, %o2
    ld [%o2], %o3

    ! Add the numbers
    add %o1, %o3, %o4

    ! Store the result
    set result, %o5
    st %o4, [%o5]

    ! Exit the program
    mov 1, %g1
    ta 0
```

Each case study demonstrates the unique aspects and syntactic differences across various architectures while performing the same fundamental task, providing a practical framework for understanding assembly language in context.

Chapter 7

Memory Management

This chapter provides an in-depth look at memory management in assembly language, covering memory addressing modes, segment and offset addressing, and the structure and operations of the stack and heap. It addresses memory protection, paged and segmented memory models, virtual memory, and direct memory access (DMA). The chapter also explores cache memory principles and management, memory-mapped I/O, and strategies for optimizing memory usage in assembly programs.

7.1 Introduction to Memory Management

Memory management is fundamental to the efficient and effective execution of programs in assembly language. It involves the dynamic allocation and deallocation of memory segments, ensuring that memory is utilized in an optimal manner. Understanding memory management is essential for tasks ranging from simple stack manipulations to complex dynamic memory allocations.

In assembly language, memory management can be broadly categorized into several key areas: memory addressing modes, segment and offset addressing, stack and heap operations, memory protection, virtual memory, and direct memory access. Each of these areas plays a critical role in the overall management of memory in a system.

The architecture of computational systems dictates the specific mechanisms and strategies employed for memory management. Central to this discussion are the concepts of memory addressing modes, which define how instructions specify the location of their operands.

Consider the following basic example in x86 assembly. Suppose we want to load a value from memory into a register. The instruction might look like this:

Listing 7.1: ASCII Character Encoding Example

```
MOV AX, [BX]
```

Here, the MOV instruction transfers the data located at the memory address specified by the BX register into the AX register. This is an example of indirect addressing, where the address of the data is held in a register.

Understanding the structure and operations of memory segments is crucial. A segment is a contiguous block of addresses in memory, and in x86 architecture, segments are accessed using segment registers like CS (Code Segment), DS (Data Segment), SS (Stack Segment), and ES (Extra Segment). Segment addressing combines a segment base address with an offset to access specific memory locations.

For example:

Listing 7.2: ASCII Character Encoding Example

```
MOV AX, 0x1234 ; Load AX with immediate value
MOV DS, AX ; Set data segment
MOV BX, 0x5678 ; Load BX with offset
MOV AX, [DS:BX] ; Load AX from DS segment with BX offset
```

In this series of instructions, we first load the AX register with an immediate value and then set the DS (Data Segment) register. Subsequently, we load BX with an offset value and finally access memory in the data segment at the location specified by BX.

The stack is another critical area in memory management. It is used for temporary storage and supports operations like function calling and local variable storage. The stack utilizes data structures based on Last In, First Out (LIFO) principles.

Appending to the stack example, consider the following x86 instructions for function calls and returns:

Listing 7.3: ASCII Character Encoding Example

```
PUSH AX ; Save AX on stack
CALL myFunction ; Call subroutine
```

```
myFunction:
    ; Subroutine code
    POP AX ; Restore AX from stack
    RET ; Return from subroutine
```

Here, PUSH saves the current value of the AX register on the stack before the function call. Inside the function, the POP instruction restores the AX register before returning control to the calling function with the RET instruction.

Dynamic memory allocation, often managed via the heap, involves allocating and freeing memory at runtime. Unlike the stack, which grows and shrinks in a pre-defined order, heap memory can be allocated and freed in arbitrary order, allowing for flexible memory usage. Consider the following pseudocode for dynamic memory allocation:

Listing 7.4: ASCII Character Encoding Example

```
; Allocation example (pseudo-assembly, syntax may vary)
MOV EAX, size_to_allocate ; Move size into EAX
CALL malloc ; Call malloc function to allocate memory
MOV allocated_ptr, EAX ; Store allocated memory pointer
```

In this example, malloc (a typical function used in higher-level languages) is called to allocate a block of memory of the specified size, and the pointer to the allocated memory is stored in allocated_ptr.

Memory protection mechanisms ensure that a process does not access the memory allocated to another process without permission. Modern processors support various hardware-based protection schemes like segmentation and paging to enforce these rules.

In paged memory models, memory is divided into fixed-size pages, and a page table keeps track of page mappings. Each page can be marked with access control bits for read, write, and execute permissions. This is pivotal for maintaining system stability and security.

Virtual memory extends physical memory by using disk space, allowing programs to use more memory than physically available. The memory management unit (MMU) handles translation between virtual addresses and physical addresses, effectively abstracting this complexity from the programmer.

Direct Memory Access (DMA) enables peripherals to access system memory independently of the CPU, allowing for efficient data transfers without burdening the processor.

Efficient memory management is critical in assembly language programming, directly influencing the performance and reliability of software systems. Understanding these concepts provides the foundation for advanced techniques and optimizations in assembly programming.

7.2 Memory Addressing Modes

Memory addressing modes provide the programmer with various methods to specify the operands for the instructions. They are crucial for efficient memory access and utilization. In assembly language, understanding the different addressing modes enables the programmer to write more optimized and flexible code. We will discuss several common addressing modes used in assembly language programming.

Immediate Addressing Mode: In immediate addressing mode, the operand is specified explicitly in the instruction itself. This means that the data to be manipulated is part of the instruction rather than being stored in a memory location.

Listing 7.5: ASCII Character Encoding Example

```
// Example of Immediate Addressing Mode in Assembly
mov ax, 5 ; Move the value 5 into register AX
```

In the example above, 5 is the immediate value, directly provided as part of the instruction.

Register Addressing Mode: With register addressing mode, the operand is held in an internal processor register. This mode provides very fast access to data as no memory access is required.

Listing 7.6: ASCII Character Encoding Example

```
// Example of Register Addressing Mode in Assembly
mov bx, ax ; Move the value from register AX to register BX
```

Here, the content of AX is moved to BX. Both AX and BX are registers.

Direct Addressing Mode: In direct addressing mode, the address of the operand is directly specified in the instruction. This mode is straightforward but tends to be slower due to memory access.

Listing 7.7: ASCII Character Encoding Example

```
// Example of Direct Addressing Mode in Assembly
mov ax, [1234h] ; Move the value stored at memory address 1234h into AX
```

The instruction has $1234\mathrm{h}$ as the operand's address, indicating the processor to fetch the value from this memory address.

Indirect Addressing Mode: Indirect addressing mode uses a register to hold the address of the operand. This offers more flexibility than direct addressing and allows for efficient memory manipulation.

Listing 7.8: ASCII Character Encoding Example

```
// Example of Indirect Addressing Mode in Assembly
mov si, 3000h ; Move the address 3000h into register SI
mov ax, [si] ; Move the value from the address stored in SI (3000h) to AX
```

Here, $3000h$ is moved into SI register, and then the value at that address is moved into AX.

Indexed Addressing Mode: In indexed addressing, the effective address of the operand is determined by adding a constant value (offset) to the contents of a register. This is particularly useful for array processing and table lookups.

Listing 7.9: ASCII Character Encoding Example

```
// Example of Indexed Addressing Mode in Assembly
mov bx, 4 ; Offset value
mov si, 2000h ; Base address
mov ax, [si + bx] ; Move the value from memory address (2000h + 4) into AX
```

The effective address here is $2000h + 4$, and its value is moved into AX.

Base Plus Index Addressing Mode: This form of addressing uses both a base register and an index register to calculate the effective address. It is useful in accessing multi-dimensional arrays and data structures.

Listing 7.10: ASCII Character Encoding Example

```
// Example of Base Plus Index Addressing Mode in Assembly
mov bx, 5 ; Index value
mov bp, 1000h ; Base address
mov ax, [bp + bx] ; Move the value from memory address (1000h + 5) into AX
```

$1000h$ is the base address and 5 is the index, making the effective address $1000h + 5$.

Base Plus Index with Offset Addressing Mode: This is an extension of the base plus index mode, where an additional constant value (offset) is added to the sum of a base register and an index register to form the effective address.

Listing 7.11: ASCII Character Encoding Example

```
// Example of Base Plus Index with Offset Addressing Mode in Assembly
mov bx, 3 ; Index value
```

```
mov bp, 2000h ; Base address
mov ax, [bp + bx + 4] ; Move the value from memory address (2000h + 3 + 4) into AX
```

$2000h + 3 + 4$ gives the effective address, which is then accessed to move its value into AX.

In understanding these addressing modes, we see that they provide various ways to efficiently locate and manipulate operands. Each mode has its use-case scenarios that fit the program's need for speed, memory efficiency, and complexity.

7.3 Segments and Offset Addressing

Segments and offset addressing are crucial concepts within assembly language that facilitate efficient and flexible memory management. These concepts allow the coder to access specific memory locations within the larger addressable space, providing a structured and organized approach to memory allocation and utilization.

A memory segment in the context of assembly language refers to a contiguous block of memory that has a defined starting point and length. Each segment is identified by a segment selector, which is employed in conjunction with offsets to form a complete address. The CPU, particularly those designed with the x86 architecture, uses segments to simplify memory management, allowing the division of memory into logically separate sections.

When dealing with segment and offset addressing, it is crucial to understand how these components interact. A segment register holds the base address (or starting address) of the segment, while the offset is a value added to this base address to access a specific memory location within that segment. Combining these two produces a complete physical address. The typical segment registers in an x86 processor include CS (Code Segment), DS (Data Segment), SS (Stack Segment), and ES (Extra Segment), each serving distinct roles in the memory management process.

Listing 7.12: ASCII Character Encoding Example

```
MOV AX, 1234H ; Load 1234H into AX register
MOV DS, AX ; Set DS (Data Segment) to 1234H
MOV BX, 5678H ; Load 5678H into BX register (offset)
MOV [BX], AL ; Access memory at DS:BX, store AL in that location
```

In the example above, the data segment (DS) is loaded with the value

1234H, which serves as the base address of the segment. The offset 5678H is then moved into the BX register. By accessing the memory at DS:BX, we correctly address the physical memory location corresponding to the sum of the base address (1234H) and the offset (5678H).

The practical significance of segment and offset addressing is highlighted in scenarios where memory organization and efficient address calculation play essential roles. For instance, segment registers can be easily modified to point to different memory areas, allowing dynamic data access needed in high-performance applications and while manipulating large data structures. Moreover, segment override prefixes can be used to specify that an instruction should use a segment other than the default. This is particularly useful when dealing with data storage or specific memory areas located within different segments.

Listing 7.13: ASCII Character Encoding Example

```
MOV AX, [ES:BX] ; Use ES segment instead of DS for the memory operand
```

In this example, the ES register is explicitly used instead of the default DS for accessing memory. Segment override prefix thus ensures flexibility, allowing multiple data segments to be accessed efficiently within a program.

Understanding the limitations and advantages of segment and offset addressing is equally important:

- **Memory Organization:** Segments offer an organized approach, helping to separate different types of data such as code, stack, or heap data, which simplifies program maintenance and debugging.
- **Extended Addressability:** The combination of segment and offset addresses allows a 16-bit system to effectively address a 20-bit or even 32-bit memory space, significantly extending its capabilities.
- **Performance Considerations:** Over-reliance on segment manipulation can increase overhead due to the cost of segment register loads, which should be minimized where possible for optimal performance.

The underlying mechanics rely heavily on how the CPU translates these segmented addresses into linear or effective addresses. In protected mode, for instance, segments are defined by a descriptor in the Global

Descriptor Table (GDT) or Local Descriptor Table (LDT), which includes not only the base address but also the segment's limit and access control information.

Listing 7.14: ASCII Character Encoding Example

```
CLI ; Clear interrupts
MOV AX, 0x10 ; Data segment selector value from GDT
MOV DS, AX
MOV ES, AX
MOV FS, AX
MOV GS, AX
...
LIDT [IDT_ADDR] ; Load Interrupt Descriptor Table
```

The example above illustrates the setup required in protected mode. Moving data segment selector values into DS, ES, FS, and GS registers, which are loaded from the GDT. This setup is critical for establishing a functional memory model under different operating conditions.

Offset addressing, combined with segment registers, provides a robust mechanism for managing complex addressing needs in assembly programming. Ensuring proper use and understanding of these methods can significantly enhance the control and efficiency of assembly language programs.

7.4 The Stack: Structure and Operations

The stack is a fundamental data structure used extensively in assembly language programming for managing function calls, local variables, and control flow. Understanding its structure and operations is crucial for efficient memory management and program execution.

The stack is a contiguous block of memory that operates on a Last-In-First-Out (LIFO) principle. This means that the most recently pushed (added) value is the first one to be popped (removed). The two primary operations on the stack are PUSH and POP. The PUSH operation places a value onto the stack, and the POP operation removes a value from the stack.

Listing 7.15: ASCII Character Encoding Example

```
PUSH AX ; Push the contents of register AX onto the stack
POP BX ; Pop the top value from the stack into register BX
```

PUSH and POP instructions are essential for saving and restoring the state of the CPU during function calls. When a function is called, the current execution context – which includes the instruction pointer, base pointer, and other relevant registers – is saved onto the stack. The function can then operate, and once it completes, the saved context is restored, ensuring a seamless return to the caller function.

The stack pointer (SP) register tracks the top of the stack. In x86 architecture, the stack grows downwards, meaning that new values pushed onto the stack decrease the SP register value. Conversely, popping values from the stack increases the SP register. The stack segment (SS) register points to the segment containing the stack.

Consider an example where a function is called, modifying the stack:

Listing 7.16: ASCII Character Encoding Example

```
CALL MyFunction ; Call the function MyFunction

; Inside the function MyFunction:
MyFunction:
    PUSH BP ; Save base pointer on the stack
    MOV BP, SP ; Establish a new base pointer
    SUB SP, 10 ; Allocate space for local variables
    ; Perform function tasks
    MOV SP, BP ; Restore stack pointer
    POP BP ; Restore base pointer
    RET ; Return from the function
```

In this example, the CALL instruction saves the return address onto the stack. Inside the function, the original base pointer (BP) is saved, and a new base pointer is established using the stack pointer (SP). Space for local variables is allocated by adjusting the SP value. Upon function completion, the stack pointer and base pointer are restored to their original values, and the function returns to the caller using the RET instruction, which pops the return address from the stack.

Local variables within functions are typically accessed relative to the base pointer. For instance:

Listing 7.17: ASCII Character Encoding Example

```
MOV AX, [BP-4] ; Access local variable 1
MOV BX, [BP-6] ; Access local variable 2
```

Stack frames are created to manage function calls and local variables efficiently. Each function call generates a new stack frame, maintaining a clear structure for nesting calls. The base pointer (BP) serves as a reference point for accessing parameters and local variables within these frames.

When dealing with interrupts and exceptions, the stack plays a critical role in preserving the state of the CPU. Upon an interrupt, the current state (including registers, flags, and return address) is pushed onto the stack. Once the interrupt service routine executes, the state is restored by popping these values off the stack, ensuring consistent system behavior.

Stack management is pivotal in optimizing memory usage. Mismanagement can lead to stack overflow or underflow conditions, which cause program instability or crashes. For example, a stack overflow occurs when there is insufficient space in the stack segment to accommodate new data, often resulting from deep or infinite recursion.

Advanced assembly programming techniques exploit the stack for efficient function calls, parameter passing, and local variable storage. Optimizing these operations can lead to significant improvements in performance and resource utilization. Understanding the intricacies of the stack's structure and operations provides a solid foundation for advanced assembly language programming and effective memory management techniques.

7.5 The Heap: Dynamic Memory Allocation

Dynamic memory allocation in an assembly language program is managed via the heap. The heap is a significant region of the memory, allowing for flexibility and management of memory during the runtime of the program. Unlike stack memory, which follows a strict last-in, first-out (LIFO) behavior, heap memory is dynamically allocated and freed as needed. This provides a powerful mechanism for handling complex data structures like linked lists, trees, and graphs, which require non-contiguous memory spaces.

Heap Management Basics The heap resides in the larger addressable memory space and grows towards higher memory addresses. Memory allocation and deallocation in the heap are generally handled by system calls to the operating system.

A typical assembly implementation of heap management might involve system calls to functions such as malloc (memory allocation), free (memory deallocation), and realloc (resizing the allocated memory block). Below is an example of how dynamic memory allocation can be handled in assembly language by utilizing these functions.

Listing 7.18: ASCII Character Encoding Example

```
section .data
    ; size of memory to allocate (in bytes)
    mem_size dd 100

section .bss
    ; variable to store the pointer to allocated heap memory
    mem_ptr resb 4

section .text
    global _start

_start:
    ; System call to allocate memory (Linux x86)
    mov eax, 45 ; syscall number for brk (allocate memory)
    mov ebx, 0 ; 0 indicates to allocate
    int 0x80 ; interrupt to invoke syscall

    ; Check if allocation was successful
    test eax, eax
    jz allocation_failed

    ; Store the address of allocated memory
    mov [mem_ptr], eax

    ; System call to exit program
    mov eax, 1 ; syscall number for exit
    xor ebx, ebx ; exit code 0
    int 0x80

allocation_failed:
    ; Handle allocation failure
    mov eax, 1 ; syscall number for exit
    mov ebx, 1 ; exit code 1 (failure)
    int 0x80
```

In this example, a block of memory of size 100 bytes is allocated, and the address of this memory block is stored in the mem_ptr variable. Note that the brk system call is used here as an example for illustrative purposes. On different systems or for more sophisticated memory management, functions like malloc and free would generally be used, which are part of the C standard library.

Memory Allocation Strategies Dynamic memory allocators use various strategies to manage the heap efficiently. Common strategies include:

- **First-Fit Allocation:** Finds the first block of memory that is large enough to satisfy the allocation request.
- **Best-Fit Allocation:** Searches the entire list of available blocks and selects the smallest block that is sufficient for the allocation request.

- **Worst-Fit Allocation:** Allocates memory from the largest available block to leave moderately sized blocks available for future requests.

These strategies affect both the performance and the fragmentation of the heap. A fragmented heap has many small, unusable gaps between allocated blocks, which can lead to inefficient use of memory.

Releasing Memory Proper management of memory heap involves not only allocating memory but also ensuring that it is released when it is no longer needed. Failing to free memory results in memory leaks, which can eventually exhaust the available memory, leading to program crashes or poor performance.

The following code snippet demonstrates how to free allocated heap memory in assembly language.

Listing 7.19: ASCII Character Encoding Example

```
section .text

free_memory:
    mov eax, 91 ; syscall number for munmap (free memory) in Linux x86
    mov ebx, [mem_ptr] ; pointer to memory block to free
    mov ecx, [mem_size] ; size of memory block
    int 0x80 ; interrupt to invoke syscall

    ; Check if deallocation was successful
    test eax, eax
    jz deallocation_failed

    ; Successful deallocation
    jmp done

deallocation_failed:
    ; Handle deallocation failure

done:
    ; Continue with rest of the program
```

In the example, the munmap system call is used to free the allocated memory block. This needs to be done carefully to avoid illegal memory access. Ensuring deallocation of memory that is no longer in use also prepares the program to manage further dynamic memory allocation requests efficiently.

Implications for Assembly Programming Proficiently handling dynamic memory allocation in assembly language demands a thorough understanding of the underlying memory management mechanisms provided by the operating system. It must also take into account:

- **Minimizing Fragmentation:** By using efficient allocation strategies and merging free memory blocks when possible.
- **Error Handling:** Prevention of memory leaks and ensuring your program can handle allocation and deallocation failures gracefully.
- **Concurrency Issues:** Ensuring that allocations and deallocations do not interfere with each other in multi-threaded environments, potentially requiring the implementation of locks or other synchronization mechanisms.

By understanding and implementing these principles of dynamic memory management, an assembly language programmer can create robust, efficient programs that make optimal use of system memory resources.

7.6 Memory Protection and Access Control

Memory protection and access control are critical aspects of memory management in modern computer systems. These mechanisms are implemented to ensure the integrity and security of memory by preventing unauthorized access or modifications. This section explores the principles and techniques used to achieve memory protection and enforce access control policies.

At the core of memory protection is the ability to distinguish between different types of memory access, such as read, write, and execute, and to apply appropriate permissions to various memory regions. This is typically managed by the operating system and supported by the hardware through features like memory management units (MMUs) and segmentation.

Memory Protection Mechanisms

Memory protection mechanisms are designed to prevent processes from accessing memory regions that they do not own. This is achieved through the use of access control lists (ACLs), capability-based systems, and page tables.

- Access Control Lists (ACLs): ACLs are used to specify which users or system components have permission to access specific resources, including memory regions. Each entry in an ACL indicates a permission associated with an identifier, typically corresponding to a user or process.
- Capability-based Systems: These systems use tokens, known as capabilities, which grant specific types of access to resources. Each capability defines a set of access rights and is assigned to a process, ensuring that only processes with the appropriate capabilities can access protected memory regions.
- Page Tables: In virtual memory systems, page tables map virtual addresses to physical addresses. Each entry in a page table includes access control information, such as read/write permissions and user/supervisor mode controls. The MMU uses this information to enforce access restrictions.

Below is an example of setting up page table entries with access control bits in assembly language:

Listing 7.20: ASCII Character Encoding Example

```
// Define page table entry macro
#define PTE_P 0x001 // Present
#define PTE_W 0x002 // Writeable
#define PTE_U 0x004 // User accessible

// Initialize page table entries
mov eax, page_table_base
mov [eax], PTE_P | PTE_W | PTE_U // User readable and writeable
mov [eax+4], PTE_P | PTE_W // Supervisor readable and writeable
```

Protection Rings and Privilege Levels

Modern CPUs support multiple protection levels, commonly referred to as rings. These rings are designed to enforce privilege separation between the operating system kernel and user applications.

- Ring 0: This is the most privileged level, typically reserved for the operating system kernel and low-level hardware control.
- Ring 1 and Ring 2: These intermediate rings are not commonly used but can be designated for device drivers or privileged services.
- Ring 3: This is the least privileged level, used for user applications.

Transitioning between rings is controlled by the CPU, ensuring that higher-privilege code can control lower-privilege code but not vice versa. Here is an example of an assembly instruction that checks the current privilege level (CPL):

Listing 7.21: ASCII Character Encoding Example

```
mov eax, cs // Move the current code segment register to eax
and eax, 0x3 // Mask all but the lowest 2 bits to get the CPL
```

Memory Segmentation

Memory segmentation divides the memory into segments, each with its base address and limit. Segmentation facilitates the enforcement of access restrictions based on segment descriptors stored in segment tables like the Global Descriptor Table (GDT) and Local Descriptor Table (LDT).

Here is an example of setting up a segment descriptor in the GDT:

Listing 7.22: ASCII Character Encoding Example

```
gdt_entry:
    .word 0xffff // Limit (15:0)
    .word 0x0000 // Base (15:0)
    .byte 0x00 // Base (23:16)
    .byte 0x9a // Access byte: executable, accessed
    .byte 0xcf // Limit (19:16) and flags: 32-bit, 4K pages
    .byte 0x00 // Base (31:24)
```

Hardware Support for Memory Protection

Hardware support for memory protection often includes features like:

- MMU (Memory Management Unit): The MMU translates virtual addresses to physical addresses and enforces access control based on the information in page tables.
- NX (No-Execute) Bit: This bit, present in page table entries, marks regions of memory as non-executable, providing protection against certain types of attacks such as buffer-overflow exploits.
- SMEP/SMAP (Supervisor Mode Execution Prevention / Access Prevention): These features prevent the CPU from executing or accessing user-space memory while operating in supervisor mode, enhancing security.

Here is an example of enabling the NX bit:

Listing 7.23: ASCII Character Encoding Example

```
// Enable NX bit in EFER register (Extended Feature Enable Register)
mov ecx, 0xc0000080 // EFER MSR address
rdmsr // Read EFER
or eax, 0x800 // Set NXE bit (bit 11)
wrmsr // Write back to EFER
```

Access Control Policies

Access control policies define the rules that govern access to memory and other resources. Common policies include:

- Discretionary Access Control (DAC): Allows resource owners to specify access rights for other users or processes.
- Mandatory Access Control (MAC): Enforces access policies determined by the system, independent of resource owners. Policies are often based on security labels.
- Role-Based Access Control (RBAC): Assigns permissions to roles rather than individual users, simplifying management in complex systems.

This section has detailed the fundamental concepts, mechanisms, and hardware support for memory protection and access control, providing a comprehensive understanding required to manage memory securely and effectively in assembly language programming.

7.7 Paged and Segmented Memory Models

In computer architecture, memory management is vital for ensuring efficient use of physical memory and safeguarding the memory space allocated to different processes. This section delves into two fundamental memory management models: paged and segmented memory. These models are instrumental in addressing memory allocation, protection, and efficient access.

Paged Memory Model

The paged memory model divides the physical memory into fixed-size blocks called pages. Correspondingly, the memory is logically divided into blocks of the same size, referred to as page frames. This model simplifies memory management by ensuring that both logical and physical memory are treated in a uniform manner.

The following pseudocode illustrates the basic principles of paged memory management:

Algorithm 3: Address Translation in Paged Memory

Data: Process logical address $\$A$

Result: Physical address $\$B$

```
$P ← PageNumber($A);
$D ← OffsetWithinPage($A);
$F ← PageTable[$P];
$B ← BaseAddress($F) + $D;
```

$\mathrm{PageNumber}(\$A)$ computes the page number from the logical address $\$A$, whereas $\mathrm{OffsetWithinPage}(\$A)$ derives the offset within the selected page. The $\mathrm{PageTable}[\$P]$ retrieves the frame number associated with the page from the page table, and finally, $\mathrm{BaseAddress}(\$F)$ maps to the base address of the frame. Adding the offset $\$D$ to this base address yields the physical address $\$B$.

Advantages of Paged Memory Model:

- **Efficiency:** By using fixed-size pages, the model simplifies memory allocation and management.
- **Protection:** Each page can be independently protected, minimizing the risk of one process accessing another's address space.
- **Swapping:** It facilitates the swapping of pages between physical memory and disk storage, supporting virtual memory.

Drawbacks of Paged Memory Model:

- **Internal Fragmentation:** Due to fixed page sizes, memory allocated to a page may not be fully utilized, resulting in wasted space.
- **Page Table Overhead:** The need for a page table introduces additional memory overhead, particularly in systems with large address spaces.

Segmented Memory Model

In contrast to fixed-size pages, the segmented memory model divides the memory into variable-sized segments, each corresponding to a logical unit such as a function, data array, or a module. Each segment has a specific base and limit address, which define its presence in the physical memory.

Here is an algorithm for segment-based address translation:

Algorithm 4: Address Translation in Segmented Memory

Data: Segment number \$S, logical address \$A
Result: Physical address \$B

```
$L ← SegmentTable[$S].Limit;
if $A < $L then
    $Base ← SegmentTable[$S].Base;
    $B ← $Base + $A;
end
else
    Raise segmentation fault;
end
```

SegmentTable[\$S].Limit fetches the limit of the segment, ensuring the address \$A does not exceed this limit to prevent segmentation faults. If valid, SegmentTable[\$S].Base retrieves the base address, and adding \$A to this base address produces the physical address \$B.

Advantages of Segmented Memory Model:

- **Logical Organization:** Allows for a more logical organization of memory, closely mirroring the program structure.
- **Protection and Sharing:** Segments can be independently protected and shared among processes.
- **Dynamic Sizing:** Segments can dynamically resize, offering greater flexibility in memory usage.

Drawbacks of Segmented Memory Model:

- **External Fragmentation:** Variable-sized segments can lead to fragmented memory and inefficient usage.
- **Complexity:** Management of variable-sized segments is more complex than fixed-size pages.

Integrating Paged and Segmented Models

Many modern systems employ a combination of both paged and segmented memory models to leverage the advantages of each. In these hybrid models, each segment is divided into pages, allowing the logical organization of segments while maintaining the efficiency of paging.

Illustrating this integrated model:

Listing 7.24: ASCII Character Encoding Example

```
; Initialize segment table
SegmentTable:
  .base: 0x0040
  .limit: 0x0020

; Sample page table for a segment
PageTable:
  Page 0: Frame 4
  Page 1: Frame 7
```

In this example, SegmentTable provides base and limit information, while PageTable maps logical pages of a segment to physical frame numbers.

```
Logical Address: Segment 0, Page 1, Offset 0x0012
Physical Address: Frame 7, Offset 0x0012
```

By integrating segments and pages, this dual approach strikes a balance, enhancing both memory protection and management efficiency. The combination ensures that memory allocation is both logical and efficient, supporting complex and large-scale applications.

Understanding the intricacies of paged and segmented memory models is fundamental to mastering memory management in assembly language, underpinning more advanced concepts discussed in subsequent sections.

7.8 Virtual Memory and Paging

Virtual memory is an abstraction that provides each process with its own address space, seemingly distinct from the physical memory of the machine. This technique enables efficient and safe memory usage by allowing processes to operate in isolated environments. Virtual memory relies on two primary mechanisms: paging and segmentation. This section delves into paging, a core concept underpinning modern virtual memory systems.

Paging divides the virtual address space and the physical memory into fixed-sized blocks. In the virtual address space, these blocks are termed pages, while in the physical memory, they are referred to as page frames. A critical component of paging is the page table, which maps virtual pages to physical page frames.

To comprehend paging, consider the virtual address generated by the CPU. This address needs to be translated to a physical address before accessing physical memory. The process of mapping a virtual address to a physical address is accomplished through the page table. A virtual address is typically divided into two parts: the page number and the offset. The page number is used to index into the page table, where a corresponding page frame number is retrieved, while the offset specifies the exact location within the page frame.

Listing 7.25: ASCII Character Encoding Example

```
# Define the virtual address format
virtual_address = page_number | offset

# Example virtual address and page table entries
virtual_address = 0x1234
page_table[0x12] = 0x9AB

# Translate virtual address to physical address
page_number = 0x12
offset = 0x34
page_frame_number = page_table[page_number]
physical_address = (page_frame_number << OFFSET_BITS) | offset
```

In this example, the virtual address 0x1234 is split into page_number = 0x12 and offset = 0x34. The page table entry for page number 0x12 points to page frame 0x9AB, allowing translation to physical address 0x9AB34.

```
Virtual Address: 0x1234
Page Number: 0x12
Offset: 0x34
Page Frame Number from Page Table: 0x9AB
Physical Address: 0x9AB34
```

A central advantage of paging is that it facilitates efficient memory use, as non-contiguous pages of a process can be mapped to physical page frames, enhancing flexibility and avoiding fragmentation. The process responsible for managing the page tables and performing the translation is typically handled by the kernel and supported by the Memory Management Unit (MMU) hardware.

Page tables can become extensive, particularly with large address spaces, so hierarchical paging structures are employed to mitigate this. A common approach is multi-level paging, where multiple page tables are used in a hierarchically structured manner to manage the mappings efficiently.

Algorithm 5: Multi-Level Paging Translation

Data: Virtual address
Result: Physical address

extract $P1, P2, ..., Pn$, and offset from the virtual address;
current_table ← base_physical_address_of_P1_table;
for *each* $P1, P2, ..., Pn$ *except* offset **do**
    entry ← current_table[Pnext];
    current_table ← entry_address;
end
physical_address ← current_table + offset;

In this algorithm, a hierarchical multi-level paging approach is depicted. The virtual address is broken down into various components such as $P1$, $P2$, etc., representing different levels of page tables, finally concluding with an offset. The current table is initialized to the base physical address of the $P1$ table and iteratively updated until the physical address is computed by adding the offset to the final page table entry.

Advancements in paging include techniques like demand paging, where pages are loaded only when required, and copy-on-write, which optimizes memory usage by delaying the creation of copies of memory pages until modifications are necessary. Understanding these principles aids in grasping how virtual memory systems manage physical memory and optimize performance for complex and resource-intensive applications.

7.9 Direct Memory Access (DMA)

Direct Memory Access (DMA) is a crucial feature for efficient data transfer in systems where minimizing CPU intervention is essential. DMA allows peripherals to directly read from and write to memory without the continuous involvement of the CPU, significantly improving the data throughput and freeing the CPU to perform other tasks.

DMA Controller: The DMA operation is managed by a DMA controller, a hardware component responsible for handling memory access such as transferring data between memory and a peripheral device. The primary functions of a DMA controller include addressing memory, managing data transfer, and sending interruption signals to the CPU upon transfer completion.

DMA Operation: The process begins when a peripheral device needs to read from or write to memory. Instead of engaging the CPU for each byte, the peripheral sends a request to the DMA controller. The DMA controller, upon receiving the request, takes over the bus from the CPU and manages the data transfer.

DMA operation involves several key steps:

- The peripheral issues a DMA request to the DMA controller.
- The DMA controller requests control of the system bus from the CPU.
- Once the CPU acknowledges the request, the DMA controller takes over the bus.
- Using addresses specified in its control registers, the DMA controller performs the read or write operations.
- Upon completion, the DMA controller releases the bus and notifies the CPU via an interrupt.

Algorithm 6: DMA Transfer Process

Input : Source memory address, Destination memory address, Transfer size, Control signals

Output : Completion interrupt

```
while Transfer size > 0 do
    DMA controller receives a request signal from the peripheral;
    DMA controller requests bus access from the CPU;
    if CPU grants bus access then
        DMA controller reads from source address;
        DMA controller writes to destination address;
        Transfer size is decremented;
    else
        DMA controller waits;
DMA controller releases the bus;
DMA controller generates an interrupt to notify the CPU;
```

Types of DMA Transfers: There are three main types of DMA transfers: Burst Mode, Cycle Stealing Mode, and Transparent Mode.

- **Burst Mode:** The DMA controller gains control of the bus and transfers an entire block of data in one contiguous operation. It holds onto the bus until the whole transfer is complete, ensuring maximal transfer speed but potentially causing latency for other bus users.
- **Cycle Stealing Mode:** The DMA controller transfers one word of data at a time, releasing the bus back to the CPU after each transfer. This method allows the CPU to regain control of the bus in between DMA operations, reducing the latency for other operations but at the cost of reduced data transfer speed.
- **Transparent Mode:** The DMA controller transfers data only when the CPU is not using the system bus, leading to the least interference with the CPU but potentially the slowest data transfer rate, depending on the CPU's activity.

DMA Configuration: Configuring a DMA channel typically involves specifying several parameters in the controller's control registers:

- Source Address: The starting address from which data will be read.
- Destination Address: The starting address to which data will be written.
- Transfer Count: The number of bytes (or words) to transfer.
- Control Signals: Such as the direction of transfer (read or write), mode of transfer (burst, cycle stealing, transparent), and interrupt enabling.

Here is a basic assembly routine for setting up a DMA controller:

Listing 7.26: ASCII Character Encoding Example

```
; Example routine to configure and start a DMA transfer
; Assumptions: DMA controller registers are mapped at specific IO addresses

MOV AX, SourceAddress ; Load the source address
OUT DX, AX ; Send to DMA controller source register
MOV AX, DestinationAddress ; Load the destination address
OUT DX, AX ; Send to DMA controller destination register
MOV AX, TransferCount ; Load the count of bytes to transfer
OUT DX, AX ; Send to DMA controller transfer count register
MOV AX, ControlValue ; Load control values (mode, direction)
OUT DX, AX ; Send to DMA controller control register
STI ; Set interrupt flag to enable interrupts
HLT ; Halt CPU till interrupt occurs
```

In this example, the SourceAddress, DestinationAddress, and TransferCount are placeholders for actual addresses and count values. The ControlValue sets the transfer mode and enables the DMA controller. The STI instruction enables interrupts, permitting the DMA controller to signal the CPU upon completing the data transfer.

The utilization of DMA is especially advantageous in scenarios requiring high-speed data transfers, such as streaming data to and from storage devices, real-time data acquisition systems, and implementing memory-to-memory transfers with minimal CPU intervention. This efficiency underscores the significance of mastering DMA techniques for optimizing assembly language programs and the broader system performance.

7.10 Cache Memory: Principles and Management

Cache memory is a critical component of modern computer architectures, designed to bridge the gap between the slower main memory and the faster central processing unit (CPU). It temporarily stores copies of frequently accessed data from the main memory, significantly enhancing system performance by reducing the average time to access memory.

Cache Memory Hierarchy: Computer systems typically employ a multi-level cache hierarchy, each level providing varying sizes and speeds of storage. The hierarchy generally includes:

- L1 Cache: The smallest and fastest cache, located closest to the CPU cores. It is often split into separate instruction and data caches.
- L2 Cache: Larger and slower than L1, but faster than the main memory. It serves as a secondary cache for both instructions and data.
- L3 Cache: The largest and slowest cache in the hierarchy, shared across multiple CPU cores to facilitate inter-core communication and data sharing.

Basic Principles of Cache Operation: Cache memory operates based on the principles of *temporal locality* and *spatial locality*.

- Temporal Locality: Frequently accessed data tends to be referenced multiple times within a short time duration.
- Spatial Locality: Data located nearby recently accessed memory addresses are likely to be accessed soon.

When a CPU seeks data, it first checks the L1 cache. If the data is not present (*cache miss*), the search progresses to L2 and then to L3 caches before ultimately accessing the main memory. A *cache hit* occurs when the data is found within the cache levels.

Cache Organization and Mapping: Cache memory is organized into blocks (or lines) and set up in different architectures for efficient data management. The three primary cache mapping techniques used are:

- Direct Mapped Cache: Each block of main memory maps to only one cache line. The simplicity of this mapping reduces hardware complexity but may lead to frequent conflicts.
- Fully Associative Cache: Any block of main memory can be loaded into any line of the cache. This technique minimizes conflicts but increases search time and hardware complexity.
- Set Associative Cache: A hybrid approach, where the cache is divided into a number of sets. Each block of main memory maps to exactly one set, but within that set, a block can be placed in any line. This is a compromise solution between direct-mapped and fully associative caches.

Below is an example program illustrating how cache mapping might be simulated in assembly language:

Listing 7.27: ASCII Character Encoding Example

```
// Pseudocode of Set Associative Cache Simulation
// Assume each set has 2 lines, and the cache has 4 sets
// Memory addresses are represented in hexadecimal format

ORG 1000H ; Start of program
MOV AX, 1234H ; Example address to access
CALL CacheAccessProcedure ; Cache access simulation

CacheAccessProcedure:
    MOV BX, AX ; Move address to BX
    AND BX, 0FH ; Extract set index (lower 4 bits)

    ; Check if data exists in the set
    ; Simulate the associative cache behavior
    ; Here we assume predefined sets and lines
```

```
    ; Set 0 simulation
    CMP BX, 0H
    JNE NOT_SET_0
        ; Check line 0 and line 1 of Set 0
        ; Further logic to simulate set 0 cache access

    NOT_SET_0:
    ; Continue with Set 1, Set 2, up to the number of sets
RET
```

Cache Replacement Policies: When a cache miss occurs, and the cache is full, a block of cache must be replaced. The efficiency of cache memory is heavily influenced by the replacement policy employed:

- Least Recently Used (LRU): Replaces the cache block that has not been used for the longest time.
- First-In-First-Out (FIFO): Replaces the oldest block in the cache.
- Random Replacement: Randomly selects a block to replace, which can sometimes balance workload efficiently.

The pseudocode for an LRU replacement policy is depicted below:

Algorithm 7: LRU Cache Replacement Policy

```
Input: New memory block to be accessed
Output: Cache updated with new block
AccessCache(NewBlock);
Set = GetCacheSet(NewBlock);
if Set is full then
    VictimBlock = GetLRUBlock(Set);
    Replace(VictimBlock, NewBlock);
    UpdateAccessOrder(NewBlock);
end
else
    InsertBlock(Set, NewBlock);
end
```

Cache Write Strategies: Two primary strategies for handling write operations in cache memory are *write-through* and *write-back*:

- Write-Through: Every write to the cache simultaneously updates the main memory, ensuring data consistency but potentially increasing latency.

- Write-Back: Writes are initially made only to the cache, with a write to the main memory deferred until the cache block is replaced. This reduces latency but requires careful management of data consistency.

The effectiveness of cache memory in a system depends on several factors such as hit rate, miss penalty, cache size, and line size. Optimizing these parameters is crucial for achieving efficient memory performance.

7.11 Memory-Mapped I/O

In assembly language programming, **Memory-Mapped I/O** (MMIO) is a technique that integrates input/output device control with the memory system. This integration allows data to flow between an I/O device and a processor using the processor's regular load and store instructions. MMIO is an efficient method for device communication, avoiding the need for separate instructions for accessing devices.

The memory address space includes specific addresses reserved for peripherals, known as *I/O addresses*. These addresses are mapped to device registers rather than to regular memory. Each of these registers performs specific tasks such as sending or receiving data, setting up control flags, or polling status flags.

Here, we will delve into how this mapping works at a low level and how it is implemented in assembly language.

Listing 7.28: ASCII Character Encoding Example

```
section .data
    ; Define variables and constants

section .bss
    ; Allocate memory for buffers and state information

section .text
    global _start

_start:
    mov eax, [address] ; Read from memory-mapped I/O address
    ; Perform operations with the read value
    mov [address], eax ; Write back to memory-mapped I/O address
```

In the snippet above, address refers to a memory location reserved for an I/O device register. When the processor executes the mov instruction, it either reads from or writes to the device register as if it were regular memory.

To clarify, consider an example where a processor communicates with a memory-mapped UART (Universal Asynchronous Receiver/Transmitter). The UART's base address, say $0x4000$, contains several registers:

- $0x4000$ – UART data register
- $0x4004$ – UART status register
- $0x4008$ – UART control register

Read and write operations to these memory addresses can be handled the same way as any other memory operation in assembly language.

Listing 7.29: ASCII Character Encoding Example

```
UART_BASE equ 0x4000
UART_DATA equ UART_BASE + 0x0
UART_STATUS equ UART_BASE + 0x4
UART_CONTROL equ UART_BASE + 0x8

section .text
    global _start

_start:
    ; Polling example: waiting for UART to be ready to send data
    poll_uart:
        mov eax, [UART_STATUS]
        test eax, 0x01 ; Check if the UART is ready
        jz poll_uart ; If not ready, loop

    ; Sending data to UART
    mov eax, 'A' ; Load data (to be transmitted) into eax
    mov [UART_DATA], eax ; Write data to UART data register
```

In the above code, the processor first polls the UART_STATUS register till the UART is ready (indicated by bit 0). Once it is ready, it sends a character 'A' by writing to the UART_DATA register.

Advantages of using Memory-Mapped I/O include:

- Simplified Instruction Set: Memory and I/O devices use the same instructions for data transfer, reducing the complexity of the instruction set.
- Integration: Simplifies hardware design by integrating memory and peripheral devices under a unified address map.
- Performance: Allows faster data transfer between CPU and I/O devices as regular memory access mechanisms are utilized.

However, it also presents some challenges:

- Address Space Consumption: Portions of the address space are dedicated to I/O devices, which can limit the available space for system memory.
- Memory Protection Complexity: Ensuring that peripheral registers mapped to memory space are properly protected requires additional consideration in the memory management unit (MMU).

MMIO is pivotal in embedded systems and systems programming, offering a streamlined and efficient path for hardware control. As memory speeds have improved, MMIO remains a relevant technique for ensuring optimal CPU to peripheral communication. Understanding how to map and manipulate these addresses is fundamental for developing low-level, performance-sensitive applications.

7.12 Optimizing Memory Usage in Assembly Programs

Effective memory optimization in assembly programming is paramount to achieving efficient, high-performance applications. This section delves into various methodologies and strategies for optimizing memory usage, focusing on techniques specific to assembly language.

One of the primary considerations in optimizing memory usage is minimizing the footprint of data and instructions. This involves careful selection of addressing modes, as well as optimizing data structures and flow control.

Addressing Modes Optimization: Selecting the appropriate addressing mode can significantly impact both the speed and memory consumption of an application. Consider the following addressing modes in x86 assembly:

- Immediate Addressing - Directly uses constant values within instructions, which increases instruction size.
- Register Addressing - Uses CPU registers for operations, which aids in reducing memory access times.
- Direct Addressing - Accesses memory location directly, suitable for static data.

- Indirect Addressing - Provides flexibility by referencing memory locations via pointers.

By favoring Register Addressing where possible, you can minimize memory accesses and thus decrease overall memory usage. The following example illustrates this concept:

Listing 7.30: ASCII Character Encoding Example

```
; Example of Register Addressing optimization
mov eax, [var1] ; Load var1 into register eax
add eax, [var2] ; Add var2 to the value in eax
mov [result], eax ; Store the result back into memory
```

Reducing Code Bloat: Another optimization strategy is to minimize code bloat by using efficient branching and looping constructs. Unnecessary instructions should be eliminated, and loops should be unrolled where feasible for performance gains. Consider comparing the ordinary loop with an unrolled loop:

Listing 7.31: ASCII Character Encoding Example

```
; Ordinary loop
mov ecx, 10
loop_start:
    add eax, [array + ecx*4]
    dec ecx
    jnz loop_start
```

Unrolling the loop can reduce the number of branch instructions, thus optimizing execution:

Listing 7.32: ASCII Character Encoding Example

```
; Unrolled loop
add eax, [array + 36]
add eax, [array + 32]
add eax, [array + 28]
add eax, [array + 24]
add eax, [array + 20]
add eax, [array + 16]
add eax, [array + 12]
add eax, [array + 8]
add eax, [array + 4]
add eax, [array]
```

Data Structure Optimization: Optimizing data structures to align with memory boundaries can prevent wastage and improve access speed. Padding bytes may be added to ensure that structures are aligned to specific boundaries, such as 4 or 8 bytes, which aligns with most processor cache lines.

Listing 7.33: ASCII Character Encoding Example

```
; Structure with padding for alignment
section .data
aligned_struct:
    db 0x01 ; 1 byte
    db 0x00, 0x00, 0x00 ; 3 bytes padding
    dd 0x12345678 ; 4 bytes (DWORD)
```

Stack and Heap Management: Efficient management of stack and heap memory can also lead to significant optimizations. The stack is typically faster but limited in size, making it suitable for function calls and small automatic variables. The heap, managed via system calls, is more suitable for dynamic memory needs but incurs a higher overhead.

When optimizing stack usage, reuse registers whenever possible to minimize local variable allocations. For heap management, implementing custom memory allocators tailored to the application's needs can reduce fragmentation and overhead.

Below is an example of optimal stack usage:

Listing 7.34: ASCII Character Encoding Example

```
; Function utilizing stack efficiently
push ebp
mov ebp, esp
sub esp, 8 ; allocate space for two local variables
mov dword [ebp-4], 10 ; first variable
mov dword [ebp-8], 20 ; second variable
; perform operations
add [ebp-4], [ebp-8]
mov eax, [ebp-4]
mov esp, ebp
pop ebp
ret
```

Inline Functions and Macros: Using inline functions and macros can inline frequently used blocks of code without the overhead of function calls. This is particularly useful in tight loops and performance-critical sections.

An example of a macro in assembly:

Listing 7.35: ASCII Character Encoding Example

```
%macro ADD_VALUES 2
    add %1, %2
%endmacro

section .text
    ; Using the macro
    ADD_VALUES eax, ebx
```

Efficient memory optimization in assembly programs is achieved through meticulous planning and careful consideration of code, data structures, and memory management techniques. Employing these strategies can lead to substantial reductions in memory usage and improvements in execution speed.

Chapter 8

Input and Output in Assembly Language

This chapter details input and output operations in assembly language, including the use of BIOS and DOS interrupts for I/O, as well as port-mapped and memory-mapped I/O methods. It covers handling keyboard input and displaying text on the screen, file operations such as reading and writing files, and interfacing with printers and peripheral devices. Practical examples and applications of I/O operations are provided to illustrate these concepts.

8.1 Introduction to Input and Output

The Input/Output (I/O) operations in assembly language are critical functionalities because they allow a program to interact with external devices and users. Understanding these operations is paramount for developing applications that communicate effectively with hardware components such as keyboards, displays, printers, disks, and other peripheral devices. This section provides the foundational knowledge required to grasp how I/O operations are implemented and utilized in assembly language programming.

At its core, I/O operations facilitate data exchange between the central processing unit (CPU) and the peripheral devices. This exchange can occur through various methods, including interrupt-driven I/O, polling, and direct memory access (DMA). In assembly language, I/O operations typically involve either port-mapped I/O or memory-mapped I/O, with specific instructions used to send and receive data.

Whereas high-level programming languages abstract the complexities of I/O operations, assembly language programmers must explicitly manage the low-level details. These details include configuring device registers, handling interrupts, and optimizing data transfer processes to enhance performance.

To begin, consider an explanation of the fundamental I/O concepts:

- **I/O Ports:** I/O ports are used to facilitate communication between the CPU and peripheral devices. Each port is identified by a unique address, and these addresses are used to read from or write to the specific device.
- **Interrupts:** Interrupts are signals sent by devices to the CPU to indicate that they require attention. They allow devices to operate asynchronously with the processor, reducing the need for constant polling.
- **BIOS and DOS Interrupts:** In assembly language, certain interrupt vectors provided by BIOS and DOS are used to perform standard I/O functions. These interrupts abstract some low-level operations, simplifying the process of interacting with hardware.
- **Polling:** Polling is a method where the CPU repeatedly checks the status of a device at regular intervals to determine whether it needs service. This can be CPU-intensive but is straightforward to implement.
- **Direct Memory Access (DMA):** DMA is a system that allows peripherals to directly read from and write to memory without needing CPU intervention for each byte transferred, allowing for more efficient data handling.

For practical understanding, below is an example of writing a single character to the screen using BIOS interrupt in assembly language. This simple operation leverages interrupt 0x10, function 0x0E, which outputs a character to the teletype (TTY) display:

Listing 8.1: ASCII Character Encoding Example

```
section .data
    char db 'A' ; Character to display
```

```
section .text
    global _start

_start:
    ; Load the character to be displayed into the AL register
    mov al, [char]

    ; Load 0x0E into AH register to use BIOS TTY output function
    mov ah, 0x0E

    ; Set the page number (0 in this case)
    mov bh, 0x00

    ; Load the appropriate video page and display the character
    int 0x10

    ; Terminate the program (for an OS like DOS)
    mov ax, 0x4C00
    int 0x21
```

In this example, the mov al, [char] instruction loads the character 'A' into the AL register. Setting AH to 0x0E selects the BIOS interrupt function for teletype output, and int 0x10 calls this interrupt to display the character on the screen.

Next, let us examine how input can be read from the keyboard using BIOS interrupt 0x16, function 0x00, which reads a keystroke:

Listing 8.2: ASCII Character Encoding Example

```
section .bss
    key resb 1 ; Reserve 1 byte for the key input

section .text
    global _start

_start:
    ; Call BIOS to read a keystroke into the AX register
    mov ah, 0x00
    int 0x16

    ; Store the character part of AX into key
    mov [key], al

    ; Optional: Display the key using BIOS TTY output
    mov ah, 0x0E
    mov al, [key]
    int 0x10

    ; Terminate the program (for an OS like DOS)
    mov ax, 0x4C00
    int 0x21
```

Here, the int 0x16 interrupt call waits for a key press and stores the ASCII code of the pressed key in the AL register. The program then moves this value into the memory location key, and for demonstration purposes, it prints the character to the screen with another BIOS interrupt call.

These examples are simplified for clarity but encapsulate the essentials of I/O operations in assembly language. As we advance, the later sections provide more profound insights into using DOS interrupts for I/O and discuss port-mapped versus memory-mapped I/O in-depth. Each concept and example incrementally builds on the previous material, ensuring a comprehensive understanding of assembly language input and output operations.

8.2 Basic Concepts of I/O in Assembly Language

Input and output (I/O) operations in assembly language are fundamental for interacting with the hardware components of a computer system. To effectively perform I/O operations, a programmer must understand the low-level mechanisms and instructions specific to assembly language. Assembly language provides direct access to the hardware, allowing precise control over I/O devices. This section delves into the essential concepts and instructions pertaining to I/O operations in assembly language.

Types of I/O Operations: Assembly language I/O operations can be broadly categorized into two types:

- **Port-Mapped I/O:** I/O ports are special addresses dedicated to communication with peripheral devices. The processor uses specific instructions, such as IN and OUT, to read from and write to these ports.
- **Memory-Mapped I/O:** In this approach, device control registers are mapped to specific memory addresses. Standard memory instructions like MOV are used to interact with the devices.

Understanding the distinction between these types is crucial for writing efficient and effective assembly code. Port-mapped I/O uses a separate address space for I/O operations, while memory-mapped I/O shares the address space with regular memory.

Port-Mapped I/O: In port-mapped I/O, devices are accessed through dedicated ports, each identified by an address. The IN and OUT instructions are used to facilitate communication. The general syntax for these instructions is as follows:

Listing 8.3: ASCII Character Encoding Example

```
; IN instruction to read from an input port
IN AL, DX ; Read a byte from port specified in DX into AL

; OUT instruction to write to an output port
OUT DX, AL ; Write a byte from AL to the port specified in DX
```

The ports are referenced by 16-bit addresses. For example, the keyboard might be mapped to a specific port, such as 0x60, and communication with the keyboard is done through this port.

Memory-Mapped I/O: In memory-mapped I/O, devices appear as if they are part of the system memory. This allows the use of standard memory instructions for I/O operations. Memory-mapped I/O does not require special instructions; instead, it relies on the addressing of specific memory locations. For example:

Listing 8.4: ASCII Character Encoding Example

```
; Example of memory-mapped I/O
MOV AX, [0xFF00] ; Read from a device register at address 0xFF00 into AX
MOV [0xFF02], AX ; Write the value in AX to a device register at address 0xFF02
```

Here, addresses $0xFF00$ and $0xFF02$ are assumed to be mapped to device control registers. The processor treats these addresses just like any other memory address.

Synchronization and Polling: I/O operations often require synchronization to ensure that data is read from or written to the device correctly. A common method is polling, where the CPU repeatedly checks the status of a device until it is ready for communication.

Consider the following example for a port-mapped I/O device:

Listing 8.5: ASCII Character Encoding Example

```
WAIT_READY:
  IN AL, 0x64 ; Read the status register of the device
  TEST AL, 0x01 ; Test if the device is ready (assuming ready bit is 0x01)
  JZ WAIT_READY ; If not ready, keep polling
```

Interrupt-Driven I/O: Unlike polling, interrupt-driven I/O allows devices to signal the CPU when they are ready to perform an operation. An interrupt is generated by the device, causing the CPU to execute an interrupt handler routine. This method is more efficient as it allows the CPU to perform other tasks while waiting for the device to be ready.

Data: Device raises an interrupt
Result: CPU executes interrupt handler

```
interrupt_handler:
    Read data from the device port;
    Perform necessary operations;
    Acknowledge and clear the interrupt;
    Return from interrupt;
```

Direct Memory Access (DMA): DMA allows devices to transfer data directly to or from memory without continuous CPU intervention. This method is especially useful for large data transfers, improving system efficiency by freeing the CPU to perform other tasks. The DMA controller manages these transfers, initiating and completing them while the CPU is only involved at the beginning and end of the process.

By understanding these foundational concepts, you will be equipped to handle more complex I/O operations and effectively communicate with the various peripherals connected to your system.

8.3 Using BIOS Interrupts for I/O

BIOS interrupts provide a fundamental interface for input and output operations in assembly language, allowing direct communication with hardware devices at a low level. BIOS, or Basic Input/Output System, is firmware used to perform hardware initialization during the booting process and provide runtime services for operating systems and programs. This section focuses on leveraging BIOS interrupts to perform essential I/O tasks, such as handling keyboard input and managing screen output.

The primary mechanism for invoking BIOS services is through software interrupts. An interrupt is a signal to the processor emitted by hardware or software indicating an event that needs immediate attention. In the context of BIOS, the INT instruction is used to generate a software interrupt.

Listing 8.6: ASCII Character Encoding Example

```
MOV AH, 0x0E ; Function to write character to TTY
MOV AL, 'A' ; The ASCII character to print
INT 0x10 ; Call BIOS video service
```

In the above code snippet, the operation uses INT 0x10 to invoke the

BIOS video service, which handles screen outputs. The AH register is set to 0x0E to specify the function of writing a character to the teletypewriter (TTY). The AL register holds the ASCII value of the character to be displayed. Here, 'A' will be printed to the screen.

Below is a list of commonly used BIOS interrupt functions for various I/O operations:

- INT 0x10 - Video services
- INT 0x13 - Disk services
- INT 0x16 - Keyboard services
- INT 0x14 - Serial communication services

To retrieve a keystroke from the keyboard, INT 0x16 is typically used. This interrupt provides several functions for keyboard operations, such as reading a keystroke, checking for a keystroke, etc.

For instance, to read a keystroke from the keyboard, the following code can be utilized:

Listing 8.7: ASCII Character Encoding Example

```
MOV AH, 0x00 ; Function to read a keystroke
INT 0x16 ; Call BIOS keyboard service
MOV [key], AL; Store the ASCII of the key read
```

In this snippet, INT 0x16 with AH set to 0x00 reads a keystroke from the keyboard and places the ASCII code of the pressed key into the AL register. The value can then be stored or processed accordingly.

For disk operations, such as reading sectors from a disk, INT 0x13 is employed. Here's an example of reading a sector from a floppy disk:

Listing 8.8: ASCII Character Encoding Example

```
MOV AH, 0x02 ; Function to read sectors
MOV AL, numSectors ; Number of sectors to read
MOV CH, trackNumber ; Track number
MOV CL, sectorNumber; Sector number
MOV DH, headNumber ; Head number
MOV DL, driveNumber ; Drive number
INT 0x13 ; Call BIOS disk service
JC errorHandler ; Jump to error handler if carry flag is set
```

This code issues a read sector command with INT 0x13, specifying the number of sectors, track number, sector number, head number, and drive number. The carry flag (CF) is checked afterward to handle any potential errors.

Serial communication is managed through INT 0x14, where various functions such as initializing the serial port, sending a character, or receiving a character can be executed. To initialize a serial port, the code would appear as follows:

Listing 8.9: ASCII Character Encoding Example

```
MOV AH, 0x00 ; Function to initialize the serial port
MOV AL, 0x03 ; Line control settings
MOV DX, 0x00 ; Serial port number (COM1)
INT 0x14 ; Call BIOS serial service
```

In this context, INT 0x14 is used with AH set to 00 to initialize the serial port. The AL register holds the line control settings, and DX specifies the port number (COM1).

Understanding and utilizing BIOS interrupts for I/O operations allows for direct and efficient communication with hardware components, essential for tasks requiring precise control or in environments without a more robust operating system interface.

8.4 Using DOS Interrupts for I/O

DOS (Disk Operating System) provides a set of interrupts, primarily interrupt 21h, which handle various input/output operations. This allows the programmer to leverage standard DOS system calls to perform tasks such as reading input from the keyboard, writing output to the screen, and managing files. Utilizing DOS interrupts simplifies programming by abstracting complicated hardware-level I/O processes behind easy-to-use software interrupts.

Invoking DOS Interrupts: To initiate a DOS interrupt, the Intel assembly language instruction INT is used, followed by the interrupt vector number. For example, INT 21h invokes the DOS interrupt 21h. Prior to calling the interrupt, appropriate values must be set in relevant CPU registers such as AH, AL, BX, CX, etc., depending on the specific service being requested.

Example of Writing a Character to Screen:

Listing 8.10: ASCII Character Encoding Example

```
MOV AH, 02h ; Function 02h - Character output
MOV DL, 'A' ; Character to output
```

```
INT 21h ; DOS interrupt
```

Upon invoking the above code, the character 'A' appears on the screen. Here, AH is loaded with 02h to indicate the desired service (character output), and DL holds the ASCII value of the character to be printed.

Example of Reading a Character from Keyboard:

Listing 8.11: ASCII Character Encoding Example

```
MOV AH, 01h ; Function 01h - Character input without echo
INT 21h ; DOS interrupt
MOV AL, AL ; Character read is now in AL
```

In this case, function 01h is used to read a single character from the keyboard. The character read is placed into the AL register.

String Output: To output a string, DOS provides function 09h. The string must be terminated with a $ character.

Listing 8.12: ASCII Character Encoding Example

```
MOV AH, 09h ; Function 09h - String output
MOV DX, OFFSET message ; Offset of the message
INT 21h ; DOS interrupt

message DB 'Hello, World$',0
```

This code prints the string "Hello, World" to the screen. The DX register is loaded with the address of the string to be printed.

File Operations: DOS interrupts simplify file handling with a series of dedicated functions.

Creating or Opening a File:

Listing 8.13: ASCII Character Encoding Example

```
MOV AH, 3Ch ; Function 3Ch - Create file
MOV CX, 0 ; File attribute (normal file)
MOV DX, OFFSET filename ; File name
INT 21h ; DOS interrupt
JC error ; Check for error (carry flag set)

filename DB 'testfile.txt', 0
```

This snippet creates a new file named testfile.txt. If the file already exists, it is overwritten. The file handle for subsequent operations is returned in the AX register if successful.

Reading from a File:

Listing 8.14: ASCII Character Encoding Example

```
MOV AH, 3Fh ; Function 3Fh - Read from file
MOV BX, [filehandle] ; File handle
MOV CX, 10 ; Number of bytes to read
MOV DX, OFFSET buffer ; Buffer for data
INT 21h ; DOS interrupt

filehandle DW 0
buffer DB 10 DUP(?)
```

Here, function 3Fh reads up to 10 bytes from the file associated with filehandle into buffer. Upon completion, the actual number of bytes read is returned in AX.

Writing to a File:

Listing 8.15: ASCII Character Encoding Example

```
MOV AH, 40h ; Function 40h - Write to file
MOV BX, [filehandle] ; File handle
MOV CX, 12 ; Number of bytes to write
MOV DX, OFFSET buffer ; Buffer containing data
INT 21h ; DOS interrupt

filehandle DW 0
buffer DB 'Hello, file!', 0
```

Function 40h writes data from buffer to the file referred to by filehandle. The count of bytes to be written is specified in CX.

Closing a File:

Listing 8.16: ASCII Character Encoding Example

```
MOV AH, 3Eh ; Function 3Eh - Close file
MOV BX, [filehandle] ; File handle
INT 21h ; DOS interrupt

filehandle DW 0
```

This code closes the file referenced by filehandle using function 3Eh. It is crucial to close files properly to ensure data integrity.

Error Handling: DOS interrupts typically return error codes in the AX register if the carry flag is set. Proper error handling ensures robustness in assembly programs.

Overall, DOS interrupts offer comprehensive and accessible methods for managing various I/O operations, significantly easing the task of I/O control within assembly language programs. The syntactical simplicity of DOS interrupt calls enables efficient input and output handling through intuitive software interfaces.

8.5 Port-Mapped I/O

Port-Mapped I/O, also known as peripheral I/O, is an essential method for communication between the CPU and peripheral devices in assembly language programming. This method uses dedicated I/O ports to interact with various hardware components. The I/O ports operate in a separate address space from the general memory, allowing the processor to read from and write to peripheral devices independently of the system memory.

Port-mapped I/O uses specific instructions to access hardware registers. These instructions are typically the IN and OUT instructions, which differ from the MOV instructions used for memory operations. The IN instruction is used to read data from an input port, while the OUT instruction is used to send data to an output port.

Listing 8.17: ASCII Character Encoding Example

```
; Read 8-bit data from port 0x60 (keyboard input buffer)
mov dx, 0x60
in al, dx

; Write 8-bit data to port 0x61
mov dx, 0x61
out dx, al
```

In this example, the mov dx, 0x60 instruction loads the port address 0x60 into the DX register, then the IN instruction reads a byte of data from the port 0x60 into the AL register. Similarly, the mov dx, 0x61 instruction loads the port address 0x61 into the DX register, and the OUT instruction writes the value from AL into the port 0x61.

The choice of ports and the meaning of the data they represent depend on the specific hardware in use. For example, standard PC hardware often uses port 0x60 for keyboard input and port 0x61 for various system control tasks.

In cases requiring interaction with multiple devices, managing these port addresses and ensuring data integrity becomes crucial. Usually, devices use distinct port addresses to avoid conflicts. Understanding the hardware specifications and chipset documentation is critical for identifying the correct port addresses.

Listing 8.18: ASCII Character Encoding Example

```
; Assume printer data port is at 0x378 and status port is at 0x379

; Check if printer is ready (bit 7 of the status port, 0x379, should be 1)
mov dx, 0x379
```

```
in al, dx
test al, 0x80
jz not_ready

; Send ASCII 'A' to printer data port 0x378
mov dx, 0x378
mov al, 'A'
out dx, al
not_ready:
; Handle not ready case here
```

In the printer example, the status port (0x379) is checked before sending data. The IN instruction reads the printer status byte into AL, and the TEST instruction checks if the printer is ready by evaluating bit 7 of the status byte. If the printer is ready, ASCII character 'A' is sent to the printer data port (0x378).

To effectively use Port-Mapped I/O, it is imperative to understand the hardware architecture and the functions of specific ports. For instance, to control a parallel port or a serial port, one must consult the technical documentation that defines the roles and bit patterns of each I/O port involved.

Specialized I/O control methods, such as waiting for device readiness and handling interrupts, further exemplify the complexities of port-mapped I/O. Interrupt-driven I/O allows the CPU to perform other tasks while waiting for the peripheral device to become ready. When the device is ready, it sends an interrupt signal to the CPU, triggering an interrupt service routine (ISR) to handle the I/O operation.

Listing 8.19: ASCII Character Encoding Example

```
; Enable interrupts and configure PIC (Programmable Interrupt Controller)

; Enable hardware interrupts
sti

; Remap IRQ0-15 to INT 32-47 as per standard PIC remapping
mov al, 0x20 ; ICW1: edge triggered, cascaded mode, ICW4 needed
out 0x20, al
out 0xA0, al
mov al, 0x20 ; ICW2: master PIC vector offset
out 0x21, al
mov al, 0x28 ; ICW2: slave PIC vector offset
out 0xA1, al

; ICW3 and ICW4 configurations follow...
```

This interrupt-driven example initializes the Programmable Interrupt Controller (PIC) to handle hardware interrupts. The sti instruction enables interrupts, and the subsequent code remaps IRQ lines to avoid conflicts with processor exceptions.

Understanding port-mapped I/O and its associated instructions is fundamental to controlling hardware devices at a low level. Mastery of these concepts will enable the development of efficient and effective assembly language programs for interfacing with a wide range of peripheral devices.

8.6 Memory-Mapped I/O

Memory-mapped I/O is a technique in assembly language where the same address space is shared between memory and peripheral devices. This allows both the CPU and devices to access hardware registers as if they were regular memory locations. This approach simplifies the design and addressing, providing a direct and efficient mechanism for I/O operations.

When using memory-mapped I/O, specific addresses in the address space are reserved for peripheral devices. Accessing these addresses will trigger hardware interactions rather than typical memory reads or writes. Here, we explore the fundamental principles and provide practical examples.

Address Space Configuration

In a memory-mapped I/O configuration, the system's address space is divided between RAM, ROM, and peripheral device registers. Typically, the addresses for these devices are defined in the system's hardware specifications. For instance, in many microcontrollers, specific ranges of the address space are dedicated to functions like timers, communication ports, and digital I/O pins.

The simplified model can be represented as:

```
+--------------------+
|       ROM          |
+--------------------+
|       RAM          |
+--------------------+
| Peripheral Devices |
+--------------------+
```

Accessing Memory-Mapped Registers

To interact with memory-mapped I/O devices, the assembly code needs to perform read and write operations to specific memory addresses. The exact addresses are usually provided in the hardware documentation. The following example demonstrates how to write to and read from a memory-mapped I/O register.

Consider a hypothetical system where an LED is controlled by an 8-bit I/O register located at address 0xFF00. Writing a value of 1 to this register turns on the LED, and writing 0 turns it off.

Listing 8.20: ASCII Character Encoding Example

```
; Define the address for the I/O register
LED_CONTROL_REGISTER equ 0xFF00

section .data

section .text

; Turn LED on
mov dx, LED_CONTROL_REGISTER
mov al, 1
out dx, al

; Turn LED off
mov dx, LED_CONTROL_REGISTER
mov al, 0
out dx, al

; Read LED status
mov dx, LED_CONTROL_REGISTER
in al, dx
```

In this example, LED_CONTROL_REGISTER is a constant representing the memory address of the LED control register. The mov instruction sets up the address, and the out instruction sends the value to the LED control register. The in instruction reads the current state of the register.

Advantages of Memory-Mapped I/O

Memory-mapped I/O offers several advantages:

- **Simplified Addressing:** Using standard memory instructions for I/O operations simplifies the programming model since no special I/O instructions are required.
- **Uniform Access:** Both data and I/O registers are accessed using the same instructions, making the process more intuitive.
- **Flexibility:** It's easier to implement complex data transfers, such as block moves, directly with standard memory instructions.

Potential Issues and Considerations

Despite its advantages, memory-mapped I/O also has limitations:

- **Address Space Utilization:** Since I/O addresses consume parts of the total address space, less space is available for main memory.

- **Access Timing:** Accesses to peripheral devices may have different timing characteristics compared to regular memory, necessitating careful timing analysis.
- **Complexity in Address Decoding:** The hardware must distinguish between regular memory accesses and I/O operations, which can complicate the address decoding logic.

Example: Interfacing with a Serial Port

Let us consider an example where we interface with a serial port at addresses 0x3F8 through 0x3FF, commonly used for COM1 on x86 systems. Here, we will write a byte to the serial port.

Listing 8.21: ASCII Character Encoding Example

```
; Define the base address of the serial port
SERIAL_PORT_BASE equ 0x3F8

section .data
    message db 'A', 0

section .text
    ; Write a character to the serial port
    mov dx, SERIAL_PORT_BASE
    mov al, [message]
    out dx, al
```

In this code, SERIAL_PORT_BASE is a constant representing the base address of the serial port. We move the character 'A' from the message variable into the al register and write it to the port.

Memory-mapped I/O is an essential technique in low-level programming that allows efficient and straightforward peripheral device management. Understanding and utilizing this method is crucial for developing systems that require direct hardware control. By carefully mapping I/O devices into the memory space, one can simplify software design, though it requires an understanding of the underlying hardware architecture.

8.7 Keyboard Input Handling

Keyboard input handling in assembly language involves directly accessing the hardware and software interfaces that manage keyboard interactions. The keyboard, an essential input device, operates via a series of interrupts that communicate key presses and their corresponding actions to the processor. Understanding how to manage keyboard input precisely necessitates a thorough comprehension of BIOS interrupts and the processor's interaction with the keyboard controller.

BIOS Interrupt 16h is pivotal for keyboard input manipulation. This interrupt provides various services to read and control the keyboard. The most commonly used function is $16h$ with subfunction $00h$, which reads a character from the keyboard. When a key is pressed, BIOS places the key's scan code into a buffer, and the corresponding ASCII value is returned through registers.

Listing 8.22: ASCII Character Encoding Example

```
MOV AH, 00h ; BIOS keyboard service to read character
INT 16h ; Call BIOS keyboard service
MOV [char], AL ; Store the ASCII value in 'char'
```

The registers involved are: - AH is set to $00h$ to specify the function. - AL receives the ASCII value of the key pressed. - The scan code can also be retrieved from AH after the interrupt call.

In addition to reading a character, BIOS provides other services related to keyboard input:

- $AH = 01h$: Check for a keystroke, returning zero flag if no key is pressed. - $AH = 02h$: Get the keyboard shift flags.

To check for a keystroke without blocking program execution, use the $16h$ with subfunction $01h$:

Listing 8.23: ASCII Character Encoding Example

```
MOV AH, 01h ; BIOS keyboard service to check keystroke
INT 16h ; Call BIOS keyboard service
JZ NoKeyPressed ; Jump if zero flag is set (no key pressed)
MOV [char], AL ; Store the ASCII value in 'char' if key is pressed
NoKeyPressed:
```

For detailed keyboard control, understanding the *keyboard buffer* and handling *interrupts* directly can be beneficial. The keyboard buffer, typically located at memory segment $0040h$ offset $001Eh$, stores the scan codes of keys pressed. The head and tail pointers of this circular buffer indicate the current state of keyboard input.

Listing 8.24: ASCII Character Encoding Example

```
MOV AX, 0040h ; Segment address of BIOS Data Area (BDA)
MOV ES, AX
MOV BX, ES:[001Eh] ; Head pointer of keyboard buffer
```

```
MOV CX, ES:[001Ch] ; Tail pointer of keyboard buffer
```

Handling keyboard interrupts directly using INT 09h requires writing an Interrupt Service Routine (ISR). This ISR intercepts the keyboard interrupt, processes the key press, and optionally passes control back to the original ISR. ISRs must ensure that they save and restore the state of the CPU registers and handle the End Of Interrupt (EOI) signal.

Listing 8.25: ASCII Character Encoding Example

```
KbdISR:
PUSH AX ; Save registers
PUSH BX
IN AL, 60h ; Read scan code from port 60h
MOV [ScanCode], AL ; Store scan code
OUT 20h, 20h ; Send End Of Interrupt (EOI) to PIC
POP BX ; Restore registers
POP AX
IRET ; Return from interrupt
```

IN AL, 60h reads the scan code of the key pressed from the keyboard controller port 60h, and OUT 20h, 20h signals the end of interrupt to the Programmable Interrupt Controller (PIC).

To interface seamlessly at a higher level, the DOS interrupts can also be leveraged. DOS interrupt 21h with subfunction 0Ah can be used to read a string from the keyboard, allowing for more complex input buffering and line editing capabilities.

Listing 8.26: ASCII Character Encoding Example

```
MOV AH, 0Ah ; DOS function to read string
MOV DX, OFFSET buffer ; Point to buffer
INT 21h ; Call DOS service
```

The buffer for this function should be structured as follows: - The first byte is the maximum buffer size. - The second byte is the number of characters actually read upon return. - The subsequent bytes contain the inputted characters.

Understanding and utilizing these methods and interfaces provide comprehensive control over keyboard input in assembly language. Handling keyboard input efficiently ensures responsive and user-friendly applications, critical in both systems programming and embedded applications development.

8.8 Displaying Text on the Screen

Displaying text on the screen in assembly language involves using the system's interrupt handling mechanisms to directly interface with the hardware. The primary methods for achieving this include BIOS and DOS interrupts, each of which provides functions to control text output.

The easiest way to begin displaying text on the screen is by making use of the DOS interrupt int 21h. This interrupt has various functions, among which function 09h is particularly useful for displaying strings. When using this function, the string to be displayed must be terminated by a $ character.

Listing 8.27: ASCII Character Encoding Example

```
; Sample code to display a string using DOS interrupt 21h

section .data
    message db 'Hello, world!$', 0

section .text
    global _start

_start:
    ; Load the address of the message into the DX register
    mov dx, message
    ; Load AH with 09h to specify the print string function
    mov ah, 09h
    ; Call the DOS interrupt 21h
    int 21h
    ; Exit the program
    mov ax, 4C00h
    int 21h
```

Running the above program will output the string Hello, world! to the screen. The $ character marks the end of the string as required by DOS function 09h.

While using int 21h is straightforward and available on DOS systems, a more universal approach involves using the BIOS interrupt int 10h. The BIOS interrupt provides a myriad of services for directly interfacing with the screen, including functions for cursor positioning and character output.

Function 0Eh of interrupt int 10h allows for teletype (TTY) output, meaning it prints a single character at the current cursor position and then increments the cursor. Below is an example of how to use BIOS interrupt int 10h to display a character on the screen:

Listing 8.28: ASCII Character Encoding Example

```
; Sample code to display characters using BIOS interrupt 10h

section .data
    message db 'Hello, BIOS!'

section .text
    global _start

_start:
    ; Load the address of the message into the SI register
    lea si, [message]

print_loop:
    ; Load the next character from the string into AL
    lodsb
    ; Check if we have reached the end of the string (null terminator)
    cmp al, 0
    je done
    ; Load AH with 0Eh to specify the teletype function
    mov ah, 0Eh
    ; Call the BIOS interrupt 10h
    int 10h
    ; Repeat until the end of the string
    jmp print_loop

done:
    ; Exit the program
    mov ax, 4C00h
    int 21h
```

This program outputs the string Hello, BIOS! to the screen, using a loop to process each character individually through BIOS interrupt int 10h. The loop continues until it encounters the null terminator at the end of the string.

Using BIOS interrupts offers more functionality and direct control compared to DOS interrupts. For example, with BIOS, you can position the cursor at any screen location before printing by using interrupt int 10h, function 02h:

Listing 8.29: ASCII Character Encoding Example

```
; Sample code to position the cursor and display a character using BIOS interrupt 10h

section .data
    message db 'Positioned Text!'

section .text
    global _start

_start:
    ; Position cursor to row 10, column 5
    mov ah, 02h ; Function: Set Cursor Position
    mov bh, 0 ; Page number
    mov dh, 10 ; Row number (10)
    mov dl, 5 ; Column number (5)
    int 10h ; Call BIOS interrupt 10h
```

```
    ; Load the address of the message into the SI register
    lea si, [message]

print_loop:
    ; Load the next character from the string into AL
    lodsb
    ; Check if we have reached the end of the string (null terminator)
    cmp al, 0
    je done
    ; Load AH with 0Eh to specify the teletype function
    mov ah, 0Eh
    ; Call the BIOS interrupt 10h
    int 10h
    ; Repeat until the end of the string
    jmp print_loop

done:
    ; Exit the program
    mov ax, 4C00h
    int 21h
```

This program first sets the cursor position to row 10 and column 5 of the screen before printing the message. It utilizes function 02h of int 10h to control cursor positioning.

The strategies discussed emphasize low-level control provided by BIOS and DOS interrupts, essential for text display in assembly language. They also show the advantages of using BIOS for additional functionality such as cursor management. The examples presented demonstrate key concepts required for advanced manipulation of text output on the screen, crucial for creating more sophisticated assembly language programs.

8.9 File Operations: Reading and Writing Files

File operations are critical not only in high-level programming languages but also in assembly language, where direct control over file manipulation is required. This section details how to read from and write to files using DOS interrupts, which provide a higher-level interface than directly accessing hardware or BIOS-level functions.

Reading from a File

Reading data from a file in assembly language involves several steps. The key DOS interrupt for file I/O is int 21h, which provides various services for file handling. The function for reading from a file is identified by setting register AH to 3Fh.

1. **Open the File**: Use function 3Dh of int 21h to open the file. Set AH to 3Dh, AL to the access mode (00h for read-only), and DX to the address of the filename. The function returns a file handle in AX.

Listing 8.30: ASCII Character Encoding Example

```
mov ah, 3Dh ; DOS function for opening a file
mov al, 0 ; Access mode: read-only
mov dx, offset filename ; Filename address
int 21h ; Call DOS interrupt
jnc file_opened ; Jump if no error
mov ah, 09h ; If error, display error message
mov dx, offset error_msg
int 21h
file_opened:
mov bx, ax ; Save the file handle
```

2. **Read the File**: Use function 3Fh to read from the file. Set BX to the file handle, CX to the number of bytes to read, and DX to the address of the buffer to store the data.

Listing 8.31: ASCII Character Encoding Example

```
mov ah, 3Fh ; DOS function for reading from a file
mov bx, filehandle ; File handle
mov cx, 100 ; Number of bytes to read
mov dx, offset buffer ; Buffer to store data
int 21h ; Call DOS interrupt
jnc read_successful ; Jump if no error
mov ah, 09h ; If error, display error message
mov dx, offset read_error_msg
int 21h
read_successful:
; Data is now in the buffer
```

3. **Close the File**: It is important to close the file after operations are completed. Use function 3Eh to close the file by setting BX to the file handle.

Listing 8.32: ASCII Character Encoding Example

```
mov ah, 3Eh ; DOS function for closing a file
mov bx, filehandle ; File handle
int 21h ; Call DOS interrupt
```

Writing to a File

Writing data to a file follows a similar protocol. The function for writing to a file is identified by setting register AH to 40h.

1. **Create or Open the File**: Use function 3Ch or 3Dh of int 21h to create a new file or open an existing file for writing. Set AH to 3Ch to create a file or 3Dh to open a file, AL to the access mode (01h for write-only), and DX to the address of the file name. The function returns a

file handle in AX.

Listing 8.33: ASCII Character Encoding Example

```
mov ah, 3Ch ; DOS function for creating a file
mov cx, 0 ; File attribute: normal
mov dx, offset filename ; Filename address
int 21h ; Call DOS interrupt
jc file_open_error ; Jump if error
mov filehandle, ax ; Save the file handle
```

2. **Write to the File**: Use function 40h to write to the file. Set BX to the file handle, CX to the number of bytes to write, and DX to the address of the data buffer.

Listing 8.34: ASCII Character Encoding Example

```
mov ah, 40h ; DOS function for writing to a file
mov bx, filehandle ; File handle
mov cx, length ; Number of bytes to write
mov dx, offset buffer ; Address of data to write
int 21h ; Call DOS interrupt
jnc write_successful ; Jump if no error
mov ah, 09h ; If error, display error message
mov dx, offset write_error_msg
int 21h
write_successful:
; Data is written to the file
```

3. **Close the File**: As with reading, use function 3Eh to close the file by setting BX to the file handle.

Listing 8.35: ASCII Character Encoding Example

```
mov ah, 3Eh ; DOS function for closing a file
mov bx, filehandle ; File handle
int 21h ; Call DOS interrupt
```

Detailed and precise execution of these steps ensures successful reading from and writing to files in assembly language, facilitating robust file manipulation.

8.10 Working with Printers

Interfacing with printers in assembly language involves understanding how to send data to the printer and control various printer functions. This requires using specific interrupts and port-based communication, as described in this section.

Printers are typically interfaced through port-mapped I/O. Each printer is assigned a set of I/O ports, and by writing to these ports, commands and data can be sent to the printer.

The legacy parallel port, also known as the LPT (Line Printer Terminal) port, has historically been used to connect printers. LPT ports are designated as LPT1 (usually at I/O address 0x378), LPT2 (at 0x278), and so forth.

Printing a character involves two main steps:

- Sending the character to the data port.
- Signaling the printer to print the character.

First, data is written to the data port, typically 0x378 for LPT1. Then, a control signal is sent to the control port, typically 0x37A for LPT1, to trigger the actual printing process.

Before proceeding with the assembly code, it is important to understand the port addresses and their significance:

- Data port (0x378 for LPT1): Used to send data (characters) to the printer.
- Status port (0x379 for LPT1): Used to read the status of the printer.
- Control port (0x37A for LPT1): Used to send control signals to the printer.

Here is an example assembly program for printing a single character 'A' using the LPT1 port:

Listing 8.36: ASCII Character Encoding Example

```
MOV DX, 0x378 ; LPT1 data port address
MOV AL, 'A' ; Character to print
OUT DX, AL ; Send character to data port

MOV DX, 0x37A ; LPT1 control port address
MOV AL, 0x0D ; Control signal: Strobe + Init high
OUT DX, AL ; Send control signal

NOP ; Small delay
NOP ; Small delay

MOV AL, 0x0C ; Control signal: Strobe high
OUT DX, AL ; End strobe
```

In this code, the character 'A' is sent to the data port at address 0x378. A control signal is then sent to the control port at address 0x37A to trigger the print operation.

The control port values in the example:

- $0x0D$: Strobe (bit 0) and Init (bit 2) high.
- $0x0C$: Strobe signal goes high to low, completing the strobe pulse.

To print a string, this process must be repeated for each character in the string. Here is a more complex example that prints a null-terminated string:

Listing 8.37: ASCII Character Encoding Example

```
PRINT_STRING:
    MOV SI, STRING ; Point to the string
NEXT_CHAR:
    LODSB ; Load next character into AL
    OR AL, AL ; Check if end of string (null terminator)
    JZ DONE ; If zero, end of string, jump to DONE

    MOV DX, 0x378 ; LPT1 data port address
    OUT DX, AL ; Send character to data port

    MOV DX, 0x37A ; LPT1 control port address
    MOV AL, 0x0D ; Control signal: Strobe + Init high
    OUT DX, AL ; Send control signal

    NOP ; Small delay
    NOP ; Small delay

    MOV AL, 0x0C ; Control signal: Strobe high
    OUT DX, AL ; End strobe

    JMP NEXT_CHAR ; Repeat for next character

DONE:
    RET

STRING DB 'Hello, Printer!', 0
```

This routine uses string addressing through SI and relies on the LODSB instruction to load each character from the string into the accumulator AL.

Apart from the basic port communication to print characters, it is essential to handle printer status. The status port provides feedback from the printer about its state, including readiness to receive data, errors, and acknowledgments. Here is a simplified status check before sending each character:

Listing 8.38: ASCII Character Encoding Example

```
WAIT_FOR_PRINTER:
    MOV DX, 0x379 ; LPT1 status port address
```

```
CHECK_STATUS:
    IN AL, DX ; Read status byte
    TEST AL, 0x80 ; Check busy flag (bit 7)
    JNZ CHECK_STATUS ; If busy, keep checking

    RET
```

This routine reads the status port and checks the busy flag. If the printer is busy, it loops until the printer is ready.

For error handling, the status port can also be checked for other flags, such as out of paper or printer error, to make the program more robust.

Working with modern printers often involves higher-level protocols and interfaces like USB or network connections, typically abstracted via operating system drivers. However, understanding the fundamentals of port communication provides a foundation for more advanced interfacing techniques.

Understanding printer interfacing at a low level in assembly language provides critical insights into hardware interactions, laying the groundwork for more complex I/O operations and system programming.

8.11 Interfacing with Peripheral Devices

Interfacing with peripheral devices in assembly language involves direct communication with hardware components other than the central processing unit (CPU) and the main system memory. This section delves into the fundamental principles and practical examples of peripheral device interfacing using assembly language. Peripheral devices can include, but are not limited to, printers, scanners, network cards, and storage devices. The interaction typically occurs through port-mapped or memory-mapped I/O operations, which have been covered in preceding sections.

Port-Mapped I/O involves accessing hardware devices using specific I/O ports. Each device is assigned a unique port address, and communication is accomplished via IN and OUT instructions. Here is an example of reading from a port:

Listing 8.39: ASCII Character Encoding Example

```
MOV DX, 0x60 ; port address of the keyboard controller
IN AL, DX ; read data from port 0x60 into AL register
```

In this example code, the command MOV DX, 0x60 loads the port address of the keyboard controller into the DX register. The IN instruction is then used to read the data from the specified port into the AL register.

Memory-Mapped I/O involves interacting with devices mapped into the address space of the system memory. Devices are accessed using regular memory instructions, such as MOV. Here is an example of writing to a memory-mapped device:

Listing 8.40: ASCII Character Encoding Example

```
MOV AX, 0x1234 ; some data
MOV [0xFF00], AX ; write data to the device memory address
```

In this example, the MOV instruction writes the data located in register AX to the memory address 0xFF00, which corresponds to a memory-mapped device.

Printer Interfacing:

For example, consider a parallel printer connection. Printers connected via parallel ports generally follow the Centronics standard. The Centronics port interface involves a base address, typically 0x378, with additional control and status registers. Data is sent to the printer one byte at a time via the data register (base address), while the control register (base address + 2) helps manage the handshake process.

Listing 8.41: ASCII Character Encoding Example

```
MOV DX, 0x378 ; printer data port
MOV AL, 0x41 ; ASCII code for 'A'
OUT DX, AL ; send character 'A' to printer

;;; handshake process
MOV DX, 0x37A ; control register
IN AL, DX ; read control register
OR AL, 0x01 ; set strobe bit
OUT DX, AL ; send strobe signal
```

In this code:

- The MOV DX, 0x378 sets the data port address of the printer. - The MOV AL, 0x41 loads the ASCII value of 'A' into AL. - OUT DX, AL sends this data to the printer. - The subsequent lines handle the strobe signal to inform the printer that data is available.

Interfacing with Network Cards:

Network cards are often accessed through network device drivers. However, lower-level programming can involve direct port access for network initialization and data transmission. For instance, NICs (Network Interface Cards) based on the National Semiconductor 8390 chip have a set of registers mapped to I/O ports.

Listing 8.42: ASCII Character Encoding Example

```
MOV DX, 0x300 ; base address of the NIC
MOV AL, 0x11 ; some initialization command
OUT DX, AL ; send init command to NIC
```

This snippet sends an initialization command to a NIC at port address 0x300.

Handling Interrupt Requests:

Peripheral devices often use interrupts to signal the CPU about the completion of tasks or availability of data. IRQs (Interrupt Requests) allow devices to asynchronously notify the CPU, improving efficiency compared to polling methods.

For instance, a serial communication device might signal data availability through an interrupt. This requires setting up an interrupt handler:

Listing 8.43: ASCII Character Encoding Example

```
.386
.MODEL SMALL
.STACK 100h

.DATA
msg DB 'Data received from serial port', 0Dh, 0Ah, '$'

.CODE

   ORG 100h
start:
   MOV AX, @data
   MOV DS, AX

   ; Begin initialization
   MOV DX, 0x3F8 ; COM1 base port
   MOV AL, 0x80 ; Enable DLAB
   OUT DX, AL
   MOV DX, 0x3F8 ; Baud rate divisor (low byte)
   MOV AL, 0x0C ; Set baud rate to 9600
   OUT DX, AL
   MOV DX, 0x3F9 ; Baud rate divisor (high byte)
   MOV AL, 0x00
   OUT DX, AL
   MOV DX, 0x3FB ; Line control register
   MOV AL, 0x03 ; 8 bits, no parity, 1 stop bit
   OUT DX, AL
   MOV DX, 0x3FA ; Interrupt enable register
   MOV AL, 0x01 ; Enable received data interrupt
   OUT DX, AL

   ; Set up Interrupt Vector Table
   CLI
   MOV AX, 0x0000
   MOV DS, AX
   MOV WORD PTR [0x10 * 4], offset serial_irq_handler
```

```
    MOV WORD PTR [0x10 * 4 + 2], CS
    STI

    ; Enable interrupts
    MOV AL, 0x01
    OUT 0x21, AL

    ; Main Program Loop
    MOV DX, 0x3F8
wait:
    IN AL, DX
    TEST AL, 0x01
    JZ wait

serial_irq_handler:
    ; Code to handle serial interrupt
    MOV AH, 09h
    LEA DX, msg
    INT 21h
    IRET
END start
```

In this assembly code:

- The program initializes the serial port, sets the baud rate, and configures line control. - It enables the received data interrupt for the serial port. - The interrupt vector table is configured to point to the serial_irq_handler. - An example interrupt handler echoes a message on the screen each time data is received.

Handling peripheral devices efficiently in assembly language requires understanding both hardware architecture and software integration. By mastering port-mapped and memory-mapped I/O, and utilizing proper interrupt handling techniques, precise control over peripheral devices can be achieved, fulfilling both simple and complex application requirements.

8.12 Examples and Applications of I/O Operations

This section emphasizes concrete examples demonstrating how input and output operations can be effectively implemented in assembly language. Building upon the theoretical concepts discussed, we delve into practical applications critical for mastering the intricacies of I/O processes.

Example 1: Keyboard Input and Screen Output Using BIOS Interrupts

The following code demonstrates how to read a character from the keyboard and display it on the screen utilizing BIOS interrupts.

Listing 8.44: ASCII Character Encoding Example

```
section .data
    msg db 'You pressed: $'

section .bss
    input_char resb 1

section .text
    global _start

_start:
    ; Call BIOS interrupt to read a character from the keyboard
    mov ah, 0x00 ; INT 16h function 00h - Read character
    int 0x16 ; BIOS interrupt call
    mov [input_char], al ; Store the input character

    ; Display static message
    mov ah, 0x09 ; INT 21h function 09h - Display string
    mov dx, msg
    int 0x21 ; DOS interrupt call

    ; Display input character
    mov dl, [input_char]
    mov ah, 0x02 ; INT 21h function 02h - Display character
    int 0x21 ; DOS interrupt call

    ; Exit the program
    mov ah, 0x4C ; INT 21h function 4Ch - Exit
    int 0x21 ; DOS interrupt call
```

Executing this assembly program prompts the user for a keystroke, captures this input, and subsequently displays both a predefined message and the input character on the screen.

```
You pressed: A
```

Example 2: Reading a File Using DOS Interrupts

This example illustrates reading the content of a file and outputting it to the screen. We utilize DOS interrupts to achieve this.

Listing 8.45: ASCII Character Encoding Example

```
section .data
    filename db 'example.txt', 0
    buffer_size equ 128
    buffer resb buffer_size

section .text
    global _start

_start:
    ; Open the file
    mov ah, 0x3D ; INT 21h function 3Dh - Open file
    mov al, 0 ; Read-only mode
```

```
    mov dx, filename
    int 0x21 ; DOS interrupt call
    jc open_error ; Jump if carry flag is set (error)
    mov bx, ax ; File descriptor

    ; Read from the file
    mov ah, 0x3F ; INT 21h function 3Fh - Read file
    mov cx, buffer_size
    mov dx, buffer
    int 0x21 ; DOS interrupt call
    jc read_error ; Jump if carry flag is set (error)

    ; Display the content of the buffer
    mov si, buffer
    print_buffer:
        lodsb ; Load string byte into AL
        cmp al, 0 ; Compare AL with zero terminator
        je done ; If end of buffer, end loop
        mov ah, 0x0E ; BIOS interrupt to print character
        int 0x10 ; BIOS interrupt call
        jmp print_buffer

    done:
    ; Close file
    mov ah, 0x3E ; INT 21h function 3Eh - Close file
    int 0x21 ; DOS interrupt call

    ; Exit program
    mov ax, 0x4C00 ; Terminate program
    int 0x21 ; DOS interrupt call

open_error:
    ; Handle file open error (implementation specific)
    jmp done

read_error:
    ; Handle read error (implementation specific)
    jmp done
```

If the file "example.txt" contains the following text:

```
Hello, World!
```

The output upon running the program would be:

```
Hello, World!
```

Example 3: Writing to a File Using DOS Interrupts

In this example, we write a string to a file using DOS interrupts.

Listing 8.46: ASCII Character Encoding Example

```
section .data
    filename db 'output.txt', 0
    msg db 'Hello from assembly!', 0

section .text
    global _start

_start:
```

```
    ; Create a new file (or truncate if it exists)
    mov ah, 0x3C ; INT 21h function 3Ch - Create file
    mov cx, 0 ; File attributes (normal)
    mov dx, filename
    int 0x21 ; DOS interrupt call
    jc create_error ; Jump if carry flag is set (error)
    mov bx, ax ; File descriptor

    ; Write to the file
    mov ah, 0x40 ; INT 21h function 40h - Write file
    mov cx, 19 ; Number of bytes to write
    mov dx, msg ; Pointer to data
    int 0x21 ; DOS interrupt call
    jc write_error ; Jump if carry flag is set (error)

    ; Close file
    mov ah, 0x3E ; INT 21h function 3Eh - Close file
    int 0x21 ; DOS interrupt call

    ; Exit program
    mov ax, 0x4C00 ; Terminate program
    int 0x21 ; DOS interrupt call

create_error:
    ; Handle file creation error (implementation specific)
    jmp terminate

write_error:
    ; Handle write error (implementation specific)
    jmp terminate

terminate:
    mov ax, 0x4C00
    int 0x21
```

After execution, the content of "output.txt" would be:

```
Hello from assembly!
```

Example 4: Interfacing with Peripheral Devices

For this practical application, we will interface with a simple parallel port to control an LED.

Listing 8.47: ASCII Character Encoding Example

```
section .data
    port_address equ 0x378

section .text
    global _start

_start:
    ; Light up the LED
    mov dx, port_address
    mov al, 0xFF ; ASCII 255, which sets all bits to high
    out dx, al ; Output the value to the data port

    ; Wait for a short period (implementation specific delay)
    ; Turn off the LED
    mov al, 0x00 ; Set all bits to low
```

```
out dx, al ; Output to the data port

; Exit program
mov ax, 0x4C00
int 0x21
```

In this code, port_address corresponds to the base address of a parallel port commonly used for interfacing with simple peripheral devices like LEDs.

Output and functionality for this example depend on the correct hardware setup, which typically involves connecting an LED and a resistor to one of the pins of the parallel port's data registers.

These detailed examples exhibit practical use cases of assembly language for performing I/O operations. They demonstrate reading from and writing to files, interacting with hardware through ports, and handling user inputs to produce meaningful outputs, encompassing a comprehensive understanding critical to proficient assembly language programming.

Chapter 9

Debugging and Optimization

This chapter focuses on the techniques and tools for debugging and optimizing assembly language programs. It covers the use of common debugging tools, setting breakpoints, single-stepping through code, and inspecting registers and memory contents. The chapter also addresses common assembly errors and their resolution. On the optimization front, it introduces basic principles, register allocation, loop and branch optimization, and profiling for performance analysis, supplemented by real-world examples.

9.1 Introduction to Debugging

Debugging in assembly language is a fundamental skill that requires a structured approach and familiarity with various tools. In assembly language, bugs can be particularly challenging due to the low-level nature of the language and the direct manipulation of hardware resources. This section will introduce the essential concepts and tools necessary for effective debugging.

The primary objective of debugging is to identify and rectify errors in a program. Assembly language programs, due to their proximity to hardware, are susceptible to a wide array of errors, such as incorrect use of registers, faulty memory accesses, and logic errors. To detect and correct these errors, developers utilize specialized debugging tools known as debuggers.

A debugger is a software utility that allows a programmer to control the execution of a program, inspect its state, and understand its behavior more thoroughly. The use of a debugger involves setting breakpoints, stepping through code, and examining the state of the CPU registers and memory. Furthermore, debuggers can also evaluate the call stack and monitor memory allocation and usage.

The initiation of debugging often begins with symptom identification, where the developer notes the incorrect behavior of the program. Using a debugger, breakpoints can be set at strategic locations in the code to halt execution and examine the program state. This process helps isolate the exact instruction or set of instructions causing the issue.

Listing 9.1: ASCII Character Encoding Example

```
section .data
    msg db 'Hello, world!',0 ; Message to display

section .text
    global _start

_start:
    mov rax, 1 ; System call number for sys_write
    mov rdi, 1 ; File descriptor 1 is stdout
    mov rsi, msg ; Address of string to output
    mov rdx, 13 ; Number of bytes
    syscall ; Invoke the system call

    mov rax, 60 ; System call number for sys_exit
    xor rdi, rdi ; Exit code 0
    syscall ; Invoke the system call
```

In the provided example, if an error occurs that prevents the message from being printed correctly, a debugger can be used to examine each instruction's effect on the CPU's state. This often involves the following steps:

- Setting Breakpoints: Breakpoints are set to pause the program execution at specific points, facilitating examination of the state at those points.
- Stepping Through Code: Single-stepping allows the developer to execute the program one instruction at a time, closely observing changes in registers and memory.
- Inspecting Register Contents: Examining and modifying the con-

tents of general-purpose and special-purpose registers to determine and correct erroneous values.

- Memory Examination: Observing the contents of memory locations to ensure data is being correctly read from and written to the expected memory addresses.

The following is an example of using the GNU Debugger (GDB) to set a breakpoint and step through the example code:

Listing 9.2: ASCII Character Encoding Example

```
(gdb) break _start
Breakpoint 1 at 0x8048080
(gdb) run
Starting program: /path/to/program

Breakpoint 1, 0x08048080 in _start ()
(gdb) step
(gdb) info registers
rax 0x1 1
rdi 0x1 1
rsi 0x804a000 0x804a000
rdx 0xd 13
...
```

Upon encountering the breakpoint, the developer can utilize commands like info registers to view the contents of the CPU registers. The step command allows single-step execution, making it easier to pinpoint erroneous instructions.

Beyond identifying faulty instructions, debugging tools also permit the analysis of the program's flow and data handling. The debugger can display the contents of specific memory addresses, track variable changes, and manage breakpoints for more efficient debugging sessions.

```
08048080:   B8 01 00 00 00        mov    $0x1,%eax
08048085:   BF 01 00 00 00        mov    $0x1,%edi
0804808A:   BE 00 A0 04 08        mov    $0x804a000,%esi
0804808F:   BA 0D 00 00 00        mov    $0xd,%edx
...
```

Memory inspection is crucial, particularly in assembly language, where direct memory access and pointer manipulation are common. The ability to view and manipulate memory directly helps diagnose and correct issues related to faulty memory operations, such as buffer overflows and incorrect data writes.

Ultimately, a proficient understanding of debugging not only aids in resolving bugs but also enhances a developer's conceptual grasp of the assembly language and the hardware it controls. The iterative process of setting breakpoints, stepping through code, inspecting registers, and examining memory empowers developers to delve deeply into their programs, ensuring robust and efficient code execution. Mastery of these techniques forms the foundational skill set necessary for advanced debugging and optimization tasks covered in subsequent sections of this chapter.

9.2 Common Debugging Tools: Debuggers and Disassemblers

Debugging assembly language programs can be challenging due to the low-level nature of the language and the lack of high-level abstractions. To assist in this complex process, several specialized debugging tools have been developed. Among the most important are debuggers and disassemblers.

Debuggers are powerful tools that allow you to examine and manipulate the execution of a program in real-time. They provide capabilities such as setting breakpoints, stepping through code, inspecting register values, and modifying memory contents. On the other hand, disassemblers convert machine code back into assembly language, providing a human-readable format useful for both debugging and understanding how compilers translate high-level code into assembly.

1. Debuggers

A debugger is a software tool that allows you to control the execution of a program. Debuggers offer various features to aid in identifying and resolving bugs:

- **Breakpoints** - Allow the program to be paused at specific points.
- **Single-stepping** - Execute the program one instruction at a time.
- **Watchpoints** - Monitor changes to specified variables or memory locations.
- **Register and Memory Inspection** - View and modify the contents of CPU registers and memory.
- **Stack Traces** - Examine the call stack to diagnose issues related to function calls.

Consider the following example using the GNU Debugger (GDB). The code we are debugging is a simple program that adds two numbers. We will set a breakpoint at the addition instruction, run the program, and inspect the register values before and after the addition.

Listing 9.3: ASCII Character Encoding Example

```
; Simple addition program in assembly

section .data
    num1 db 5
    num2 db 3
    result db 0

section .text
    global _start

_start:
    mov al, [num1]
    add al, [num2]
    mov [result], al

    ; Exit the program
    mov eax, 1 ; sys_exit
    int 0x80
```

To debug this program with GDB, we would proceed with the following steps:

```
$ nasm -f elf64 addition.asm
$ ld -o addition addition.o
$ gdb addition
(gdb) break *0x08048074
(gdb) run
(gdb) info registers
(gdb) nexti
(gdb) info registers
(gdb) x/1xb &result
```

In the above GDB session: 1. We break at the instruction at address 0x08048074, which corresponds to the add instruction. 2. Run the binary. 3. Check the CPU registers before the addition. 4. Execute the next instruction (nexti). 5. Check the CPU registers again to observe changes. 6. Examine the memory location of result to verify the outcome of the addition.

2. Disassemblers

A disassembler translates machine code back into assembly language, offering insights into how the code operates at the hardware level. This is particularly useful when working without the original source code or when analyzing the output of a compiler.

One common disassembler is the objdump tool in Unix-like systems.

Given an executable, objdump can produce a disassembly listing.

Consider the same simple addition program compiled and then analyzed using objdump:

```
$ nasm -f elf64 addition.asm
$ ld -o addition addition.o
$ objdump -d addition
```

```
Producing the output:
\begin{FittedVerbatim}
08048060 <_start>:
 8048060: b0 05                 mov    al,0x5
 8048062: 02 05 03 00 00 00     add    al,BYTE PTR ds:0x3
 8048068: a2 00 00 00 00        mov    BYTE PTR ds:0x0,al
 804806d: b8 01 00 00 00        mov    eax,0x1
 8048072: cd 80                 int    0x80
```

In the disassembly output, each line shows a memory address, the machine code bytes, and the corresponding assembly instruction. From this output, one can correlate the machine code with specific assembly instructions. This capability is essential for debugging, as it provides visibility into what the CPU is executing.

Combining the usage of debuggers and disassemblers can significantly enhance the debugging process. Debuggers allow for interactive exploration, manipulation, and monitoring of a running program, while disassemblers provide a static view of the program's executable structure. Utilizing both tools effectively leads to a more thorough understanding and efficient resolution of issues in assembly language programs.

9.3 Setting Breakpoints and Watchpoints

Breakpoints and watchpoints are essential tools in the debugging process. They allow developers to halt program execution at specified points or when certain conditions are met, enabling an in-depth examination of the program's state. This section discusses how to set and utilize breakpoints and watchpoints effectively within assembly language debugging.

Breakpoints are specific locations in the code where the debugger will pause execution. To set a breakpoint, one typically uses the debugger command interface or a graphical user interface associated with the debugger. In assembly language debugging, setting breakpoints typically involves specifying the exact memory address or instruction where execution should pause.

Consider the following example of an assembly program segment that adds two numbers:

Listing 9.4: ASCII Character Encoding Example

```
section .data
    num1 db 10
    num2 db 20
    result db 0

section .text
    global _start

_start:
    mov al, [num1]
    add al, [num2]
    mov [result], al

    ; Exit
    mov eax, 1
    int 0x80
```

To debug this program, we may want to set a breakpoint at the add instruction to verify that the value in al is correctly modified. Using gdb, a popular debugger for assembly language, you would set the breakpoint by specifying the memory address of the add instruction:

Listing 9.5: ASCII Character Encoding Example

```
(gdb) break *0x08048063
```

After running the program in the debugger with the run command, execution will pause at the breakpoint, allowing the inspection of registers and memory contents at this point.

Watchpoints, on the other hand, are conditions that pause program execution when the value of a specified variable or memory location changes. This is particularly useful in assembly debugging when you need to track changes to specific data in memory, such as variables or array elements.

Returning to the previous example, suppose we suspect that the value of num1 unexpectedly changes during execution. We can set a watchpoint on num1 to halt execution whenever it is modified:

Listing 9.6: ASCII Character Encoding Example

```
(gdb) watch num1
```

When the program modifies num1, gdb will pause, and this will allow you to investigate what caused the change.

Effective usage of breakpoints and watchpoints often involves combining them with other debugging commands. Here are a few standard commands and their typical functions within gdb:

- info breakpoints: Lists all the breakpoints that have been set.
- disable [num]: Temporarily disables the breakpoint specified by num.
- enable [num]: Re-enables a previously disabled breakpoint.
- delete [num]: Removes the breakpoint specified by num.
- info watchpoints: Lists all the watchpoints that have been set.
- awatch [expr]: Sets a watchpoint that pauses execution when the expression expr is written to.
- rwatch [expr]: Sets a watchpoint that pauses execution when the expression expr is read from.

Consider this assembly function that manipulates an array. Debugging such functions often involves numerous breakpoints and watchpoints due to the complexities involved:

Listing 9.7: ASCII Character Encoding Example

```
section .data
    array db 1, 2, 3, 4, 5
    len equ 5

section .text
    global _start

_start:
    mov ecx, len ; Set loop counter
    lea esi, [array] ; Load address of array into ESI

loop:
    add byte [esi], 1 ; Increment each array element
    inc esi ; Move to the next element
    loop loop ; Loop until ECX is 0

    ; Exit
    mov eax, 1
    int 0x80
```

You can use watchpoints to monitor the values in the array as they change during the loop execution:

Listing 9.8: ASCII Character Encoding Example

```
(gdb) break *0x08048058 ; Set breakpoint at the start of the loop
(gdb) run
(gdb) watch *(char[5])array
```

This will halt execution each time an element of the array is modified, facilitating inspections and ensuring that the changes occur as expected.

The command:

Listing 9.9: ASCII Character Encoding Example

```
(gdb) continue
```

resumes execution until the next breakpoint or watchpoint condition is met. This iterative process of setting breakpoints and using watchpoints, along with the tools provided by the debugger, helps identify and rectify errors that are otherwise difficult to diagnose.

Ensuring a thorough understanding of setting and using breakpoints and watchpoints is essential for proficient debugging in assembly language. These techniques provide granular control over the program execution, significantly enhancing the ability to troubleshoot and refine code systematically.

9.4 Single-Stepping Through Code

Single-stepping through code is an essential debugging technique that allows the programmer to execute one instruction at a time and observe the immediate effects on the processor's state. This granular level of control simplifies the process of identifying errors in logic and verifying the correct execution of instructions. Single-stepping is particularly vital in assembly language due to the direct correlation between instructions and processor actions.

To begin single-stepping, one typically uses a debugger, which provides an interface for executing instructions individually. Below are the key commands and actions involved in single-stepping with a debugger such as 'gdb' (GNU Debugger).

Listing 9.10: ASCII Character Encoding Example

```
(gdb) step
```

The step command executes the next instruction in the program. If the instruction is a function call, step enters the function and allows the user to walk through each instruction within it.

Listing 9.11: ASCII Character Encoding Example

```
(gdb) next
```

The next command, on the other hand, executes the next instruction but treats function calls as a single instruction, stepping over the function rather than into it. This can be particularly useful when you are certain that a function is working correctly and wish to proceed without delving into it.

Listing 9.12: ASCII Character Encoding Example

```
(gdb) stepi
```

Alternatively, the stepi command executes exactly one machine instruction rather than a single source line. This is an even more fine-grained approach which is beneficial when debugging at the assembly level or when dealing with complex compiler optimizations.

```
Example:
(gdb) stepi
0x08048456 in main ()
(gdb) stepi
0x08048457 in main ()
```

To illustrate, consider an assembly snippet involving a basic arithmetic operation:

Listing 9.13: ASCII Character Encoding Example

```
mov eax, 5
add eax, 3
sub eax, 2
```

When single-stepping through this code, the debugger will provide feedback on the state of the eax register after each instruction is executed.

```
(gdb) stepi
0x080483f4 in main ()
(gdb) print $eax
$1 = 5
(gdb) stepi
0x080483f5 in main ()
(gdb) print $eax
$2 = 8
(gdb) stepi
0x080483f6 in main ()
(gdb) print $eax
$3 = 6
```

Above, the print $eax command displays the current value of the eax register immediately after each instruction, which helps verify that the program logic is functioning correctly.

Single-stepping is also instrumental in identifying improper memory accesses. By examining the values in registers and memory at each stage, subtle bugs such as erroneous pointer arithmetic can be detected and corrected. Consider a scenario with a memory access issue:

Listing 9.14: ASCII Character Encoding Example

```
mov eax, [ebx]
add eax, [ecx]
```

Using the commands:

Listing 9.15: ASCII Character Encoding Example

```
(gdb) stepi
0x08048400 in main ()
(gdb) print $ebx
$1 = 0xffffd0fc
(gdb) x/1wx $ebx
0xffffd0fc: 0x00000005
(gdb) stepi
0x08048401 in main ()
(gdb) print $ecx
$2 = 0xffffd100
(gdb) x/1wx $ecx
0xffffd100: 0x00000003
```

Here, x/1wx $ebx inspects the contents of the memory address held in ebx, ensuring the fetched data is as expected before use.

Algorithmic approach to manual single-stepping for systematic debugging:

```
Function SingleStepDebugging(start_addr, end_addr):
    while current_addr ≤ end_addr do
        Execute instruction at current_addr;
        Display register contents and memory state;
        if(memory_access_issue) break;
        Move to the next instruction (current_addr++);
```

The manual process entails starting from a specified address, executing each instruction, observing changes in state, and specifically checking for anomalies in memory accesses. This approach allows for thorough and systematic debugging of individual instructions and their effects.

By utilizing single-stepping within a debugger, programmers harness the ability to observe and control program flow at an instruction level, vital for debugging assembly code. This technique serves as a foundational tool in the broader context of debugging and optimization, leading to a more robust and reliable final program.

9.5 Inspecting and Modifying Registers

In this section, we delve into the crucial aspect of debugging and optimizing assembly language programs: the inspection and modification of CPU registers. Registers are pivotal in the execution of assembly instructions, acting as the fastest memory locations that hold data, addresses, and control information. Understanding how to effectively inspect and modify these elements can significantly enhance debugging efficiency and program performance.

Inspecting Registers:

When debugging assembly programs, it is essential to examine the content of various registers to understand the current state of the execution. This involves identifying and interpreting the values held in general-purpose registers (GPRs), segment registers, control registers, and status registers.

To inspect the registers, we commonly use a debugger, such as GNU Debugger (GDB). The commands vary slightly between different debugging tools, but the underlying principles remain consistent.

Listing 9.16: ASCII Character Encoding Example

```
(gdb) info registers
```

The output of this command displays the current values of all general-purpose registers. For instance:

```
eax    0x0    0
ebx    0x1    1
ecx    0x3    3
edx    0x4    4
esi    0x5    5
edi    0x6    6
```

This output snapshot provides a detailed view of each GPR. By examining these values, you can determine what data is being processed and identify any discrepancies or unexpected values that might highlight logical errors or miscalculations in the code.

Additionally, to inspect specific sets of registers in GDB:

Listing 9.17: ASCII Character Encoding Example

```
(gdb) info all-registers
```

This command extends the output to include additional register categories such as floating-point registers and segment registers. Developing a familiarity with register contents is vital for understanding instruction execution flow.

Modifying Registers:

There are scenarios in debugging where modifying a register's value can help simulate and test specific conditions or recover from an erroneous state, facilitating control flow testing and conditional logic validation.

Within GDB, the set command allows for register modification:

Listing 9.18: ASCII Character Encoding Example

```
(gdb) set \$eax = 0x9
```

To verify this change:

Listing 9.19: ASCII Character Encoding Example

```
(gdb) info registers
```

```
eax    0x9    9
ebx    0x1    1
ecx    0x3    3
edx    0x4    4
esi    0x5    5
edi    0x6    6
```

The new value 0x9 in the \$eax register confirms the modification. Such changes can be instrumental in manipulating program state and behavior during debugging sessions.

In addition to modifying GPRs, you can alter segment and control registers. However, exercise caution, as improper changes can lead to system instability or crashes, particularly with control registers that manage specific CPU features.

Listing 9.20: ASCII Character Encoding Example

```
(gdb) set \$cs = 0x10
```

Understanding the implications of altering segment registers is crucial as they define the addressing context for segments. Therefore, refrain from modifying control registers in most scenarios unless there is a clear understanding and specific need.

Example of Practical Usage:

Consider a scenario where an assembly program malfunctions based on conditional jumps relying on the ZF (zero flag) within the EFLAGS register. Inspecting this flag upon hitting a breakpoint can provide insight into whether an anticipated zero result occurred:

Listing 9.21: ASCII Character Encoding Example

```
(gdb) info registers eflags
```

```
eflags         0x202      [ IF ]
```

If the ZF is not set (IF), and it should be, you can force the condition and proceed to the instruction execution:

Listing 9.22: ASCII Character Encoding Example

```
(gdb) set \$eflags = \$eflags | 0x40
```

Re-inspect to verify changes:

Listing 9.23: ASCII Character Encoding Example

```
(gdb) info registers eflags
```

```
eflags         0x242      [ IF ZF ]
```

This output indicates ZF is now active. The program can now proceed as if the zero condition were true, enabling further testing and validation.

In mastering these tools and techniques, programmers gain a powerful capability to control their program's execution at a granular level, facilitating effective identification and resolution of issues, thereby improving overall program stability and performance.

9.6 Examining and Changing Memory Contents

Examining and modifying memory contents are essential tasks in debugging assembly language programs. These tasks allow developers to understand the state of the program at any given point in time and adjust as necessary to control program behavior or fix bugs.

Memory inspection involves checking the current values stored in specific memory addresses. This can help identify issues such as buffer overflows, incorrect data storage, and other memory-related errors. Modification, on the other hand, allows you to change the contents of memory directly, which can be used to test how the program behaves with different data or to immediately correct values without recompiling the program.

Memory Inspection:

Most debugging tools provide commands to inspect memory contents at specific addresses. In a typical debugger, you might use commands like examine to display memory contents.

Listing 9.24: ASCII Character Encoding Example

```
(gdb) x/x 0x600104
0x600104: 0x00000001
```

In this example, x/x is a GDB command used to examine memory. The x indicates the format (x for hexadecimal), and 0x600104 is the address being examined. The output shows that the value at memory address 0x600104 is 0x00000001.

Multiple formats can be used to display memory:

- x/x: Display in hexadecimal.
- x/d: Display in signed decimal.
- x/u: Display in unsigned decimal.
- x/o: Display in octal.
- x/t: Display in binary.
- x/s: Display as string.
- x/i: Display as machine instructions.

The number of units to be displayed can also be specified. For example, x/5x will display five consecutive memory addresses in hexadecimal.

Listing 9.25: ASCII Character Encoding Example

```
(gdb) x/5x 0x600104
0x600104: 0x00000001 0x2 0x3 0x4 0x5
```

Memory Modification:

To modify memory, most debuggers use commands like set. For example, to set the value of a specific memory address in GDB:

Listing 9.26: ASCII Character Encoding Example

```
(gdb) set {int}0x600104 = 42
(gdb) x/x 0x600104
0x600104: 0x0000002a
```

Here, set {int}0x600104 = 42 changes the contents of address 0x600104 to 42. The type specifier {int} indicates that the value should be stored as a 32-bit integer. After modification, the new value is verified using the x/x command.

You can also combine memory examination and modification to diagnose and fix problems dynamically. For example, if you notice incorrect values being stored during a program run, you can use conditional breakpoints and watchpoints to halt execution when specific conditions are met and immediately inspect and correct the memory.

Watchpoints:

Watchpoints are a powerful feature in debuggers to monitor memory locations. Unlike breakpoints, which halt execution at specific code lines, watchpoints trigger when the value at a specific memory address changes:

Listing 9.27: ASCII Character Encoding Example

```
(gdb) watch *(int*)0x600104
Hardware watchpoint 1: *(int*)0x600104
```

Once a watchpoint is set, execution stops whenever the watched address is written to:

```
Hardware watchpoint 1: *(int *) 0x600104

Old value = 41
New value = 42
main () at sample.c:10
10      sample.c: No such file or directory.
```

In this example, the watchpoint on 0x600104 stops execution when the value changes from 41 to 42, providing information about the line and context where the change occurred.

Summary of Commands:

- x/NFMT ADDR: Examine memory at ADDR in format FMT (e.g., hexadecimal, decimal).
- set {TYPE}ADDR = VALUE: Set the value at ADDR to VALUE with type TYPE.
- watch EXPR: Set a watchpoint to stop execution when EXPR is accessed.
- rwatch EXPR: Set a read watchpoint for EXPR.
- awatch EXPR: Set an access watchpoint for EXPR.

Examining and modifying memory contents provide direct insights and control, facilitating efficient debugging and program refinement.

9.7 Using Stack Traces to Debug Procedures

When debugging procedures in assembly language, understanding the call stack is crucial. The call stack stores information about active subroutines or functions in a program, and a stack trace provides a snapshot of the call stack at a particular point in time. This section delves into the mechanics of using stack traces to debug procedures effectively.

To utilize stack traces, we must first understand the fundamental components of the call stack. The call stack typically consists of:

- Return Address: The address where control should return after a subroutine call.
- Frame Pointer (FP): A register that points to the base of the stack frame for the current function.
- Stack Pointer (SP): A register that points to the top of the current stack.
- Local Variables: Temporary storage for the current function's local variables.
- Arguments: Parameters passed to the function.

During the debugging process, a stack trace allows you to view the sequence of function calls that led to the current execution point. This is particularly useful for identifying where an error or unexpected behavior originates.

Listing 9.28: ASCII Character Encoding Example

```
(gdb) backtrace
#0 my_function () at myfile.asm:42
#1 0x0804841a in another_function () at anotherfile.asm:56
#2 0x080483fc in main () at main.asm:34
```

The above stack trace output indicates that the program is currently executing my_function at line 42 of myfile.asm. This function was called by another_function at line 56 of anotherfile.asm, which in turn was called by the main function at line 34 of main.asm.

By interpreting stack traces, you can trace back the sequence of function calls and identify any discrepancies between the expected and actual flow of execution. For instance, if a function was called with incorrect parameters or if a procedure was not supposed to be called at all, stack traces help pinpoint the source of the issue.

To further illustrate, consider a scenario where a stack trace reveals an unexpected call sequence:

Listing 9.29: ASCII Character Encoding Example

```
(gdb) backtrace
#0 faulty_function () at errorfile.asm:78
#1 0x0804852b in intermediary_function () at interfile.asm:102
#2 0x0804845d in legitimate_function () at legitfile.asm:60
```

Here, the presence of faulty_function at the top of the stack trace hints at an anomaly in its invocation. By examining the calls in the order from top to bottom, you realize intermediary_function called faulty_-function, leading to the issue.

To explore and manipulate the call stack, debuggers provide commands such as frame, up, and down. The frame command allows you to select and inspect a particular stack frame:

Listing 9.30: ASCII Character Encoding Example

```
(gdb) frame 1
```

In the above command, frame 1 selects the frame at index 1, corresponding to another_function. Subsequently, you can examine local variables and arguments associated with this frame:

Listing 9.31: ASCII Character Encoding Example

```
(gdb) info locals
```

The info locals command lists the local variables of the current frame, aiding in corroborating their values and identifying any discrepancies.

Navigating between frames can also be done using the up and down commands to move up and down the call stack, respectively:

Listing 9.32: ASCII Character Encoding Example

```
(gdb) up
```

Listing 9.33: ASCII Character Encoding Example

```
(gdb) down
```

These commands facilitate examining the call hierarchy and analyzing how data flows through the call stack.

Another useful technique is to harness the power of conditional breakpoints. By setting a breakpoint with a specific condition, you can pause execution precisely when a particular state is encountered:

Listing 9.34: ASCII Character Encoding Example

```
(gdb) break my_function if x > 10
```

The above command sets a breakpoint at my_function but only if the variable x exceeds 10. This approach minimizes disruption by focusing on the exact conditions that manifest the bug, leading to more efficient debugging.

Many modern debugging tools provide graphical interfaces that visualize stack traces, making it easier to interpret and navigate. Tools like GDB with frontends like gdbgui and IDE-integrated debuggers (e.g., Visual Studio or Eclipse) provide a more user-friendly experience compared to traditional command-line interfaces.

Using stack traces in debugging procedures enables the systematic identification of erroneous function calls, misallocated memory, and other execution anomalies in an assembly language program.Interpret and track call sequences methodically, you can enhance the reliability and performance of your assembly code.

9.8 Debugging Common Assembly Errors

Assembly programming, by its nature, is more prone to errors compared to high-level languages due to its low-level operations and lack of abstraction. This section will address frequent mistakes encountered while programming in assembly and provide strategies for effective debugging.

Assembly errors can be broadly categorized into syntax errors, logical errors, and runtime errors. Understanding these categories and their distinct characteristics will significantly enhance one's debugging skills.

Syntax errors are the most straightforward to identify. These occur due to incorrect usage of the assembly language syntax. Common syntax errors include:

- Misplacement of operands
- Incorrect mnemonics
- Missing or extra commas and brackets

Consider the following code snippet which illustrates a syntax error due to incorrect operand placement.

Listing 9.35: ASCII Character Encoding Example

```
mov ax, [bx+si+4]
```

In many assembly dialects, the code above will produce an error since the addressing mode used with the mov instruction is invalid. The correct syntax may vary depending on the assembler, but a typical correction could be as follows:

Listing 9.36: ASCII Character Encoding Example

```
mov ax, [bx+si]
add ax, 4
```

Logical errors are more insidious and often more challenging to detect. These occur when the program compiles and runs but does not produce the expected results. Logical errors typically stem from a misunderstanding of the instruction set architecture (ISA) or flawed algorithm implementations. One common logical error is incorrect handling of jump instructions. For instance, consider this loop intended to sum elements in an array:

Listing 9.37: ASCII Character Encoding Example

```
mov cx, 10 ; Loop counter
lea si, array ; Load address of array
mov ax, 0 ; Initialize the sum to 0

sum_loop:
    add ax, [si] ; Add current element to sum
    add si, 2 ; Move to the next element (assuming 16-bit elements)
    loop sum_loop ; Decrement cx and jump if not zero
```

If the code does not yield the correct sum, a potential logical error might be mishandling of the loop counter or array indexing. Reviewing the values in the registers after each iteration with a debugger can uncover such mistakes.

Runtime errors, arising during the execution, can vary significantly and may lead to program crashes. Common runtime errors include segmentation faults and illegal instructions. These typically result from issues like dereferencing invalid memory addresses or executing invalid opcodes. Tools like GDB (GNU Debugger) or LLDB can help identify and resolve such errors. Consider the following scenario:

Listing 9.38: ASCII Character Encoding Example

```
mov eax, 0x12345678
mov ebx, [eax]
```

If eax contains an address that is not valid for the data segment, this will cause a segmentation fault. Using GDB, you can set a breakpoint and inspect the value of eax before the faulting instruction.

Listing 9.39: ASCII Character Encoding Example

```
gdb a.out
(gdb) break *0x0804841e
Breakpoint 1 at 0x804841e
(gdb) run
Starting program: /path/to/a.out

Breakpoint 1, 0x0804841e in main ()
(gdb) info registers eax
eax 0x12345678 305419896
(gdb) x/4x $eax
0x12345678: Cannot access memory at address 0x12345678
```

The above GDB session reveals the invalid address access attempt.

Efficiently passing from noticing an error to fully resolving it necessitates the use of common assembly language debugging strategies, including:

- **Careful inspection of registers and flags**: Ensure that all registers and condition flags are correctly set after each instruction.
- **Analyzing stack behavior**: Verify that push and pop operations maintain stack balance.
- **Monitoring memory access**: Ensure that memory accesses are within valid bounds.
- **Step-by-step execution using breakpoints**: Identifying the exact point where the program deviates from expected behavior.

Monitoring the state of the CPU and its registers during execution is particularly vital. Consider the following sequence:

Listing 9.40: ASCII Character Encoding Example

```
start:
    mov eax, 5 ; Initialize eax
    mov ebx, 10 ; Initialize ebx
    sub eax, ebx ; Subtract ebx from eax
    jz equal ; Check if result is zero
    ; more code
equal:
    ; some code for when eax == ebx
```

Here, if jz does not transfer control when expected, inspecting the Zero Flag (ZF) will reveal whether the subtraction resulted in zero.

By utilizing these meticulous techniques and tools, the debugging process can become a systematic and more predictable endeavor. Avoiding common pitfalls and understanding common error patterns simplify the journey to a correctly functioning program.

9.9 Introduction to Optimization

Optimization in assembly language programming aims to enhance the performance and efficiency of code by reducing its execution time, minimizing its memory usage, or achieving a balance between the two. This section lays the groundwork for understanding optimization principles, essential for developing high-performance applications.

Assembly language allows for direct manipulation of hardware resources, providing opportunities for fine-grained optimization unavailable in higher-level languages. However, achieving optimal performance requires a deep understanding of both the hardware architecture and the intricacies of the assembly language.

Key Objectives of Optimization:

- **Minimizing Execution Time:** Reducing the number of clock cycles required for program execution.
- **Reducing Memory Usage:** Lowering the program's memory footprint to enhance efficiency and suitability for memory-constrained environments.
- **Power Efficiency:** Decreasing the power consumption, essential for battery-operated devices.
- **Resource Utilization:** Making efficient use of CPU registers, cache, and other resources to avoid bottlenecks.

Effective optimization often requires a balanced approach, considering the trade-offs between different objectives. For example, an attempt to minimize execution time might increase memory usage, and vice versa.

Basic Strategies for Code Optimization:

- **Eliminating Redundancies:** Removing unnecessary instructions that do not contribute to the final output.
- **Instruction Scheduling:** Reordering instructions to avoid pipeline stalls and make efficient use of CPU resources.
- **Inlining Functions:** Eliminating the overhead of function calls by inserting the body of functions directly into the caller code.
- **Loop Optimization:** Enhancing loops by reducing the number of iterations or optimizing redundant computations within loops.
- **Register Allocation:** Efficiently using CPU registers to minimize memory access, which is usually slower.

To build a foundational understanding of these principles, consider the following example, which illustrates basic optimization tactics in assembly code:

Listing 9.41: ASCII Character Encoding Example

```
; Original code
MOV AX, [DATA]
MOV BX, [DATA]
ADD AX, BX

; Optimized code
MOV AX, [DATA]
ADD AX, [DATA]
```

In the original code, the value at memory location $[\mathrm{DATA}]$ is loaded into both AX and BX registers before performing the addition. This redundancy is eliminated in the optimized version, where the memory value is loaded once and added directly to AX. This not only reduces memory access but also reduces overall instruction count, improving execution time.

The concepts of **reducing instruction count** and **minimizing memory access** are central to effective assembly language optimization. However, the complexity of real-world applications necessitates deeper strategies and a robust understanding of the CPU architecture.

Analytical Approach to Optimization:

- **Profiling:** Utilize profiling tools to identify bottlenecks and performance-critical sections within the code.
- **Benchmarking:** Conduct benchmarks to measure the performance impact of various optimization techniques.
- **Algorithm Analysis:** Evaluate algorithms for their complexity and scalability, selecting the most efficient algorithm for a given task.

Profiling tools provide insights into the execution time distribution across different parts of the code, highlighting areas where optimization can have the most significant impact. For instance, if profiling reveals that a loop is a major contributor to the total execution time, focus efforts on loop unrolling or other loop optimization techniques to achieve the greatest performance improvement.

Instruction Count Before Optimization: 1500
Instruction Count After Optimization: 1000
Time Reduction: 33.3%

Another optimization technique involves efficient use of CPU registers. Consider that accessing data from registers is significantly faster than accessing it from memory. Therefore, careful planning of register usage can lead to substantial performance gains.

Listing 9.42: ASCII Character Encoding Example

```
; Inefficient register usage
MOV AX, [DATA1]
MOV BX, [DATA2]
ADD AX, BX
MOV [RESULT], AX

; Optimized register allocation
MOV AX, [DATA1]
ADD AX, [DATA2]
MOV [RESULT], AX
```

In this example, the original code uses two registers, AX and BX, for intermediate storage. The optimized version utilizes only one register for the addition operation, reducing the required instructions and enhancing CPU resource utilization.

A deep understanding of the specific CPU's architecture can further drive optimization. In superscalar processors, multiple instructions can be executed simultaneously. Aligning code to take advantage of this parallel execution capability, such as by interleaving independent instructions, can maximize throughput.

Assembly language optimization is a meticulous task requiring thorough knowledge of hardware architecture and careful benchmarking. By applying the fundamental principles and techniques discussed, one can significantly improve the performance and efficiency of assembly programs, paving the way for writing high-performance applications tailored to specific hardware constraints.

9.10 Basic Principles of Code Optimization

Code optimization in assembly language involves a set of strategies to make code run more efficiently by improving its execution speed and reducing its memory footprint. These principles rely on an in-depth understanding of how the CPU executes instructions and how memory accesses are performed. Understanding the basics of code optimization provides a foundation for writing high-performance assembly code. This section discusses several key principles: minimizing instruction count, efficient register usage, minimizing memory accesses, avoiding pipeline stalls, and utilizing parallelism.

Minimizing Instruction Count

The number of instructions executed directly affects the performance of a program. Reducing the instruction count can often lead to significant improvements in execution time. Common strategies include:

- Peephole Optimization: This involves examining short sequences of instructions (the peephole) and replacing them with more efficient ones. For example, a sequence that loads a value into a register and then immediately moves that value to another register can often be reduced to a single move operation if the architecture supports it.

  Listing 9.43: ASCII Character Encoding Example

  ```
  ; Before Optimization
  MOV AX, [value]
  MOV BX, AX

  ; After Optimization
  MOV BX, [value]
  ```

- Inlining Simple Procedures: Calling a procedure involves several instructions for saving the current state and jumping to the procedure code. For small procedures, it can be more efficient to inline the procedure code directly within the caller, thus avoiding the overhead of the call and return instructions.

Listing 9.44: ASCII Character Encoding Example

```
; Calling a simple increment procedure
CALL Increment

; Inlined increment operation
INC AX
```

Efficient Register Usage

Registers are the fastest form of storage available to the CPU. Efficient use of registers can greatly enhance performance. Techniques include:

- Register Allocation: Maximizing the use of registers to hold frequently accessed data can minimize slower memory accesses. This involves careful planning to avoid register spills, where values must be temporarily stored in memory due to a lack of available registers.

Listing 9.45: ASCII Character Encoding Example

```
; Suboptimal register usage
MOV AX, [var1]
ADD AX, [var2]
MOV [result], AX

; Improved usage by keeping intermediate results in registers
MOV AX, [var1]
MOV BX, [var2]
ADD AX, BX
MOV [result], AX
```

- Avoiding Register Conflicts: Ensuring that registers are used in a way that minimizes conflicts and the need to save and restore data can also improve efficiency.

Listing 9.46: ASCII Character Encoding Example

```
; Incorrect usage causing spills
MOV CX, [value1]
CALL Procedure
MOV [value2], CX

; Optimized by saving and restoring only when necessary
PUSH CX
MOV CX, [value1]
CALL Procedure
POP CX
MOV [value2], CX
```

Minimizing Memory Accesses

Memory accesses are significantly slower than register accesses. Techniques for minimizing memory access include:

- Data Locality: Ensuring that data that is accessed together is stored together in memory can take advantage of the CPU cache, which significantly reduces memory access times.

Listing 9.47: ASCII Character Encoding Example

```
; Non-optimal memory access pattern
MOV AX, [array1]
MOV BX, [array2]

; Improved locality by accessing sequentially
MOV AX, [array1]
MOV BX, [array1 + 2]
```

- Loop Unrolling: This involves replicating the body of a loop multiple times to reduce the overhead of loop control instructions and improve memory access patterns.

Listing 9.48: ASCII Character Encoding Example

```
; Traditional loop
LOOP_START:
    MOV AX, [array + SI]
    ADD SI, 2
    LOOP LOOP_START

; Unrolled loop
MOV AX, [array + SI]
MOV BX, [array + SI + 2]
MOV CX, [array + SI + 4]
ADD SI, 6
; Reduced loop control overhead
```

Avoiding Pipeline Stalls

Modern CPUs use instruction pipelines to process multiple instructions simultaneously. However, certain dependencies between instructions can cause the pipeline to stall, waiting for data to become available. Optimizations to avoid stalls include:

- Instruction Scheduling: Rearranging the order of instructions to avoid dependencies can minimize the risk of pipeline stalls.

Listing 9.49: ASCII Character Encoding Example

```
; Instructions causing pipeline stall
```

```
    MOV AX, [var]
    ADD BX, AX
    MOV CX, BX

    ; Optimized by reordering to allow parallel execution
    MOV AX, [var]
    MOV CX, [another_var]
    ADD BX, AX
    ADD DX, CX
```

- Reducing Branching: Unconditional jumps and conditional branches can cause pipeline flushes. Minimizing these through techniques like loop unrolling or branch prediction can improve performance.

Listing 9.50: ASCII Character Encoding Example

```
    ; High number of branches
    CMP AX, 0
    JE ZERO_CASE
    CALL Procedure
ZERO_CASE:

    ; Reduced branching with conditional instructions
    CMP AX, 0
    JZ SHORT_SKIP
    CALL Procedure
SHORT_SKIP:
```

Utilizing Parallelism

Modern CPUs have multiple cores and support simultaneous execution of multiple threads. Taking advantage of parallelism can lead to significant performance gains.

- Instruction-Level Parallelism: By leveraging CPU features such as SIMD (Single Instruction, Multiple Data), multiple operations can be performed in parallel on different pieces of data.

Listing 9.51: ASCII Character Encoding Example

```
    ; Sequential processing
    MOVDQU XMM0, [array]
    MOVDQU XMM1, [another_array]
    PADDQ XMM0, XMM1

    ; Parallel processing with SIMD
    MOVDQU XMM0, [array]
    MOVDQU XMM1, [another_array]
    PADDQ XMM0, XMM1
    MOVDQU [result], XMM0
```

- Thread-Level Parallelism: Using multiple threads to perform different tasks simultaneously can fully utilize CPU cores and achieve higher performance.

Listing 9.52: ASCII Character Encoding Example

```
; Single-threaded computation
CALL ComputePart1
CALL ComputePart2

; Multi-threaded computation
; Thread 1 executes ComputePart1
; Thread 2 executes ComputePart2

; Main thread
WAIT_FOR_THREADS
```

Effective code optimization in assembly language balances the trade-offs between different strategies. Minimizing the instruction count, making efficient use of registers, reducing memory accesses, avoiding pipeline stalls, and utilizing parallelism all contribute to the creation of more efficient programs. This requires a deep understanding of both the target architecture and the specific requirements of the application. Detailed analysis and profiling are essential to identify bottlenecks and apply the correct optimizations to achieve the desired performance improvements.

9.11 Register Allocation and Usage

In assembly language programming, efficient use of registers is pivotal for optimal performance. Registers are the quickest form of storage available to a CPU, and their judicious allocation and utilization can drastically impact the execution speed of a program. This section delves into the principles and strategies behind effective register allocation and usage, building upon concepts previously introduced in the chapter.

The primary goal of register allocation is to minimize memory access, which is significantly slower compared to register access. To achieve this, various sophisticated techniques can be employed. This section will elucidate these techniques and how they can be implemented in assembly programming.

Register Classes and Constraints

The first step towards effective register allocation is understanding the different classes of registers and their specific constraints. Commonly used registers in x86 architecture include general-purpose registers such as EAX, EBX, ECX, and EDX. Additionally, there are specialized registers like the stack pointer (ESP), base pointer (EBP), and instruction pointer (EIP), each serving dedicated roles within the CPU.

Certain instructions may require specific registers. For example, the DIV instruction typically uses EAX and EDX for its operands. Understanding such constraints is vital for effective register allocation.

Live-Variable Analysis

Live-variable analysis is a fundamental technique used to determine the set of variables that are "live" at each point in a program. A variable is considered live if its value may be needed in the future; otherwise, it is "dead." By performing live-variable analysis, one can minimize the number of registers needed by keeping only the live variables in registers.

The output of the live-variable analysis can guide the allocation process, ensuring that each variable is bound to a register only during the live intervals.

Algorithm 8: Live-Variable Analysis

Data: Control flow graph of the program
Result: Live variable sets at each node

begin
  repeat
    foreach *node* n *in reverse order* **do**
      $out[n] \leftarrow \bigcup_{s \in succ[n]} in[s]$
      $in[n] \leftarrow use[n] \cup (out[n] \setminus def[n])$
  until *Fixed Point*

The implementation of live-variable analysis on a control flow graph (CFG) follows Algorithm **??**. This iterative process continues until the sets of live variables stabilize, reaching a fixed point.

Graph Coloring for Register Allocation

Once the live-variable analysis is performed, register allocation can be modeled as a graph-coloring problem. In this context, each node represents a variable, and an edge is drawn between two nodes if the corresponding variables are live at the same point. The goal is to assign registers (colors) to each node in such a way that no two adjacent nodes have the same color.

Here is a high-level pseudocode representation of graph coloring for register allocation:

Algorithm 9: Graph Coloring for Register Allocation

```
Data: Interference graph
Result: Register allocation for variables
begin
    while Nodes left in the graph do
        Select and remove a node with fewer than $k$
          neighbors
        Push the node into a stack
    while Stack is not empty do
        Pop a node from the stack
        Assign a color (register) to the node avoiding the
          already assigned colors to adjacent nodes
```

Algorithm 9 represents this process. The effective allocation of registers mitigates the need for spilling, where variables need to be temporarily stored in memory.

Spilling and Reloading

Spilling occurs when there are more live variables than available registers. In such cases, some variables must be stored in memory temporarily. Although spilling incurs a performance penalty due to slower memory access, it is sometimes unavoidable. The key is to minimize the number of spills and optimize the points at which spilling and reloading occur.

Here's a basic example of assembly code showing register allocation and the necessity of spilling:

Listing 9.53: ASCII Character Encoding Example

```
MOV EAX, [var1] ; Load var1 into EAX
MOV EBX, [var2] ; Load var2 into EBX
ADD EAX, EBX ; EAX = var1 + var2
MOV [result], EAX ; Store result in memory
```

In the above snippet, variables var1 and var2 are loaded into EAX and EBX, respectively. After performing the addition, the result is stored back into memory. If there were insufficient registers available, one of these variables would have to be spilled to memory, potentially using two additional instructions:

Listing 9.54: ASCII Character Encoding Example

```
MOV EAX, [var1] ; Load var1 into EAX
MOV EBX, [var2] ; Load var2 into EBX
ADD EAX, EBX ; EAX = var1 + var2
MOV [temp], EAX ; Spill EAX to memory

; Later in the code
MOV EAX, [temp] ; Reload EAX from memory
MOV [result], EAX ; Store result in memory
```

Caller-Saved and Callee-Saved Registers

Efficient register usage also requires an understanding of caller-saved and callee-saved registers. In many calling conventions, some registers are designated as caller-saved, meaning the calling function should save them before making a function call if it needs to preserve their values. Conversely, callee-saved registers must be preserved by the called function.

For instance, in the System V AMD64 ABI, registers RAX, RCX, and RDX are caller-saved, while RBX, RBP, and RSP are callee-saved.

Listing 9.55: ASCII Character Encoding Example

```
; Caller Function
PUSH RAX ; Save RAX
MOV RAX, 5 ; Prepare argument
CALL Function ; Call Function
POP RAX ; Restore RAX
RET ; Return

; Callee Function
Function:
    PUSH RBX ; Save RBX
    ...
    POP RBX ; Restore RBX
    RET ; Return
```

In this example, the caller saves RAX before the function call and restores it afterward, while the callee saves and restores RBX.

Balancing the usage of caller-saved and callee-saved registers improves the efficiency of function calls, ensuring that register allocation does not overly burden either the caller or the callee.

Effective register allocation and usage are central to high-performance assembly programming.

9.12 Optimizing Loops and Branches

Loop and branch optimization is crucial for enhancing the performance and efficiency of assembly language programs. The primary objective is to minimize the number of instructions executed within loops and branches, thereby reducing the overall execution time and resource consumption. This section delves into various strategies and techniques to achieve these optimizations effectively.

Loop Unrolling:

Loop unrolling is a technique where multiple iterations of a loop are executed within a single iteration by duplicating the loop body. This reduces the overhead caused by loop control instructions such as loop and jump. Consider the following simple loop in assembly:

Listing 9.56: ASCII Character Encoding Example

```
loop_start:
    mov eax, [esi]
    add eax, [edi]
    mov [esi], eax
    add esi, 4
    add edi, 4
    dec ecx
    jnz loop_start
```

In this example, the loop executes until ecx reaches zero, performing an addition on memory contents referenced by esi and edi. Unrolling the loop four times can transform it as follows:

Listing 9.57: ASCII Character Encoding Example

```
unrolled_loop:
    mov eax, [esi]
    add eax, [edi]
    mov [esi], eax
    mov ebx, [esi+4]
    add ebx, [edi+4]
    mov [esi+4], ebx
    mov ecx, [esi+8]
    add ecx, [edi+8]
    mov [esi+8], ecx
    mov edx, [esi+12]
    add edx, [edi+12]
    mov [esi+12], edx
    add esi, 16
    add edi, 16
    sub ecx, 4
    jnz unrolled_loop
```

Here, four iterations of the original loop are combined into one, significantly reducing the number of iterations and the overhead.

Loop Fusion:

Loop fusion merges two or more loops that operate over the same range into a single loop. This technique minimizes the overhead associated with loop control and can improve cache performance. For example:

Listing 9.58: ASCII Character Encoding Example

```
loop1:
    mov eax, [esi]
    add eax, 1
    mov [esi], eax
    add esi, 4
    dec ecx
    jnz loop1

; reset esi and ecx for the second loop

loop2:
    mov ebx, [esi]
    mul ebx, 2
    mov [esi], ebx
    add esi, 4
    dec ecx
    jnz loop2
```

This can be fused into one loop as follows:

Listing 9.59: ASCII Character Encoding Example

```
fused_loop:
    mov eax, [esi]
    add eax, 1
    mul eax, 2
    mov [esi], eax
    add esi, 4
    dec ecx
    jnz fused_loop
```

Branch Prediction:

Modern processors employ advanced mechanisms for branch prediction to enhance the efficiency of branch instructions. Providing hints to the processor can improve branch prediction accuracy and consequentially, program performance.

Consider conditional branches that are heavily biased toward one direction:

Listing 9.60: ASCII Character Encoding Example

```
cmp eax, ebx
je equal_label
mov ecx, [esi]
equal_label:
; continue execution
```

If the condition is that eax equals ebx most of the time, arrange the likely outcome directly and use a conditional jump for the unlikely path:

Listing 9.61: ASCII Character Encoding Example

```
cmp eax, ebx
jne not_equal_label
mov ecx, [esi]
jmp end_label
not_equal_label:
; handle unequal case
end_label:
; continue execution
```

Instruction Scheduling:

Reordering instructions to take advantage of instruction-level parallelism can also optimize loops and branches. For processors with multiple execution units, carefully scheduling non-dependent instructions can minimize idle cycles and enhance overall throughput. For instance:

Listing 9.62: ASCII Character Encoding Example

```
mov eax, [esi]
add eax, ebx
mov [edi], eax
; dependent entirely on result of first instruction
mov ecx, [esi+4]
add ecx, ebx
mov [edi+4], ecx
```

If the addition and memory operations are independent, schedule them as follows:

Listing 9.63: ASCII Character Encoding Example

```
mov eax, [esi]
mov ecx, [esi+4]
add eax, ebx
add ecx, ebx
mov [edi], eax
mov [edi+4], ecx
```

Eliminating Branches:

In some scenarios, it is possible to eliminate branches altogether by using conditional move instructions like cmov, thereby reducing branch mispredictions. For example:

Listing 9.64: ASCII Character Encoding Example

```
cmp eax, ebx
je equal_label
```

```
mov ecx, [esi+4]
jmp end_label
equal_label:
mov ecx, [esi]
end_label:
```

This can be transformed using a conditional move:

Listing 9.65: ASCII Character Encoding Example

```
cmp eax, ebx
cmove ecx, esi
cmovne ecx, [esi+4]
```

Efficient utilization of these techniques to optimize loops and branches can substantially enhance the performance of assembly programs. These strategies reduce instruction counts, improve cache performance, and minimize branch mispredictions - key factors in high-performance computing.

9.13 Profiling and Performance Analysis

Profiling and performance analysis are critical steps in the optimization of assembly language programs. Profiling involves measuring the performance of different parts of a program to identify bottlenecks, while performance analysis entails understanding the cause of these bottlenecks and devising appropriate solutions. This section delves into the methods and tools available for profiling and analysing the performance of assembly code.

Profiling Overview

Profiling is an empirical method to measure where a program spends its time. The goal is to collect statistics on the execution of functions, loops, and instructions within a program. These statistics help in pinpointing code sections that require optimization. The following metrics are typically collected during profiling:

- **Execution time**: The total time a section of code takes to execute.
- **Frequency**: The number of times a particular function, loop, or instruction is executed.
- **Cache misses**: The number of times data is not found in the cache, causing slower memory accesses.

Tools for Profiling

Various tools can be used for profiling assembly language programs, including hardware performance counters, software profilers, and simulators. Important tools include:

- perf: A powerful Linux tool that leverages hardware performance counters to profile applications.
- gprof: A GNU profiler that provides function-level profiling.
- Valgrind: A framework that includes various tools such as Callgrind for detailed call-graph profiling.
- Intel VTune: A performance analysis tool for Intel processors.

The following example demonstrates a simple use of perf to profile an assembly program:

Listing 9.66: ASCII Character Encoding Example

```
$ perf record -e cycles:u ./program
$ perf report
```

The above commands record performance data focusing on CPU cycles and provide a report highlighting the most time-consuming functions.

Interpreting Profiling Data

When the data is collected, the next step is to interpret it. This involves understanding the significance of the metrics. High execution times or frequency counts indicate potential areas for optimization. For example, if a loop body is executed an unusually high number of times, it may suggest inefficient iteration logic or the need for algorithmic improvement.

An illustrative example can be seen in the profiling report of a sample program:

```
Samples: 100  of event 'cycles:u', Event count (approx.): 10000000
Overhead  Command  Shared Object      Symbol
 35.00%   program  program          [.] functionA
 30.00%   program  program          [.] functionB
 15.00%   program  program          [.] functionC
  ...
```

Here, functionA consumes 35

Performance Analysis

Performance analysis is the process of understanding why a certain section of code is slow. For example, high overhead in functionA could be due to inefficient use of processor instructions, poor register allocation, or excessive cache misses. To analyse these issues, the assembly code must be carefully examined and the following considered:

- **Instruction choice**: Are there more efficient instructions available for the task?
- **Instruction ordering**: Can reordering instructions reduce pipeline stalls or improve instruction-level parallelism?
- **Register usage**: Are registers being efficiently utilized to avoid unnecessary memory accesses?
- **Memory access patterns**: Are memory accesses well-aligned and cache-friendly?

Further inspection can be augmented by using tools that provide more detailed insights, such as cache profiling with Valgrind:

Listing 9.67: ASCII Character Encoding Example

```
$ valgrind --tool=callgrind ./program
$ kcachegrind
```

The kcachegrind tool provides a graphical user interface to explore the profiling data, including cache usage statistics, function call graphs, and detailed instruction analysis.

Example of Performance Analysis

Consider the following assembly code for a simple loop and its associated performance metrics:

Listing 9.68: ASCII Character Encoding Example

```
.loop:
    mov eax, [ebx] ; 1 cycle
    add eax, 4 ; 1 cycle
    mov [ebx], eax ; 2 cycles
    add ebx, 4 ; 1 cycle
    dec ecx ; 1 cycle
    jnz .loop ; 2 cycles, unpredictable jump typically penalized
```

From the performance analysis, we observe that the ‘mov [ebx], eax‘ instruction takes 2 cycles due to a memory write, and the ‘jnz .loop‘ instruction also potentially incurs a penalty for an unpredictable jump.

One optimization could be using more registers to reduce memory writes.

Optimized Loop Example:

Listing 9.69: ASCII Character Encoding Example

```
.loop:
    mov eax, [ebx] ; 1 cycle
    add eax, 4 ; 1 cycle
    mov [ebx], eax ; 2 cycles
    lea ebx, [ebx+4] ; 1 cycle, replace add ebx, 4 with LEA for less pipeline disruption
    dec ecx ; 1 cycle
    jnz .loop ; 2 cycles, ensure ecx is predictable for better performance
```

In this example, using the LEA instruction can lead to fewer delays compared to traditional arithmetic instructions, potentially reducing pipeline stalls.

Profiling and performance analysis are iterative and empirical processes. By continually measuring and analysing the impact of changes, assembly programmers can achieve significant performance enhancements in their code.

9.14 Real-World Examples of Debugging and Optimization

In this section, we will explore practical examples that illustrate the application of debugging and optimization techniques in real-world assembly language programs. These examples aim to provide a clear understanding of how theoretical concepts are implemented in practice.

Debugging Example: Correcting an Infinite Loop

Consider an assembly program that is intended to iterate through an array of integers and sum its elements. However, the program contains a bug that causes it to enter an infinite loop. Here is the initial version of the assembly code:

Listing 9.70: ASCII Character Encoding Example

```
section .data
    array db 1, 2, 3, 4, 5
    length equ 5

section .bss
    sum resb 1

section .text
```

```
    global _start

_start:
    mov ecx, length
    mov ebx, array
    mov al, 0

loop_start:
    add al, [ebx]
    inc ebx
    loop loop_start

    mov [sum], al
    ; Exit the program
    mov eax, 1
    xor ebx, ebx
    int 0x80
```

Upon inspection and running the program, we notice that it never completes. To debug this, utilize a debugging tool such as GDB to set a breakpoint at the _start label and step through the code.

```
(gdb) break _start
Breakpoint 1 at 0x8048080
(gdb) run
Starting program: ./infinite_loop
Breakpoint 1, 0x08048080 in _start ()

(gdb) step
(gdb) nexti  # repeat until reaching the loop
```

Observe the values in ecx and ebx. A crucial observation is whether the ecx register, serving as the loop counter, is decremented properly within the loop.

The problem lies in the missing dec ecx instruction inside the loop. Correcting the loop structure ensures the counter decrements and eventually breaks out of the loop.

Listing 9.71: ASCII Character Encoding Example

```
loop_start:
    add al, [ebx]
    inc ebx
    dec ecx
    jnz loop_start
```

With these corrections, the program successfully sums the elements of the array.

Optimization Example: Loop Unrolling

Loop unrolling is an optimization technique that decreases the overhead associated with loop control by executing multiple iterations in a single loop step. Consider the same program, now optimized by unrolling the loop:

Listing 9.72: ASCII Character Encoding Example

```
section .data
    array db 1, 2, 3, 4, 5
    length equ 5

section .bss
    sum resb 1

section .text
    global _start

_start:
    mov ecx, length / 2
    mov ebx, array
    mov al, 0

loop_start:
    add al, [ebx] ; Sum elements in pairs
    add al, [ebx + 1]
    add ebx, 2 ; Move forward by 2 bytes
    dec ecx
    jnz loop_start

    ; If length is odd, add the last element
    mov ecx, length
    and ecx, 1
    jz end_sum
    add al, [ebx]

end_sum:
    mov [sum], al
    ; Exit the program
    mov eax, 1
    xor ebx, ebx
    int 0x80
```

By partially unrolling the loop, we reduce the number of iterations, effectively halving the loop overhead. This optimization improves performance, especially in cases where the array length is significantly large.

Real-World Debugging: Stack Corruption in Recursive Function

Consider an assembly program implementing a recursive function to compute the factorial of a number. The initial implementation has a stack corruption issue disrupting program execution:

Listing 9.73: ASCII Character Encoding Example

```
section .data
    num dd 5
    result resd 1

section .text
    global _start

factorial:
```

```
    push ebp
    mov ebp, esp
    sub esp, 4
    mov eax, [ebp + 8] ; get the parameter

    cmp eax, 1
    je base_case

    dec eax
    push eax
    call factorial
    add esp, 4
    mov [ebp - 4], eax

    mov eax, [ebp + 8]
    mul dword [ebp - 4]
    jmp end_factorial

base_case:
    mov eax, 1

end_factorial:
    mov esp, ebp
    pop ebp
    ret
```

To diagnose stack corruption, utilize a debugger to step through recursive calls and observe stack frame modifications. Set breakpoints at the beginning of the factorial function:

```
(gdb) break factorial
Breakpoint 2 at 0x804809c
(gdb) run
Starting program: ./factorial

Breakpoint 2, 0x0804809c in factorial ()
(gdb) nexti
```

Trace the changes in esp and register values. Notice improper stack adjustments, suggesting a problem with the stack frame's lifetimes and sizes. Correct the stack usage by ensuring balanced push and pop operations:

Listing 9.74: ASCII Character Encoding Example

```
factorial:
    push ebp
    mov ebp, esp
    sub esp, 4
    mov eax, [ebp + 8]

    cmp eax, 1
    je base_case

    dec eax
    push eax
    call factorial
    mov edx, eax
    add esp, 4
```

```
    mov [ebp - 4], edx

    mov eax, [ebp + 8]
    mul dword [ebp - 4]
    jmp end_factorial

base_case:
    mov eax, 1

end_factorial:
    add esp, 4 ; balance the stack
    mov esp, ebp
    pop ebp
    ret
```

The corrected assembly ensures stack integrity, preventing corruption across recursive calls.

Through these detailed examples, we illustrate fundamental debugging techniques and optimization strategies in assembly language programming. By methodically analyzing program behavior and enhancing code efficiency, developers can significantly improve the reliability and performance of their software.

Chapter 10

Advanced Topics in Assembly Language Programming

This chapter explores advanced topics in assembly language programming, including inline assembly in high-level languages, interfacing with C/C++, and SIMD and vector instructions. It covers parallel programming, writing device drivers, system calls, and kernel programming. Additional subjects include reverse engineering, malware analysis, cryptographic algorithms, real-time systems development, and custom instruction sets. The chapter features case studies of complex assembly programs to illustrate these advanced concepts.

10.1 Introduction to Advanced Topics

In assembly language programming, an advanced understanding encompasses the ability to transcend basic instruction manipulations by integrating assembly code with high-level languages, achieving parallelism, interfacing directly with the system hardware, and optimizing performance via specialized instruction sets. These advanced topics become pivotal for applications demanding high efficiency, precision, and deep system-level control.

Assembly language, while foundational, can be further enhanced when used together with high-level languages such as C and C++. This fusion empowers developers to utilize the efficiency of assembly for performance-critical code blocks while maintaining the readability and extensive library support of high-level languages. Inline assembly, which allows embedding assembly code directly within C/C++ programs, is one such technique that will be elaborated on in subsequent sections. Understanding how to harness inline assembly can lead to significant performance optimizations in software development.

Interfacing assembly with C/C++ goes beyond inline assembly, discussing the concepts of calling conventions, parameter passing, and stack management. Discerning these conventions is vital for creating seamless interoperability between compiled code and hand-written assembly routines. Assembly's role in initializing, managing, and manipulating hardware is underscored when developing device drivers, where programmers must often write assembly code to interact directly with hardware registers and manage low-level device operations.

A critical area touched upon involves SIMD (Single Instruction, Multiple Data) and vector instructions. These specialized instructions enable parallel data processing, which is paramount in applications such as multimedia processing, cryptographic computations, and scientific simulations. SIMD instructions pack multiple data elements into a single register and apply operations simultaneously, leveraging data-level parallelism to boost performance.

Parallel programming in assembly extends beyond SIMD, diving into multicore systems where concurrent execution threads must synchronize and communicate effectively. Here, managing synchronization primitives like mutexes and understanding memory barriers and atomic operations are essential skills for the assembly programmer. Achieving efficient parallelism ensures that applications fully exploit the computational power of modern processors.

Device drivers written in assembly serve as a translation layer between hardware and the operating system. These drivers often require low-level programming techniques to handle interrupts, direct memory access (DMA), and other hardware-driven events. The integration of assembly in writing drivers ensures minimal overhead and maximum performance, critical in high-performance applications such as real-time systems.

Furthermore, the study of system calls and kernel programming lays the groundwork for understanding how user-space applications interact with the operating system core. System call interfaces provide controlled access to kernel services, and writing kernel modules in assembly necessitates a firm grasp of operating system internals and assembly programming intricacies.

Reverse engineering and malware analysis are another realm where advanced assembly language knowledge is applied. Analyzing malware often requires dissecting executable binaries, understanding obfuscated code, and identifying malicious behaviors. Advanced assembly skills enable security professionals to deconstruct and understand complex malware structures and devise efficient countermeasures.

Cryptographic algorithms implemented in assembly benefit from direct control over the execution environment, allowing for optimizations at the instruction level. This fine-grained control is crucial in ensuring both the performance and security of cryptographic functions, such as encryption/decryption routines and hash computations.

Real-time systems development, by definition, demands predictability and low-latency responses. Assembly programming ensures that critical code paths adhere to stringent timing requirements without the overhead encountered in higher-level languages. Developers can finely tune interrupt handlers, scheduling algorithms, and task management routines to meet real-time constraints.

The exploration of custom instruction sets and extensions encapsulates the design and implementation of tailored instruction sets for specific applications. These customizations can significantly enhance processing efficiency and capability for specialized tasks. Understanding how to extend and optimize these instruction sets requires deep knowledge of both hardware architecture and assembly language programming.

Lastly, case studies of complex assembly programs provide valuable insights into practical applications and methodologies. These studies dissect sophisticated programs to illustrate how the advanced topics discussed are implemented in real-world scenarios, offering pragmatic examples and reinforcing the theoretical knowledge acquired throughout the chapter.

The in-depth examination of these advanced topics equips programmers with a robust toolkit for tackling high-performance and system-critical applications using assembly language. The following sections will delve into each of these areas, providing detailed explanations, code examples, and algorithmic insights to enhance the reader's proficiency in advanced assembly language programming.

10.2 Inline Assembly in High-Level Languages

Inline assembly allows the embedding of assembly code directly within high-level programming languages such as C and C++. This section delves into the mechanics of inline assembly, demonstrating its usage, benefits, and potential pitfalls within these high-level contexts. The primary advantage of using inline assembly is the optimization potential it offers for performance-critical code segments where high-level languages fall short.

GCC (GNU Compiler Collection) provides an accessible method for incorporating inline assembly in C/C++ programs. The basic syntax is:

Listing 10.1: ASCII Character Encoding Example

```
asm ("assembly code");
```

This form is simplistic, integrating assembly code as a string within the asm statement. However, a more powerful and commonly used form is called "extended asm."

Extended asm enhances inline assembly by allowing more explicit control over the input and output operands, as well as clobber registers. The syntax is given by:

Listing 10.2: ASCII Character Encoding Example

```
asm volatile ( "assembly template"
              : output operands
              : input operands
              : clobbers
              );
```

- assembly template: A string containing the assembly code. - output operands: A colon-separated list defining the output expressions. - input operands: A colon-separated list defining the input expressions. - clobbers: A colon-separated list of registers or memory locations that the assembly code modifies.

To illustrate, consider a simple example where inline assembly is used to add two integers and return the result:

Listing 10.3: ASCII Character Encoding Example

```
int add(int a, int b) {
    int result;
    asm ("add %1, %2; mov %2, %0"
        : "=r" (result) // output: result is assigned to a register
```

```
        : "r" (a), "r" (b) // inputs: a and b are read from registers
        : // no clobbers
    );
    return result;
}
```

In this assembly string:

- %1, %2, and %0 are placeholders for the operands. - "=r" (result) specifies that result is an output operand placed in a register. - "r" (a), "r" (b) denote that a and b are input operands, also residing in registers.

The asm volatile statement prevents the compiler from optimizing out this code segment, ensuring the embedded assembly runs as intended.

Understanding the constraints of operands is crucial. Using constraints, you can specify whether an operand should be in a specific register or memory location. Common constraints with GCC include:

- r: A general-purpose register's constraint. - m: A memory constraint. - i: An immediate integer constraint.

For example, to multiply two integers where one operand is an immediate value:

Listing 10.4: ASCII Character Encoding Example

```
int multiply_by_5(int num) {
    int result;
    asm ("imul $5, %1, %0"
        : "=r" (result) // output
        : "r" (num) // input: num in register
        : // no clobbers
    );
    return result;
}
```

Here, $5 is directly embedded in the code as an immediate operand.

Clobbers inform the compiler about registers modified by the assembly code which aren't explicitly specified as output operands. This ensures that the compiler doesn't use these registers for other tasks, avoiding unintended side effects. For instance, if the ecx register is used and modified in your assembly code, you should declare it:

Listing 10.5: ASCII Character Encoding Example

```
int calculate(int a, int b) {
    int result;
    asm ("mov %2, %%ecx; add %%ecx, %1; mov %1, %0"
        : "=r" (result)
        : "r" (a), "r" (b)
        : "%ecx" // clobber
    );
```

```
    return result;
}
```

Notice the double percentage sign (

When using inline assembly, it's imperative to ensure compatibility between high-level language constructs and the embedded assembly. The correct synchronization of registers, memory usage, and ensuring no side effects that could result from clobbering are integral to preventing erratic program behavior.

Compiler optimizations can sometimes reorder instructions or influence register allocation in unpredictable ways when inline assembly is employed. The developer must ensure the assembly code's integration does not disrupt the generated code's logical consistency.

By leveraging inline assembly, high-level language programs achieve granular control over low-level operations, paving the way for performance optimizations and an in-depth understanding of the underlying hardware. Properly harnessed, this technique bridges the gap between abstract high-level logic and efficient machine-level execution, an essential skill in advanced system programming domains.

10.3 Interfacing Assembly with C/C++

Interfacing assembly language with C/C++ can leverage the strengths of both programming paradigms, harnessing the control and efficiency of assembly with the higher-level abstraction and ease of use inherent in C/C++. This section delves into the methodologies for effective interfacing, emphasizing calling conventions, linkage, and data type alignment.

The primary considerations when interfacing assembly with C/C++ include understanding the calling conventions used by the compiler, managing the linkage between assembly routines and C functions, and ensuring proper alignment and compatibility of data types.

- **Calling Conventions**: Prescribe how parameters are passed and return values are handled between functions.
- **Linkage**: Dictates how identifiers (such as function and variable names) from different modules/pieces of code reference each other.

- **Data Type Alignment**: Ensures that data structures defined in C/C++ and assembly are consistent in memory layout.

Calling Conventions

Calling conventions define how functions receive parameters, return values, and how the stack is managed. Different compilers and operating systems may adopt different calling conventions. In x86 architecture, common conventions include __cdecl, __stdcall, and __fastcall. Understanding these conventions is essential:

- _cdecl: The caller cleans the stack. This is the default calling convention for C programs. - _stdcall: The callee cleans the stack. This convention is often used in Windows API calls. - _fastcall: Parameters are passed in registers if possible, reducing overhead.

Here is an example of interfacing a C function with assembly using the _cdecl convention:

Listing 10.6: ASCII Character Encoding Example

```
#include <stdio.h>

// Declaration of the assembly function
extern int asmFunction(int a, int b);

int main() {
    int result = asmFunction(5, 3);
    printf("The result is: %d\n", result);
    return 0;
}
```

The corresponding assembly code (using NASM syntax) could look like this:

Listing 10.7: ASCII Character Encoding Example

```
section .text
    global asmFunction
    asmFunction:
        ; Prologue
        push ebp
        mov ebp, esp

        ; Get the parameters, which are 8 bytes above EBP
        mov eax, [ebp+8]
        mov ebx, [ebp+12]

        ; Perform the addition
        add eax, ebx

        ; Epilogue
        pop ebp
        ret
```

Linkage

Linkage refers to how function names and variables declared in one module (e.g., a C file) can be accessed from another module (e.g., an assembly file). External linkage allows identifiers to be visible across multiple files.

To ensure proper linkage, use the extern "C" directive in C++ code to prevent name mangling:

Listing 10.8: ASCII Character Encoding Example

```
// C++ code
extern "C" {
    int asmFunction(int a, int b);
}
```

This directive tells the C++ compiler to use C-style naming for the specified functions.

Data Type Alignment

Data structures in C/C++ must have the same memory layout as their equivalent assembly representations. Consider the following C structure:

Listing 10.9: ASCII Character Encoding Example

```
typedef struct {
    int id;
    char name[20];
    float score;
} Student;
```

The corresponding assembly structure should account for potential padding to align data on word boundaries. Here's how you might align it in assembly:

Listing 10.10: ASCII Character Encoding Example

```
section .data
Student:
    id dd 0
    name db 20 dup(0)
    score dd 0.0
```

Proper alignment ensures that all accesses to members of the structure are consistent across both C/C++ and assembly code.

Interfacing assembly with C/C++ requires careful attention to calling conventions, linkage, and data alignment. By adhering to these principles, it is possible to create efficient and interoperable assemblies and C/C++ programs that exploit the strengths of both languages.

10.4 SIMD and Vector Instructions

Single Instruction, Multiple Data (SIMD) and vector instructions are critical components of modern assembly language programming, particularly in the context of high-performance computing and applications requiring intensive data processing. This section delves into the principles and practical applications of SIMD and vector instructions, providing examples and use cases to better illustrate their utility.

Concept of SIMD: SIMD is an approach used in computer architecture that allows a single instruction to process multiple data points simultaneously. This parallelism is achieved by applying the same operation across a vector of data, leveraging the architecture's hardware support for vectorized operations.

Vector Instructions: Vector instructions are a key aspect of SIMD. These instructions enable operations on vectors, which are arrays of data elements, in a single CPU cycle. This capability enhances the efficiency and speed of data processing tasks, particularly in applications such as image processing, scientific computations, and signal processing.

SIMD in Assembly Language: Modern CPUs, including those based on x86 and ARM architectures, support SIMD through instruction sets such as SSE (Streaming SIMD Extensions), AVX (Advanced Vector Extensions), and NEON (ARM's SIMD extension). Below is an example of using SSE instructions in assembly to perform vector addition on two arrays.

Listing 10.11: ASCII Character Encoding Example

```
section .data
    array1 dq 1.0, 2.0, 3.0, 4.0
    array2 dq 5.0, 6.0, 7.0, 8.0
    result times 4 dq 0.0

section .text
global _start
_start:
    ; Load arrays into xmm registers
    movups xmm0, [array1]
    movups xmm1, [array2]

    ; Perform addition
    addps xmm0, xmm1

    ; Store the result
    movups [result], xmm0

    ; Exit
    mov eax, 1 ; syscall: sys_exit
```

```
xor edi, edi ; status = 0
syscall
```

Understanding the Example:

- The section .data directive is used to define the data segment, where the input arrays array1 and array2 as well as the output array result are stored.
- The section .text directive denotes the beginning of the code segment where the instructions are written.
- The movups instruction loads the unaligned packed single-precision floating-point values from array1 and array2 into the registers xmm0 and xmm1, respectively.
- The addps instruction adds the packed single-precision values in xmm1 to those in xmm0.
- Finally, the resultant vector is stored back into the result array using the movups instruction.

SIMD Performance Benefits: The primary benefit of SIMD and vector instructions is performance improvement. By processing multiple data elements simultaneously, SIMD instructions reduce the number of loops and iterations necessary, which helps in minimizing the processing time. This becomes conspicuous in large-scale computations.

Consider a scenario where an array of 1000 floating-point numbers needs to be added to another array. Without SIMD, this would require 1000 separate addition operations. With SIMD, assuming a vector size of four elements, only 250 operations are needed.

Practical Use Cases:

- **Multimedia Processing:** SIMD instructions improve the performance of operations involving large datasets such as images, audio, and video by allowing the simultaneous processing of multiple pixels, samples, or frames.
- **Scientific Computing:** Algorithms for matrix multiplication, Fourier transforms, and other computational tasks benefit significantly from the parallel processing capabilities of SIMD.
- **Cryptography:** Many cryptographic algorithms involve iterative and parallelizable data transformations, making them ideal candidates for SIMD optimization.

Algorithm: Vectorized Addition Below is an algorithm for vectorized addition using SIMD.

Input : Array A of size N, Array B of size N
Output : Array C of size N

```
for i ← 0 to N − 1 Step 4 do
    Load 4 elements from A[i] into a SIMD register R1;
    Load 4 elements from B[i] into a SIMD register R2;
    Add R1 and R2 and store the result into register R3;
    Store 4 elements of R3 into C[i];
```

Limitations and Considerations: While SIMD offers substantial performance improvements, it is not without limitations:

- **Data Alignment:** SIMD operations often require data to be aligned in memory, which may necessitate additional memory management considerations.
- **Branching:** SIMD is less efficient in the presence of branching within loops, as SIMD effectiveness depends on the uniformity of operations applied to each data element.
- **Overhead:** The initial setup and management overhead for SIMD execution can offset performance gains, particularly for small datasets.

Through understanding and effectively utilizing SIMD and vector instructions, developers can achieve significant performance improvements in suitable applications. Mastery of these techniques is essential for those aiming to optimize computational code in assembly language proficiently.

10.5 Parallel Programming in Assembly

Parallel programming involves the simultaneous execution of multiple computations, which can lead to significant performance improvements on modern multicore processors. In assembly language, parallelism can be achieved through the use of SIMD (Single Instruction, Multiple Data) instructions, multi-threading, and leveraging specific parallel processing instructions provided by the processor architecture.

To begin with, understanding the concept of SIMD is crucial. SIMD instructions allow a single instruction to operate on multiple data points simultaneously. This is especially useful in operations involving large data sets, such as in image processing or scientific computations.

Consider the Intel SSE (Streaming SIMD Extensions) and AVX (Advanced Vector Extensions) instruction sets. These provide a wide range of instructions for parallel data processing. A typical use case involves the addition of two arrays of floating-point numbers. The following examples illustrate using SSE and AVX instructions to add two arrays.

Listing 10.12: ASCII Character Encoding Example

```
; Using SSE Instructions
section .data
    array1: dq 1.0, 2.0, 3.0, 4.0
    array2: dq 5.0, 6.0, 7.0, 8.0
    result: dq 0.0, 0.0, 0.0, 0.0

section .text
    global _start

_start:
    movaps xmm0, [array1] ; Load array1 into xmm0
    movaps xmm1, [array2] ; Load array2 into xmm1
    addps xmm0, xmm1 ; Perform SIMD addition
    movaps [result], xmm0 ; Store the result
```

Switching to AVX allows handling larger registers and enhancing performance further:

Listing 10.13: ASCII Character Encoding Example

```
; Using AVX Instructions
section .data
    array1: dq 1.0, 2.0, 3.0, 4.0
    array2: dq 5.0, 6.0, 7.0, 8.0
    result: dq 0.0, 0.0, 0.0, 0.0

section .text
    global _start

_start:
    vmovaps ymm0, [array1] ; Load array1 into ymm0
    vmovaps ymm1, [array2] ; Load array2 into ymm1
    vaddps ymm0, ymm0, ymm1 ; Perform SIMD addition
    vmovaps [result], ymm0 ; Store the result
```

Another key technique in parallel programming is multi-threading, which implements concurrent execution using multiple threads. Each thread can execute code independently, allowing parallel execution of tasks. To utilize multi-threading in assembly, we rely on system calls or library functions provided by the operating system, such as the

POSIX threads (pthreads) library in Linux.

The following example demonstrates creating a simple multi-threaded program using assembly and the pthreads library:

Listing 10.14: ASCII Character Encoding Example

```
section .data
    message db "Thread running",0

section .bss
    thread_id resb 8

section .text
    extern pthread_create, pthread_exit, printf
    global _start

_start:
    ; Create a thread
    mov rdi, thread_id ; Thread ID
    lea rsi, [rel thread_func] ; Function to execute
    mov rdx, 0 ; No arguments
    call pthread_create

    ; Wait for the thread to finish
    call pthread_exit

thread_func:
    ; Print a message from the thread
    lea rdi, [rel message]
    call printf
    ret
```

It is imperative to handle synchronization and avoid race conditions when dealing with shared resources in multi-threaded environments. Synchronization constructs like mutexes and semaphores can prevent such issues by controlling access to shared resources. The following example demonstrates using mutexes with pthreads:

Listing 10.15: ASCII Character Encoding Example

```
extern pthread_create, pthread_mutex_init, pthread_mutex_lock,
      pthread_mutex_unlock, printf, pthread_exit
section .data
    message db "Thread",0
    counter dq 0

mutex:
    resb 40

section .bss
    thread_id resb 8

section .text
    global _start

_start:
    ; Initialize the mutex
    lea rdi, [rel mutex]
```

```
    call pthread_mutex_init

    ; Create a thread
    mov rdi, thread_id
    lea rsi, [rel thread_func]
    mov rdx, 0
    call pthread_create

    ; Wait for the thread to finish
    call pthread_exit

thread_func:
    ; Lock the mutex
    lea rdi, [rel mutex]
    call pthread_mutex_lock

    ; Increment the counter safely
    inc qword [counter]

    ; Print a message from the thread
    lea rdi, [rel message]
    call printf

    ; Unlock the mutex
    lea rdi, [rel mutex]
    call pthread_mutex_unlock
    ret
```

Finally, advanced parallel programming techniques involve utilizing hardware-specific capabilities for synchronization and communication between threads, such as atomic operations and memory barriers. These low-level mechanisms ensure the consistency of data without the overhead of traditional locking mechanisms.

The atomic instructions provided by modern processors, such as LOCK prefix in x86 assembly, guarantee that operations on shared data are executed atomically, preventing race conditions.

A simple demonstration of an atomic operation using the LOCK prefix in x86 assembly can be seen in the increment of a shared counter:

Listing 10.16: ASCII Character Encoding Example

```
section .data
    counter dq 0

section .text
    global _start

_start:
    ; Lock and increment counter
    mov rax, 1
    lock xadd [counter], rax
```

This instruction atomically exchanges the value in rax with the value at the memory location counter and increments the counter.

By effectively combining SIMD instructions, multi-threading, synchronization techniques, and atomic operations, it is possible to harness the full power of modern multi-core processors in assembly language. Achieving efficient parallelism requires careful consideration of the hardware architecture and meticulous programming practices.

10.6 Writing Device Drivers in Assembly

Device drivers are an essential component of any operating system, serving as the interface between the hardware and the OS. Writing device drivers in assembly language allows for fine-grained control over hardware, crucial for performance-critical applications. This section delves into the intricacies of developing device drivers using assembly language, touching upon key concepts such as memory-mapped I/O, interrupt handling, and direct memory access (DMA).

A device driver must perform several specific functions:

- Initialize the hardware device.
- Handle hardware interrupts.
- Provide APIs for user-level applications or system components.
- Manage device-specific data transfers.

Memory-Mapped I/O:

Memory-mapped I/O (MMIO) is a method by which control registers of hardware devices are mapped into the system memory space. This facilitates access to hardware by reading from and writing to specific memory addresses.

Consider the following assembly code snippet demonstrating access to a memory-mapped register:

Listing 10.17: ASCII Character Encoding Example

```
MOV EAX, [0xFEC00000] ; Read from the MMIO register
MOV [0xFEC00004], EAX ; Write to another MMIO register
```

In these instructions, we load the value from a hardware register located at memory address $0xFEC00000$ into the EAX register and then write it to another register at $0xFEC00004$.

Interrupt Handling:

Hardware devices often need to interrupt the CPU to signal completion of a task or the need for attention. Handling these interrupts efficiently is a critical aspect of writing device drivers. In assembly language, this typically involves setting up an Interrupt Service Routine (ISR) and configuring the Interrupt Descriptor Table (IDT).

Listing 10.18: ASCII Character Encoding Example

```
section .data
    idt_start: dd 0 ; IDT entry start
    idt_size: dw idt_end - idt_start - 1 ; IDT Size

section .text
    ; ISR for interrupt vector 32
isr32:
    CLI ; Clear Interrupt Flag
    PUSHAD ; Save all general-purpose registers
    ; ISR Handling code here
    POPAD ; Restore all general-purpose registers
    STI ; Set Interrupt Flag
    IRET ; Return from ISR

idt_entry:
    dw isr32 ; ISR routine address low bits
    dw 0x08 ; Code segment selector in GDT
    db 0 ; Reserved byte
    db 0x8E ; Flags (Interrupt gate, present, ring 0)
    dw isr32 >> 16 ; ISR routine address high bits

    idt_end:
```

This ISR example clears the interrupt flag to prevent further interrupts during ISR execution, saves the state of the general-purpose registers, processes the interrupt, restores the state, re-enables interrupts, and then returns from the interrupt.

Direct Memory Access (DMA):

DMA is a capability that allows peripheral devices to directly read from and write to the system memory without CPU intervention, significantly enhancing data transfer performance.

Consider the following pseudo code for setting up a DMA transfer:

Listing 10.19: ASCII Character Encoding Example

```
CLI ; Disable interrupts
MOV EAX, DMA_CHANNEL ; Select DMA channel
MOV EBX, BUFFER_ADDRESS ; Memory buffer address
MOV ECX, BUFFER_SIZE ; Size of the buffer
CALL SETUP_DMA_TRANSFER ; Setup DMA transfer
STI ; Enable interrupts
```

Here, we first disable interrupts to ensure that the DMA setup process isn't interrupted. We then load the DMA channel, buffer address, and buffer size into the respective registers and call a routine to configure the DMA transfer.

Writing a Simple Device Driver:

Let us put these concepts together to write a simple device driver for a hypothetical device.

Listing 10.20: ASCII Character Encoding Example

```
section .data
    device_buffer: times 512 db 0

section .bss
    read_count resd 1

section .text
global _start

_start:
    CLI
    CALL initialize_device
    STI
    HLT ; Halt CPU, waiting for interrupts

initialize_device:
    ; Device specific initialization code
    MOV EDX, [DEVICE_COMMAND_PORT]
    MOV AL, INITIALIZE_COMMAND
    OUT DX, AL
    RET

isr_device:
    CLI
    PUSHAD
    CALL handle_device_interrupt
    MOV[EAX], read_count
    ADD EAX, 1
    JNZ continue
    POPAD
    STI
    IRET

handle_device_interrupt:
    ; Read data from the device
    MOV EDX, [DEVICE_DATA_PORT]
    IN AL, DX
    MOV[device_buffer + EAX], AL
    RET

continue:
    MOV[EAX], read_count
```

In this example, the device driver starts by disabling interrupts and initializing the device by writing to its command port. When the device generates an interrupt, the isr_device ISR services this interrupt by reading data from the device and storing it in a buffer. The initialize_device and handle_device_interrupt routines encapsulate initialization and interrupt handling logic respectively, ensuring modularity.

This section integrates various techniques to form a coherent understanding of writing device drivers in assembly language. The next step involves interfacing these low-level routines with higher-level system components to form a fully functional driver, interacting harmoniously within an operating system environment.

10.7 System Call Interface and Kernel Programming

In this section, we will delve into the system call interface and kernel programming within the context of assembly language. Understanding how to engage directly with the operating system kernel through system calls is crucial for advanced assembly language programming and building robust low-level software such as operating systems, device drivers, and embedded systems applications.

A system call provides a controlled entry point to the services offered by the operating system's kernel. These services include file operations, process control, memory management, network communication, and more. When a system call is invoked, the processor transfers control from user mode to kernel mode, enabling the program to request the OS to perform privileged operations.

To invoke a system call in assembly language, we often follow these generic steps:

- Load the respective system call number into a designated register.
- Load the necessary arguments into specific registers as defined by the architecture's calling convention.
- Execute the system call instruction, which triggers a software interrupt or makes a direct system call, depending on the architecture.
- Check the return value and handle any errors that may arise.

We will illustrate this process using the x86-64 architecture, which serves as an excellent example due to its widespread use and well-documented system call interface. Let's focus on the Linux operating system, where the syscall instruction is used to make a system call.

Here is an example that demonstrates making a system call to write a string to the standard output:

Listing 10.21: ASCII Character Encoding Example

```
section .data
    hello db 'Hello, world!', 10 ; The string to print, including a newline character
    hello_len equ $ - hello ; Calculating the length of the string

section .text
    global _start

_start:
    ; Linux write system call, which is syscall number 1
    mov rax, 1 ; syscall number for sys_write
    mov rdi, 1 ; file descriptor for stdout
    mov rsi, hello ; pointer to the string to print
    mov rdx, hello_len ; length of the string
    syscall ; make the system call

    ; Exit the program
    mov rax, 60 ; syscall number for sys_exit
    xor rdi, rdi ; exit code 0
    syscall ; make the system call
```

In this program, the syscall instruction is used to invoke the system calls. For the sys_write system call, the designated parameters are:

- rax - system call number (1 for sys_write)
- rdi - file descriptor (1 for standard output)
- rsi - pointer to the buffer (the string "Hello, world!")
- rdx - buffer size (length of the string)

The system call number for sys_exit is 60, and rdi is set to 0 to indicate a normal exit status.

Now, let's explore the handling of system calls within the kernel. Kernel programming involves writing code that runs in the kernel space and interacts directly with hardware and core OS functionalities. A simplified structure of a kernel module in Linux can be written in C with inline assembly for specific hardware interactions.

Here is an example of a basic Linux kernel module that utilizes inline assembly to perform a simple operation:

Listing 10.22: ASCII Character Encoding Example

```
#include <linux/module.h>
#include <linux/kernel.h>
#include <linux/init.h>

static int __init hello_init(void)
{
    printk(KERN_INFO "Hello, Kernel!\n");

    unsigned int eax;
    asm volatile( "cpuid"
                  : "=a"(eax)
                  : "a"(0)
                  : "ebx", "ecx", "edx" );

    printk(KERN_INFO "Output of CPUID with EAX=0: %u\n", eax);

    return 0;
}

static void __exit hello_exit(void)
{
    printk(KERN_INFO "Goodbye, Kernel!\n");
}

module_init(hello_init);
module_exit(hello_exit);

MODULE_LICENSE("GPL");
MODULE_AUTHOR("Your Name");
MODULE_DESCRIPTION("A simple example of a Linux kernel module with inline
    assembly.");
```

In this kernel module example, the function hello_init is executed when the module is loaded, and the function hello_exit is executed when the module is unloaded. Inside hello_init, we use inline assembly to execute the CPUID instruction to gather information about the CPU. The volatile keyword ensures that the assembler will not optimize this instruction away. The output is then logged using printk, a kernel-level print function.

By integrating these concepts into assembly language programming, one gains the ability to develop powerful and efficient software that interacts directly with the core operating system components. Understanding and utilizing the system call interface and kernel-level programming expands the capability of assembly language programmers, enabling them to design and optimize low-level software solutions.

10.8 Reverse Engineering and Malware Analysis

Reverse engineering and malware analysis are critical tasks in the field of cybersecurity and software development. They involve deeply understanding compiled binaries, disassembling code, and analyzing malicious software to determine its behavior, origin, and impact. This section delves into the practical applications and methods used in reverse engineering and malware analysis, focusing on the utilization of assembly language in these domains.

Reverse engineering is the process of analyzing software to deduce its design and implementation. It often involves converting binary code back into assembly language using a disassembler. The goal is to understand the software's functionality, identify vulnerabilities, or modify its behavior.

1. Disassembling Binaries

Disassemblers are tools that convert binary code into human-readable assembly language instructions. An example of a widely used disassembler is IDA Pro, which provides detailed and comprehensive analysis of binaries. Below is an example of a disassembled binary code snippet:

Listing 10.23: ASCII Character Encoding Example

```
.text:00401000 mov eax, [esp+4]
.text:00401004 add eax, [esp+8]
.text:00401008 ret
```

In this code, the function takes two arguments from the stack, adds them, and returns the result. Understanding such snippets forms the basis of reverse engineering tasks.

2. Analyzing Assembly Code

Once the binary has been disassembled, the next step is to analyze the assembly code to comprehend the software's logic. This involves identifying functions, loops, conditional branches, and other control structures. The following example shows a typical function prologue and epilogue in assembly:

Listing 10.24: ASCII Character Encoding Example

```
.text:00401010 push ebp
.text:00401011 mov ebp, esp
.text:00401013 sub esp, 16
```

```
; Function body here
.text:00401016 mov esp, ebp
.text:00401018 pop ebp
.text:00401019 ret
```

Function prologues and epilogues are standardized segments of code generated by compilers to manage the stack frame for function calls.

3. Identifying Key Structures and Patterns

Recognizing common structures and patterns is essential for effective reverse engineering. For instance:

- call and jmp instructions indicate function calls and jumps respectively. - mov instructions frequently handle data transfer between registers and memory. - cmp followed by a conditional jump such as je (jump if equal) or jne (jump if not equal) reveals decision points.

Carefully tracing these patterns helps in reconstructing the control flow and data flow of the program.

4. Malware Analysis Techniques

Malware analysis utilizes reverse engineering to dissect malicious software. There are generally two approaches: static analysis and dynamic analysis.

- **Static Analysis**: This involves inspecting the malware's code without execution. Using disassembly, one can identify suspicious patterns, hardcoded IP addresses, and commands associated with malicious activities.

```
.data:00402000 IPaddress      db '192.168.1.10'
.text:00401020                push    offset IPaddress
.text:00401025                call    connect_to_ip
```

- **Dynamic Analysis**: This involves running the malware in a controlled environment (such as a sandbox) to observe its behavior. Tools like debuggers (e.g., OllyDbg or GDB) allow setting breakpoints and stepping through code to monitor its actions.

Listing 10.25: ASCII Character Encoding Example

```
(gdb) b *0x401010
(gdb) r
(gdb) s
```

The above commands set a breakpoint at the address 0x401010 and start the program, then step through the execution.

5. Analyzing Obfuscated Code

Malware authors often obfuscate their code to hinder analysis. Common obfuscation techniques include packing, encryption, and junk code insertion. Analysts must employ deobfuscation techniques to reveal the actual code. For example:

Listing 10.26: ASCII Character Encoding Example

```
.text:00401000 mov eax, cipher_text
.text:00401005 xor eax, key
.text:00401008 ret
```

This snippet shows a simple XOR decryption routine, where cipher_text is decrypted using a key.

6. Lifting Code to Higher-Level Representations

To facilitate understanding, some tools and techniques convert assembly code to higher-level representations. For instance, tools like the RetDec decompiler attempt to reconstruct C-like pseudo-code from binaries.

```
int add(int a, int b) {
  return a + b;
}
```

This pseudo-code corresponds to the initial add function in the first disassembly example.

Understanding assembly language is crucial for reverse engineering and malware analysis. It enables determining how a program operates, uncovering vulnerabilities, and gaining insights into malicious software behaviors. Practical application of these techniques is essential for cybersecurity professionals and software engineers engaged in security-critical domains.

10.9 Cryptographic Algorithms in Assembly

Cryptographic algorithms are vital in securing information in digital communications and storage. Implementing these algorithms in assembly language can achieve high performance and efficiency, which is crucial for real-time systems and embedded devices where processing power and memory are limited. This section delves into the implementation of fundamental cryptographic algorithms in assembly language, focusing on block ciphers, stream ciphers, and hash functions.

1. Block Ciphers: The Advanced Encryption Standard (AES)

AES is a widely used symmetric encryption algorithm defined by the

National Institute of Standards and Technology (NIST). It operates on fixed-size blocks and can use keys of varying lengths. The following is a brief outline of AES implementation in assembly.

Algorithm 10: Basic AES Encryption

```
Input: A plaintext block, a key schedule
Output: The ciphertext block
AddRoundKey(state, RoundKey);
for each round in 1 to Nr-1 do
    SubBytes(state);
    ShiftRows(state);
    MixColumns(state);
    AddRoundKey(state, RoundKey);
SubBytes(state);
ShiftRows(state);
AddRoundKey(state, RoundKey);
return state
```

The AddRoundKey, SubBytes, ShiftRows, and MixColumns functions are applied iteratively across a number of rounds. Each function manipulates the 128-bit state array. Below is a simplified assembly example of the ShiftRows operation.

Listing 10.27: ASCII Character Encoding Example

```
ShiftRows:
  mov eax, [state]
  ror eax, 8
  mov [state], eax
  ret
```

2. Stream Ciphers: The Rivest Cipher 4 (RC4)

RC4 is a stream cipher known for its simplicity and speed. It generates a pseudorandom stream of bits (key stream) that is XORed with plaintext to produce ciphertext. Below is an implementation of the RC4 initialization and key generation phase.

The implementation of the RC4 key-scheduling algorithm in assembly follows:

Listing 10.28: ASCII Character Encoding Example

```
RC4_KeySched:
  mov ecx, 0
  mov ebx, 0
```

Algorithm 11: RC4 Key-Scheduling Algorithm (KSA)

Input: a key of length keylen
Output: S-box for pseudo-random generation

```
for i = 0 to 255 do
    S[i] = i;
j = 0;
for i = 0 to 255 do
    j = (j + S[i] + key[i % keylen]) % 256;
    Swap(S[i], S[j]);
return S
```

```
InitArray:
  mov [S + ecx], ecx
  inc ecx
  cmp ecx, 256
  jne InitArray

KeySchedLoop:
  mov eax, ecx
  xor eax, eax
  mov al, [S + ecx]
  add ebx, eax
  add ebx, [key + (ecx % keylen)]
  mov eax, [S + ebx]
  mov [S + ecx], eax
  mov [S + ebx], ecx
  inc ecx
  cmp ecx, 256
  jne KeySchedLoop

  ret
```

3. Hash Functions: The Secure Hash Algorithm 256 (SHA-256)

SHA-256 is a cryptographic hash function that produces a 256-bit hash value from an input message. The algorithm involves multiple rounds of bitwise operations, modular additions, and data permutations.

Below is a simplified example of the SHA-256 Sigma_1 function in assembly.

Listing 10.29: ASCII Character Encoding Example

```
Sigma_1:
  mov eax, [e]
  ror eax, 6
  mov ebx, eax
  ror eax, 11
  xor ebx, eax
  ror eax, 25
  xor ebx, eax
```

Algorithm 12: SHA-256 Compression Function

Input: Message schedule array $\mathrm{W}[0..63]$, initial hash value $\mathrm{H}[0..7]$

Output: Updated hash value $\mathrm{H}[0..7]$

```
a, b, c, d, e, f, g, h ← H[0..7];
for t ← 0 to 63 do
    T1 ← h + Σ1(e) + Ch(e, f, g) + K[t] + W[t];
    T2 ← Σ0(a) + Maj(a, b, c);
    h ← g;
    g ← f;
    f ← e;
    e ← d + T1;
    d ← c;
    c ← b;
    b ← a;
    a ← T1 + T2;
H[0..7] ← (H[0..7] + {a, b, c, d, e, f, g, h}) mod 2^32;
return H
```

```
ret
```

Implementing these cryptographic algorithms in assembly language poses challenges but offers significant speed and efficiency gains. Each algorithm is broken down into its fundamental operations to maximize performance on specific hardware architectures. Understanding and coding these algorithms at the assembly level is critical for application in security-critical and performance-sensitive environments.

10.10 Developing Real-Time Systems

Developing real-time systems in assembly language imposes stringent timing requirements that the software must adhere to with precision. Real-time systems can be categorized as either hard real-time systems, where deadlines must be strictly followed, or soft real-time systems, where it is acceptable for deadlines to occasionally be missed. This section delves deeply into the fundamental concepts, techniques, and code practices crucial for developing real-time systems.

Understanding the nature of task schedulability, interrupt handling, and timing constraints is essential. Assembly language, known for low-level hardware interaction and high performance, is ideal for real-time system development due to its predictable execution time and minimal overhead.

Task Schedulability: Determining if a set of tasks can meet their deadlines is central to real-time system design. Techniques such as Rate-Monotonic Scheduling (RMS) and Earliest Deadline First (EDF) are commonly employed to analyze and ensure schedulability.

Rate-Monotonic Scheduling (RMS) is a fixed-priority algorithm where tasks with shorter periods have higher priorities. This technique is elementary yet effective for tasks with static priorities.

Listing 10.30: ASCII Character Encoding Example

```
function rateMonotonicSchedule(tasks):
    sort(tasks by period ascending)
    for each task in tasks:
        assign priority based on task's position in sorted list
    return tasks
```

Earliest Deadline First (EDF) scheduling dynamically assigns priorities based on the upcoming deadlines, with tasks having the closest deadlines receiving the highest priority.

Listing 10.31: ASCII Character Encoding Example

```
function earliestDeadlineFirstSchedule(tasks):
    sort(tasks by deadline ascending)
    for each task in tasks:
        assign priority based on task's deadline
    return tasks
```

Interrupt Handling: Handling interrupts efficiently is crucial in real-time systems to ensure prompt responses to events. Interrupt Service Routines (ISRs) should be brief and fast. They should quickly acknowledge the interrupt, execute the required critical task, and defer any non-critical actions.

Below is an exemplary ISR in assembly for a hypothetical architecture:

Listing 10.32: ASCII Character Encoding Example

```
ISR:
    push eax ; Save register state
    push ebx

    mov eax, INTERRUPT_ID ; Process the specific interrupt
    cmp eax, TIMER_INTERRUPT
    jne .other_interrupt

    call handle_timer ; Call timer-specific handler
```

```
    jmp .exit

.other_interrupt:
    call handle_other ; Call other interrupt handler

.exit:
    pop ebx ; Restore register state
    pop eax
    iret ; Return from interrupt
```

Timing Constraints: Ensuring task deadlines are met requires precise timing control. Assembly language programs achieve this through cycle counting, hardware timers, and delay loops. It is vital to understand the clock cycles consumed by each instruction to meet the real-time requirements accurately.

Consider the use of a hardware timer to manage task timing in an assembly program:

Listing 10.33: ASCII Character Encoding Example

```
start_timer:
    mov al, 0x36 ; Command byte to initialize timer
    out 0x43, al ; Send command to control register
    mov ax, TIMER_COUNT ; Load time interval count
    out 0x40, al ; Send low byte
    mov al, ah
    out 0x40, al ; Send high byte
ret
```

To wait for a timer tick:

Listing 10.34: ASCII Character Encoding Example

```
wait_for_tick:
    in al, 0x60 ; Read status from timer port
    test al, 0x20 ; Check if tick occurred
    jz wait_for_tick ; Loop until tick occurs
ret
```

Memory Management: In real-time systems, memory management must ensure quick and deterministic access. Techniques such as fixed-size memory allocation, pre-allocated memory blocks, and direct memory access (DMA) are commonly used. Avoid dynamic memory allocation at runtime to prevent delays due to fragmentation and garbage collection.

Consider a fixed-size memory pool allocator implemented in assembly:

Listing 10.35: ASCII Character Encoding Example

```
allocate_memory:
    mov esi, mem_pool_start ; Start of memory pool
    mov ecx, mem_pool_size ; Size of memory pool
```

```
.search_loop:
    mov eax, [esi] ; Read memory block header
    test eax, eax ; Check if block is free
    jz .found ; If zero, block is free
    add esi, block_size ; Move to next block
    loop .search_loop ; Repeat until end of pool
    ret ; Return if no free block

.found:
    mov [esi], 1 ; Mark block as occupied
    mov eax, esi ; Return pointer to allocated block
ret
```

. Leveraging assembly language for the development of real-time systems demands meticulous attention to timing, scheduling, interrupt handling, and memory management to ensure the reliability and predictability required.

10.11 Custom Instruction Sets and Extensions

Custom instruction sets and extensions provide significant enhancements to the traditional instruction sets of processors, permitting software to execute more efficiently and enabling functionality that standard sets might not support. Incorporating custom instructions often involves augmenting an existing Instruction Set Architecture (ISA) with additional operations tailored to specific computational tasks or application domains. These extensions can dramatically accelerate workloads by reducing the number of instructions needed to perform complex operations.

To introduce the basic concepts of creating custom instruction sets, we shall first examine the motivation and basic mechanisms for ISA extensions. Next, we will explore practical examples and discuss how to implement these extensions in assembly language.

Motivation for Custom Instruction Sets: The primary motivations to design and incorporate custom instructions include:

- **Performance Enhancement**: Customized instructions can consolidate multiple operations into a single instruction, thus reducing the instruction count and speeding up execution.
- **Application-Specific Optimization**: Tailored instructions can optimize performance in specific applications such as digital sig-

nal processing (DSP), cryptography, or graphics, providing significant efficiency gains.

- **Reduced Code Size**: Incorporating complex operations into a single instruction reduces the program size, which is particularly beneficial for embedded systems with limited memory.

- **Energy Efficiency**: Fewer instructions and faster execution lead to energy savings, which is critical in mobile and battery-operated devices.

Designing Custom Instructions: When designing custom instructions, the following steps are typically followed:

1. **Identify the Target Operations**: Determine the computationally intensive operations within an application that are candidates for optimization.

2. **Analyze Patterns**: Examine the existing instruction patterns to identify opportunities where multiple standard instructions can be replaced with a single custom instruction.

3. **Define the Instruction Syntax**: Set the opcode, operands, and the instruction format. The opcode must be unique within the ISA, and the operands should match the intended data types and addressing modes.

4. **Modify the Processor Architecture**: Update the processor's decode, execute, and write-back units to support the new instruction.

5. **Update Assembler and Tools**: Extend the assembler, linker, and related tools to recognize and utilize the new instruction.

Practical Implementation Example: Consider optimizing a common operation in cryptographic algorithms, such as bitwise rotation often used in hash functions.

Current implementation using standard instructions:

Listing 10.36: ASCII Character Encoding Example

```
; Rotating left a 32-bit register
rol eax, 13
```

Let's define a custom instruction named ROL13 to rotate a 32-bit register left by 13 bits. Here's how to implement it:

Listing 10.37: ASCII Character Encoding Example

```
; Custom instruction ROL13
ROL13 eax
```

Architectural changes:

- **Opcode Allocation**: Assign a unique opcode for ROL13.
- **Decoder Unit**: Modify the decode logic to recognize ROL13 and generate appropriate control signals.
- **Execution Unit**: Enhance the execution unit to perform the bitwise rotation explicitly for 13 bits.

Updating assembler and tools may involve expanding the lexicon of the assembler to include the ROL13 mnemonic and ensuring the assembler generates the correct opcode for this instruction.

Instruction Set Extensions (SIMD): Single Instruction, Multiple Data (SIMD) extensions provide another illustration of comprehensive ISA enhancements. SIMD instructions operate on data vectors, performing parallel processing on multiple data points with a single instruction. This parallelism significantly enhances performance in data-intensive applications.

Example of SIMD instruction in x86 assembly:

Listing 10.38: ASCII Character Encoding Example

```
; Adding packed single-precision floating-point values
addps xmm1, xmm2
```

In this example, the addps instruction computes the sum of four packed single-precision floating-point numbers held in the xmm1 and xmm2 registers. SIMD instructions like addps enable processing multiple data elements simultaneously, hence accelerating operations such as multimedia processing and scientific computations.

Implementing SIMD Extensions: Implementing SIMD extensions involves more complex steps due to the need for parallel data path modifications:

1. **Define SIMD Datapath**: Design the datapath to handle vectors rather than scalar values, requiring multiple parallel ALUs.

2. **Update Register File**: Extend the register file to hold vector data, typically using larger registers (e.g., 128-bit or 256-bit).
3. **Instruction Design**: Create extended instructions with opcodes that support parallel data operations.
4. **Processor Pipeline Modifications**: Adapt the processor pipeline stages (fetch, decode, execute, etc.) to manage the increased data width and parallelism.

Practical implementation of these extensions ensures that specialized instructions execute efficiently by aligning with the architectural improvements within the processor. Consequently, custom instruction sets and extensions deliver optimized computational capabilities, catering to the performance and efficiency demands of specific applications.

10.12 Case Studies of Complex Assembly Programs

This section delves into case studies of complex assembly programs, showcasing the practical application of advanced assembly language programming concepts. These case studies highlight real-world scenarios where assembly programming significantly optimizes performance, reliability, and functionality. Each program is meticulously analyzed to impart a comprehensive understanding of its structure, logic, and purpose.

Case Study 1: Optimized Matrix Multiplication

Matrix multiplication is a fundamental operation in various scientific and engineering computations. Here, we examine an assembly program that performs optimized matrix multiplication leveraging SIMD (Single Instruction, Multiple Data) instructions for parallel processing.

Listing 10.39: ASCII Character Encoding Example

```
section .data
    matrix_a db 1, 2, 3, 4, 5, 6, 7, 8, 9, 10, 11, 12, 13, 14, 15, 16
    matrix_b db 16, 15, 14, 13, 12, 11, 10, 9, 8, 7, 6, 5, 4, 3, 2, 1
    result db 0, 0, 0, 0, 0, 0, 0, 0, 0, 0, 0, 0, 0, 0, 0, 0

section .text
    global _start
_start:
    ; Load matrix A
    movups xmm0, [matrix_a]
```

```
    movups xmm1, [matrix_a + 16]

    ; Load matrix B and multiply
    movups xmm2, [matrix_b]
    movups xmm3, [matrix_b + 16]
    mulps xmm0, xmm2
    mulps xmm1, xmm3

    ; Store result
    movups [result], xmm0
    movups [result + 16], xmm1

    ; Exit
    mov eax, 1
    xor ebx, ebx
    int 0x80
```

The above code snippet demonstrates the use of SSE (Streaming SIMD Extensions) instructions. The movups instruction loads unaligned data into the XMM registers, and mulps performs parallel multiplication of packed single-precision floating-point values. This approach leverages data parallelism, significantly improving computational efficiency compared to scalar operations.

Case Study 2: Real-Time Audio Processing

Real-time audio processing requires handling audio streams with minimal latency. Here, we consider an assembly program designed to apply a simple audio filter (e.g., a low-pass filter) in real-time.

Listing 10.40: ASCII Character Encoding Example

```
section .data
    audio_buffer db 256 dup(0)
    filter_coefficients db 0.5, 0.5

section .bss
    output_buffer resb 256

section .text
    global _start
_start:
    ; Load audio samples
    mov eax, audio_buffer
    mov ebx, filter_coefficients

    ; Apply filter
    mov ecx, 256 / 2
.loop:
    mov al, [eax]
    add al, [eax + 1]
    mul al, [ebx]
    mov [output_buffer + ecx], al

    add eax, 2
    loop .loop

    ; Continue processing or exit
```

```
    mov eax, 1
    xor ebx, ebx
    int 0x80
```

This code example processes audio samples in the audio_buffer by applying a filter with pre-defined coefficients stored in filter_coefficients. The samples are loaded, processed, and stored in the output_buffer. Each sample is multiplied by the corresponding filter coefficient, ensuring that the processed audio stream is output with minimal delay, meeting real-time constraints.

Case Study 3: Custom Encryption Algorithm

Encryption plays a crucial role in securing information. This case study presents an assembly implementation of a simplified symmetric encryption algorithm using XOR-based operations.

Listing 10.41: ASCII Character Encoding Example

```
section .data
    plain_text db "HELLO, WORLD!"
    key db "SECRETKEY"
    encrypted_text db 13 dup(0)

section .text
    global _start
_start:
    ; Load key and text lengths
    mov ecx, 13
    mov esi, plain_text
    mov edi, key

    ; Encrypt using XOR
.encrypt_loop:
    mov al, [esi]
    xor al, [edi]
    stosb
    inc esi
    inc edi
    loop .encrypt_loop

    ; Exit
    mov eax, 1
    xor ebx, ebx
    int 0x80
```

In this example, the plain_text is encrypted using the key. The encryption process employs XOR operations for each byte of the plain text with the corresponding byte of the key, resulting in the encrypted_text. This demonstrates the simplicity and efficiency of XOR-based encryption in assembly language, while also highlighting the need for careful key management.

Case Study 4: Fibonacci Sequence Calculation

The Fibonacci sequence is a classic example used to illustrate various programming techniques. This case study implements the calculation of the Fibonacci sequence up to a specified number of terms in assembly language, showcasing recursive and iterative approaches.

Listing 10.42: ASCII Character Encoding Example

```
section .data
    n dd 10 ; Number of terms
    fib_sequence dd 10 dup(0) ; Array to store Fibonacci sequence

section .text
    global _start
_start:
    ; Iterative Fibonacci
    mov ecx, n
    mov dword [fib_sequence], 0 ; First term
    mov dword [fib_sequence + 4], 1 ; Second term

    mov esi, 2 ; Loop counter
    mov ebx, fib_sequence

.iterative_fib:
    mov eax, [ebx + 4 * (esi - 1)]
    add eax, [ebx + 4 * (esi - 2)]
    mov [ebx + 4 * esi], eax

    inc esi
    loop .iterative_fib

    ; Exit
    mov eax, 1
    xor ebx, ebx
    int 0x80
```

The above code calculates the Fibonacci sequence iteratively. It initializes the first two terms of the sequence and then computes subsequent terms by summing the previous two. This approach avoids the overhead associated with recursive function calls, thus enhancing performance.

Each case study exemplifies critical aspects of assembly language programming, including data manipulation, parallel computation, real-time processing, encryption, and numerical computation. By dissecting these complex programs, readers can gain deeper insights into the practical implementation of advanced assembly concepts.

Made in the USA
Monee, IL
05 November 2026

67845308R00193